Cowboy Classics

Screening Antiquity

Series Editors: Monica S. Cyrino and Lloyd Llewellyn-Jones

Screening Antiquity is a cutting-edge and provocative series of academic monographs and edited volumes focusing on new research on the reception of the ancient world in film and television. Screening Antiquity showcases the work of the best-established and up-and-coming specialists in the field. It provides an important synergy of the latest international scholarly ideas about the conception of antiquity in popular culture and is the only series that focuses exclusively on screened representations of the ancient world.

Titles available in the series:

Rome *Season Two: Trial and Triumph*
Edited by Monica S. Cyrino

Cowboy Classics: The Roots of the American Western in the Epic Tradition
By Kirsten Day

Ben-Hur*: The Original Blockbuster*
By Jon Solomon

STARZ Spartacus*: Reimagining an Icon on Screen*
Edited by Antony Augoustakis and Monica S. Cyrino

Forthcoming Titles:

Broadcasting Ancient Greece on Television
Edited by Fiona Hobden and Amanda Wrigley

Cowboy Classics

The Roots of the American Western in the Epic Tradition

Kirsten Day

EDINBURGH
University Press

Edinburgh University Press is one of the leading university presses in the UK. We publish academic books and journals in our selected subject areas across the humanities and social sciences, combining cutting-edge scholarship with high editorial and production values to produce academic works of lasting importance. For more information visit our website: www.edinburghuniversitypress.com

Edinburgh University Press Ltd
13 Infirmary Street, Edinburgh, EH1 1LT

Typeset in 11/13 Sabon by
Servis Filmsetting Ltd, Stockport, Cheshire
and printed and bound by CPI Group (UK) Ltd,
Croydon CR0 4YY

A CIP record for this book is available from the British Library

ISBN 978 1 4744 0246 0 (hardback)
ISBN 978 1 3995 7153 1 (paperback)
ISBN 978 1 4744 0247 7 (webready PDF)
ISBN 978 1 4744 1516 3 (epub)

Contents

Series Editors' Preface

Screening Antiquity is a new series of cutting-edge academic monographs and edited volumes that present exciting and original research on the reception of the ancient world in film and television. It provides an important synergy of the latest international scholarly ideas about the onscreen conception of antiquity in popular culture and is the only book series to focus exclusively on screened representations of the ancient world.

The interactions between cinema, television, and historical representation is a growing field of scholarship and student engagement; many Classics and Ancient History departments in universities worldwide teach cinematic representations of the past as part of their programmes in Reception Studies. Scholars are now questioning how historical films and television series reflect the societies in which they were made, and speculate on how attitudes towards the past have been moulded in the popular imagination by their depiction in the movies. Screening Antiquity explores how these constructions came about and offers scope to analyse how and why the ancient past is filtered through onscreen representations in specific ways. The series highlights exciting and original publications that explore the representation of antiquity onscreen, and that employ modern theoretical and cultural perspectives to examine screened antiquity, including: stars and star text, directors and *auteurs*, cinematography, design and art direction, marketing, fans, and the online presence of the ancient world.

The series aims to present original research focused exclusively on the reception of the ancient world in film and television. In itself this is an exciting and original approach. There is no other book series that engages head-on with both big screen and small screen recreations of the past, yet their integral interactivity is clear to see: film popularity has a major impact on television productions and for its part, television regularly influences cinema (including film spin-offs of popular television series). This is the first academic series to identify and encourage the holistic interactivity of these two major media institutions, and the first to promote interdisciplinary research in all the fields of Cinema Studies, Media Studies, Classics, and Ancient History.

Screening Antiquity explores the various facets of onscreen creations of the past, exploring the theme from multiple angles. Some volumes will foreground a Classics 'reading' of the subject, analysing the nuances of film and television productions against a background of ancient literature, art, history, or culture; others will focus more on Media 'readings,' by privileging the onscreen creation of the past or positioning the film or television representation within the context of modern popular culture. A third 'reading' will allow for a more fluid interaction between both the Classics and Media approaches. All three methods are valuable, since Reception Studies demands a flexible approach whereby individual scholars, or groups of researchers, foster a reading of an onscreen 'text' particular to their angle of viewing.

Screening Antiquity represents a major turning point in that it signals a better appreciation and understanding of the rich and complex interaction between the past and contemporary culture, and also of the lasting significance of antiquity in today's world.

Monica S. Cyrino and Lloyd Llewellyn-Jones
Series Editors

Acknowledgments

I am grateful to series editors Monica Cyrino and Lloyd Llewellyn-Jones for the opportunity to contribute to the growing field of classical receptions through this monograph, which I am hopeful will be seen as useful. Thanks are also due to Carol Macdonald at Edinburgh University Press and to her professional staff, Dhara Patel, Adela Rauchova, Ellie Bush, and James Dale for their help and support on this project; to respondents who gave input to early versions of these papers at various conferences and lectures over the years; to students in my LSFY 102 "From Homer to Hawks: Greek and Roman Epic and Western Film" classes for sharing their insights; to my departmental colleagues who took on extra burdens during my extended sabbatical; to my student research assistants Bethany Hayenga and Diana Cleveland; and to Augustana College for generously providing the funding that allowed me to further my work in this area. A final word of gratitude to my sons Harper and Owen for their patience; to my husband Sean Chapman for his unending support of many kinds, from emotional and familial to technological, creative, and editorial; and to Monica, again, for her invaluable mentoring and her support of my work over the years.

Illustrations

Prologue

Comparisons like the one undertaken in this volume are part of a fast-growing sub-discipline known as classical receptions, an area concerned with examining the use or manifestation of classical culture in later periods in a variety of contexts – such as literature, drama, film, and visual arts – with the aim of enriching the understanding of works from both periods. This area of scholarly inquiry arose in part as a response to a related earlier movement known as the classical tradition, which also looked at manifestations of antiquity in later periods, but with the primary focus on the influence of classical works on later literary, artistic, and intellectual productions. The latter area of inquiry stems back to the work of Gilbert Highet, whose 1949 book *The Classical Tradition* sought to trace Greek and Roman influence on the canonical works of Western literature,[1] a project much in line with the still-prevalent notion that Greek and Roman antiquity provides the cornerstone and foundation of Western civilization today. In recent decades, however, a counter-movement has emerged from those who see this approach as elitist, in that it seems to frame works from antiquity as eternal, untouchable repositories of truth to which a steady stream of pale emulators aspire in vain, so that "reception" has become the preferred term for those who want to trouble this uni-directionality and challenge the impression that classical works have a fixed and immutable value.[2] The term "classical receptions" was coined in the 1990s, and since then the movement has gained momentum through the efforts of classical scholars like Lorna Hardwick and Charles Martindale.[3] Unlike the classical tradition model, classical receptions is concerned not only with the ways in which the enduring works of antiquity continue to speak to different artists, writers, and thinkers in different times and how new meanings are both derived from and made out of these ancient texts,[4] but also with how utilizing a receptions approach can provide a new lens on the *hypotext* on which it is based, suggesting new approaches or reviving those that have been neglected or marginalized.[5]

Despite its rapid growth, the classical receptions movement has not been without its detractors, such as those in other disciplines who see the undertaking of these comparisons by classicists as an unwelcome encroachment upon their territory, to which objection classics scholars like Life Blumberg are quick to respond that this turf-jumping works both ways.[6] Admittedly, however, the issue of training is a valid one: James Porter has questioned whether a non-classicist can competently conduct studies in classical receptions and, on the flip side, whether a classicist can be competent to discuss the reception of classical material in other subject areas and historical contexts,[7] while Michael Broder has acknowledged that adopting a classical receptions approach requires us to "leave our geographical and chronological safety-zones and become conversant with a fifteen-hundred-year post-classical history of classical receptions."[8] Although this is a daunting prospect, Martin Winkler has defended classicists' claims to other fields as legitimate subjects for their own analyses by arguing at length that "[c]lassical philology is the best training ground for interpretive approaches to all and any texts, literary or visual."[9] To this I would add that as scholars of many stripes have noted, enduring texts both visual and written have a multiplicity of meanings and interpretations, never limited to authorial intention or to a single historical or cultural context,[10] and I myself would argue that there is not only room for a variety of responsible critical views, such as that of the film scholar and that of one who approaches the visual text from a classics perspective, but indeed that both views are crucial parts of the scholarly conversation.

In addition to these extra-disciplinary objections, there has also been pushback from those within the classics field who criticize the emphasis on the act of receiving and the perceived implicit devaluation of the ancient works themselves.[11] Porter characterizes this sort of resistance as an "illusion that classical studies and their objects are timeless and eternal, invulnerable to the impingements of history and to contingency (all the while working to erase those impingements in an effort to uncover the unblemished truth of their object)."[12] In answer to this, some point out that the works of antiquity themselves were products of reception – many have noted Virgil's clear engagement in the process[13] – while others have pointed out that despite their literary primacy, Homer's works too not only drew on traditional folk-tales and other narrative sources, but were also a product of the interaction between the traditional story-telling strategies the ancient bards utilized and the performance context and audience response.[14]

Additional intramural objections arise in response to receptions studies that make use of lowbrow productions – most frequently, film – which strikes some as the dumbing down of an elite field and others as a desperate marketing ploy to make esoteric works more accessible and appealing to today's students. In response to the former, not just receptions scholars but even makers of many of these pop culture products have noted that canonical works like those of Homer, Virgil, and the tragedians were the popular entertainment of their own day,[15] while James Clauss has shown that examining even the campiest, most unsophisticated cinematic productions can provide valuable insights into how and why these films draw on ancient works, while uncovering serious commentary on contemporary issues at the same time.[16] To the latter charge, scholars like David Frauenfelder have defended comparisons that utilize film as pedagogically sound in that they "can begin to close the natural distance between student and material, fostering engagement and thus learning."[17] Indeed, with the use of film, the difference in medium can be of considerable pedagogical benefit, offering not only the obvious advantages of variety, time-savings, and appeal, but also helping to emphasize the visual aspects of the ancient written texts and the literary aspects of the modern visual ones, while familiarizing students with formative canonical works in both Western civilization more broadly and in American culture more specifically. More importantly, I have found that drawing on pop culture products both high and low is a valuable way not just to interest students in antiquity, but to bolster understanding – both theirs and mine – of the ancient world and our relationship to it. The most productive discussions I have had in the classroom – those rare times when every student is completely engaged, the very air energized by the synchrony of thoughts all galvanized on an issue of existential import – have all utilized touch-points between the ancient world and the one students inhabit.

In addition to the above criticisms,[18] the enthusiastic application of reception theory to cinematic products in recent years has also been subject to questions about the legitimacy of comparing ancient literary texts to modern visual productions. Many filmmakers themselves, however, have located the roots of their craft in the works of antiquity: Russian director and film theorist Sergei Eisenstein saw the art of cinema as based on a cultural past stretching all the way back to the Greeks,[19] while American director and screenwriter Sam

Peckinpah styled himself a storyteller in the tradition of Homer when he said:

> I don't make documentaries. The facts about the siege of Troy, of the duel between Hector and Achilles and all the rest of it, are a hell of a lot less interesting to me than what Homer makes of it all. And the mere facts tend to obscure the truth, anyway.[20]

Receptions scholars have also argued for the sound basis of this comparison. Winkler, for instance, has argued at length that films can and should be seen as visual "texts" that make a natural and valid comparison with literary ones.[21] Others have approached the issue from the other direction, arguing for the cinematic qualities of the ancient works under consideration in this volume: Camille Paglia asserted in her 1990 book *Sexual Personae* "that Homer is an instinctively 'cinematic' artist and that he bequeathed his long sight lines and striving, densely visualized personalities to the rest of Western literature and art,"[22] a perspective supported by Jonathan Shay when, in arguing for Achilles' social detachment after Patroclus' death, he observes that "Homer uses a dramatic device like the cinematic trick of abruptly cutting off the sound track: The Greek army vanishes, leaving Achilles alone with the Trojan soldiers that he slaughters."[23] Similarly, Fred Mench has argued that in his use of "montage, variation of viewing angle, alternation of close-up and distance shot, and the like," Virgil too employs a "kinetic visual approach" very akin to the techniques utilized by modern filmmakers, adding that "Virgil marshals not only words but images, meter, and scene in much the same way a director marshals film and score-cutting, juxtaposing, shifting focus, emphasizing breaks, or tying sequences together."[24] In teaching the Homeric epics and the *Aeneid*, I myself have found analogies with film a natural comparison and one that helps to bring the epics alive for my students, who are less used to visualizing texts both oral and literary than were ancient audiences. For instance, in Book 16 of the *Iliad*, I discuss the shift to second person as Patroclus' death approaches ("Then, Patroclus, your death became clear to you; for fearsome Apollo met you in fierce combat")[25] as a shift from a more objective distance shot encompassing the whole scene in a movie to a point-of-view shot, where we are put in Patroclus' place, seeing what he sees, a comparison I have found very effective in driving home the impact of the scene.

In addition to objections about textual versus visual, film as a legitimate subject for receptions work has come under fire due to its collaborative and commercial nature. Winkler has spoken to this first point as well, arguing that the collaborative process of filmmaking has parallels in literature and that, ultimately, the director's vision supersedes the individual wills of other contributors to the extent that he or she can be considered either the sole or principal "author."[26] But others, not only scholars of classics and cinema but filmmakers as well, insist on the collaborative nature of filmmaking, even if some products can be seen as the result of the director's singular prevailing artistic vision.[27] While two of the directors considered in this volume (Howard Hawks and John Ford) are now overwhelmingly hailed as cinematic *auteurs*, it is not my intention to argue for the validity of comparisons such as the one I am making here on this basis, but rather regardless of it. In my view, neither the popular, commercial aspect of film nor its collaborative nature justifies its wholesale exclusion from comparisons with ancient texts: Homer's works were wildly popular and performed before audiences of both the elites and the *hoi polloi*, whose tastes were undoubtedly taken into consideration – if they had not been, these products of the oral tradition would not have survived. Nor, of course, are the Homeric epics in any way to be considered the work of one man, despite their traditional attribution to "Homer"; they were changed and altered as they were handed down from bard to bard over the centuries, so that they too can be considered collaborative projects, even if the versions that have come down to us might have been shaped by a single guiding artistic vision. For his part, Virgil took both his audience and his powerful patron into consideration, as well as drawing on established mythological and narrative traditions, so that his work too was not constructed in isolation, but carries in it a variety of influences; and ancient drama, of course, was collaborative by nature, much like film.[28] For these reasons, along with those Winkler sets forth, the gulf between how a film is produced and the construction of ancient epic as a literary work is not as great as it may seem at first glance.

More important for my purposes, however, is the fact that the ancient works and modern films under consideration here, as canonical generic productions, encapsulate similar ideological strains and thus are comparable platforms for gleaning information about their respective society's values and anxieties. Indeed, it can be argued that film in general forms the core of our national dialogue and reflects our collective values in much the same way that epic did in antiquity: as Frauenfelder notes, film is a

> vivid, story-oriented genre and our most public form of popular entertainment. Because it must make money to survive, the film industry must monitor

> closely what pleases its audience. As a result, movies are endlessly reflective of our shared values, aspirations, and beliefs, which make us pay to see stories again and again.[29]

Like epic, film naturally embeds our most closely held ideological assumptions and worldviews. Thus despite the many superficial differences that make them seem odd bedfellows, mainstream cinema forms a more natural comparison with ancient epic poetry than modern genres that might initially seem a better fit, such as contemporary poetry or even epic novels.

While the ancient world as depicted in cinema has been an enormously popular subject of receptions studies, examinations of works that do not conspicuously draw on the past admittedly sit a little awkwardly in this area. Although a smattering of articles and chapters in edited volumes do focus on these sorts of comparisons, less attention has been devoted to them, perhaps in part because of the lack of developed methodologies and in part due to uncertainty over what we are doing and why we are doing it. Yet this approach warrants greater attention, as its advantages are somewhat different than those offered by contemporary works that wear their relationship to antiquity on their sleeves. I have argued elsewhere that from a pedagogical viewpoint, analyzing works whose connections with antiquity are not immediately apparent is often more productive than utilizing works more directly based on ancient sources, as beginning students often view the latter as redundant exercises while more advanced ones get caught up in identifying "inaccuracies"[30] – in both cases placing the emphasis on plot at the expense of meaning. Paglia notes that using modern productions that explicitly draw on ancient material is further complicated by the fact that "dramatizations of classical stories must take into account the European high art tradition since the Renaissance, which has produced an overwhelming number of iconic Greco-Roman images in painting and sculpture that have entered the world canon."[31] Focusing on works with no immediately identifiable connection to the ancient world, conversely, helps to shed these layers, compelling students to look for kinship in theme, character, and ideology, and from there, to extrapolate the all-important "why": why do these works from very different times, places, and cultures concern themselves with like issues and betray similar values and anxieties? What then does this tell us about ourselves, about our Greco-Roman roots, and about the human condition more generally? In my experience, utilizing works that initially seem to have no basis in antiquity helps students block out the white noise and cut to the chase (to use a term conveniently originating in film). As David Frauenfelder puts it:

> This method does not lead students first to study in a detached way how myth is received or reproduced through the ages, but to recognize that good stories have a profound effect on all cultures and that comparison of similar stories from different cultures can illuminate both sides in ways otherwise impossible.[32]

In addition, this approach brings ancient works into present relevance, whereas drawing on works that reference antiquity explicitly has the opposite effect of taking our world back to the past – a subtle but important distinction.

The pedagogical value seems clear – but is that all there is, as some scholars would contend?[33] Or can something deeper take place? Jonathan Shay's *Achilles in Vietnam* suggests that it can: this important study of how Achilles' story in the *Iliad* sheds light on the combat trauma of Vietnam War veterans by allowing us to notice things "that are so easily taken for granted that they are almost invisible"[34] is a powerful demonstration of how viewing the present through the lens of the past can have valuable real-world applications. I would also argue that broader studies which consider significant points of divergence alongside the convergences offer potential for other meaningful insights, as these are directed towards uncovering larger, more systemic relationships. Yet examination of the manifestation of themes, plots, and character types from classical narratives in seemingly unrelated films is challenging because their under-the-surface nature makes broader categorization difficult. As a result, much of the work done so far has consisted of more or less piecemeal, film-by-film examinations. A few scholars have attempted more programmatic approaches: for instance, Erling Holtsmark has outlined appearances of the *katabasis* in various film genres (including Westerns); Jane O'Sullivan has traced the Pygmalion theme through films from *Vertigo* to *Pretty Woman* and beyond; and Martin Winkler has looked at manifestations of Oedipal themes in cinema and television.[35] This thematic approach is useful in that demonstrating the pervasiveness of a particular ancient theme in modern media illustrates effectively that the ancient original functions as more than just a story; instead, it addresses anxieties common in human experience – or at least, perhaps, in patriarchal Western cultures – and thus suggests our particular cultural kinship as well as touching on something more universal and deeply human. A second approach with broader rather than one-to-one applications is the one being attempted here: a systematic examination of important thematic and ideological parallels and analogous functions present in two seemingly disparate genres. While one-to-one comparisons undoubtedly have their place, particularly in achieving specific pedagogical aims or enhancing specific works, these broader generic or thematic studies have the advantage of prompting those who engage in them to look for these themes more widely, rather than understanding them as limited to specific works. In doing so, we make more transparent the transferable nature of the critical thinking skills encouraged in this sort of analysis, as well as suggesting that our culture at large is even today implicated in the sorts of ideologies and behavior patterns that we may otherwise be tempted to see as distant and obsolete remnants of a long-gone civilization. It is my hope that as the field of classical receptions advances, this is one area that will receive additional attention in a more systematic way, providing a broader context through which connections between individual works in antiquity and in contemporary culture can be more productively viewed.

Many will remain unconvinced about the fundamental validity of comparing film with classical literature, or even of receptions work more broadly, but what is clear is that thanks to the foundational work done by scholars like Hardwick, Martindale, and Winkler – along with Jon Solomon, Maria Wyke, and Monica Cyrino, to name a few – the classical receptions movement is gaining ground and increasingly being accepted as a legitimate area of interest – some would argue a crucial one for those who wish to remain conversant with current trends in scholarship and pedagogy.[36] Benefits are many, not least the pedagogical usefulness of capitalizing on students' existing passion for and interest in popular culture productions to promote deeper understanding of the past and demonstrate its continuing relevance to the present. Receptions scholars like Joanna Paul also emphasize the "two-way dynamics of the act of reception – the capacity of a reception to not only be influenced by the 'earlier' text but also to reach back in time and in a sense reconfigure that text";[37] Michael Broder promotes the reception model as one that helps "[prepare] our students to think critically and participate actively as citizens of democratic societies in a globalized, postcolonial, multicultural world" by encouraging "creative and independent thought about such urgent categories as democracy, freedom, and justice";[38] while others stress that such studies encourage us to examine the process of myth-making and recognize that much of the power of the classical past stems from its relation to the current social, political, and moral values that it helps to legitimate.[39] In these ways and more, I personally have found my participation in classical receptions studies enriching, and I am grateful for the opportunity to contribute further to this growing field with this monograph.

NOTES

1 De Pourcq (2012: 221).
2 Hardwick (2003: 6–8) and Broder (2013: 506) credit the origins of the receptions movement to Hans Robert Jauss's theories on "the aesthetics of receptions" in the 1960s followed by Wolfgang Iser's work on reader-response. Hardwick goes on to note the work of Hans-Georg Gadamer, who argued that the meaning of a text was not essential, but dependent on the relationship between past and present. See also De Pourcq (2012: 219–21).
3 De Pourcq (2012: 221).
4 See Broder (2013: 510).
5 Hardwick (2003: 4).
6 As Blumberg noted in a 2008 conference presentation on the Sophoclean hero in Howard Hawks's Westerns, "it's not just the case that we classicists have been jumping the claim on scholars of western cinema, rather film scholars and critics have been horning in on our land for years."
7 Porter (2011: 478–9).
8 Broder (2013: 515).
9 Winkler (2009: 58; see also pp. 20–69, esp. 57–69).
10 See e.g. Wood (1996a: 164) and Eagleton (1996: 61–3, noted in Winkler 2001a: 10).
11 De Pourcq (2012: 220).
12 Porter (2011: 469).
13 Graziosi (2011: 33); Broder (2013: 510); et al.
14 See Budelmann and Haubold (2011: 19); Graziosi (2011: 26–32).
15 Peckinpah qtd. in Murray (1972: 68).
16 Clauss (2008: esp. 52–3 and 63–5).
17 Frauenfelder (2005: 210).
18 For more on these criticisms as applied to film in particular, see Paul (2011: 304).
19 Noted in Winkler (2009: 41).
20 Qtd. in Murray (1972: 72).
21 Winkler (2009: 22–34).
22 As Paglia herself succinctly put it in a subsequent article (1997: 170).
23 Shay (1994: 86).
24 Mench (2001: 219 and 228). I might note without implying agreement that Mench uses as a comparison the non-filmic sense of the *Odyssey* (2001: 228).
25 16.787–9. All translations of ancient epic are mine. Line numbers follow the Loeb editions edited by Jeffrey Henderson.

26 Winkler (2009: 34–50). Many of these arguments are expanded versions of ideas Winkler outlined in his introduction to *Classical Myth and Culture in the Cinema* (2001a: 18–20).
27 Gamel (2001: 149); Kitses (2007: 10); Zinnemann noted in Giannetti (1981: 366).
28 See Gamel (2001: 149).
29 Frauenfelder (2005: 210 n. 1).
30 Day (2014). Paul (2011: 306) notes that the "cataloguing approach," in which lists of historical inaccuracies are given without an examination of why historical authenticity should matter, why it might not matter to filmmakers or audiences, or what these differences can tell us about the receiving culture, was a pitfall of early receptions work on film in particular, but notes an improvement since Wyke (1997).
31 Paglia (1997: 169).
32 Frauenfelder (2005: 210).
33 Paul (2011: 309), following Roisman, sees examinations of works that do not refer directly to antiquity as "primarily of pedagogical value in presenting complex texts and concepts to students in innovative (and relevant) ways." Maria Wyke (2003: 441–3) has also expressed skepticism about the uses of films with non-classical settings other than "where they can expose and illuminate sustained, complex, even deliberate, evocations of antiquity that are then made to resonate with the specific significations of ancient Greece and Rome in the modern world."
34 Shay (1994: 56).
35 Holtsmark (2001); O'Sullivan (2008); Winkler (2008).
36 Winkler, for instance, positions the need "to be knowledgeable about the history of [the classical] past's influence at different times and in different media" as an obligation for all classicists (2009: 20), while Porter warns that "The risks of avoidance are incalculable" (2011: 469).
37 Paul (2011: 307); see also Hardwick (2003: 4); Hardwick and Stray (2011: 4–5).
38 Broder (2013: 505).
39 See Settis (2006); Schein (2011: 75, 84); Broder (2013: 511).

Introduction: Western Film and the Epic Tradition

In the American psyche, the "Wild West" is a mythic-historical place where the nation's values and ideologies were formed. In this violent and uncertain world, the cowboy is the ultimate hero, fighting the bad guys, forging notions of manhood, and delineating what constitutes honor as he works to build civilization out of wilderness. Tales from this mythical place are best known from that most American of media: film. In the Greco-Roman societies that form the foundation of Western civilization, similar narratives were presented in what for them was the most characteristic, and indeed most filmic, genre: epic. Like Western films, the canonical epics of classical antiquity focus on the legendary past and its warriors who worked to establish the ideological framework of their respective civilizations. These parallel cultural roles result in surprising connections between these seemingly disparate yet closely related genres.

Cowboy Classics looks at these broader generic connections and the reasons behind them through examination of some of the best examples of each: the works of Homer and Virgil – undisputed titans of Greco-Roman literature whose epics assumed near-biblical status in their own societies and are still revered as foundational masterworks of Western civilization – and five films from the Golden Age of Westerns[1] that have attained canonical status both through their critical and commercial success and through the influence they have exerted not just on later film productions in various genres, but as important components of cultural literacy in America as well. Even those who have not seen these films – or indeed, any Western movies at all – equate John Wayne with the powerful, charismatic, and intractable epitome of the Western hero as Hawks first presented him in *Red River* (1948); everyone "knows" that showdowns happen at *High Noon* (1952); for many, the cry "Shane! Come back!" (*Shane*,

1953) evokes nostalgia for lost heroes, and the exhortation to "Print the legend" (*The Man Who Shot Liberty Valance*, 1962) touches on the complicated relationship between myth, history, and America's national self-image; and moviegoers of all stripes recognize as important cinematic motifs the hero's return to a homestead burned and a family massacred, the obstinate, world-weary associations of the catch-phrase "That'll be the day," and the isolated hero framed in a doorway, even if they have never heard of John Ford's *The Searchers* (1956). These films provide the most useful comparison precisely because of their prime position on the cultural radar: like the epics of Homer and Virgil, these films have achieved pride of place because they resonate most resoundingly with American cultural anxieties, values, and ideological issues. Thus, they illustrate the principles this study examines most strikingly, helping Americans understand their roots and define their cultural identity, much as Homer and Virgil's epics did for their respective cultures.

After establishing a larger generic kinship, this book undertakes a close examination of these three epics and five films to demonstrate that Westerns, particularly as manifested in the grade-A films of the genre's Golden Age, and classical epic function as equivalent cultural narratives: each genre is anchored in a mythic-historical period from its society's past and each presents narratives that help to delineate foundational ideologies with a particular focus on notions of heroism and masculinity. At the same time, the best works from each of these genres do not present these issues unproblematically, but prompt the audience instead to question the assumptions that underlie core beliefs and value systems. Because of the parallel role these genres play, examining their intersections enhances our understanding of the mechanics at play in both and what they reveal about our cultural identities: in other words, this comparison allows us to use the American Western as a lens through which to view and better understand the more remote works of antiquity. Conversely, analyzing the dynamics at play in ancient epic as a means of shedding light on works from popular culture provides the distance that allows us to see Western films, in whose ideological undercurrents we are more directly implicated, in a more objective light. In doing so, we can more effectively take into consideration what they reveal about our own twentieth/twenty-first-century world and its relationship to the Greco-Roman civilizations that are our cultural ancestors.

BACKGROUND

My interest in looking at ancient epic and Western film as cultural counterparts began with John Ford's *The Searchers*, which, when viewed through the lens of my classical background, struck me as a Western version of Homer's *Odyssey*. I presented a paper on this comparison at the 2001 Southwest Texas Popular/American Culture Association's annual conference, and eventually developed it into an article that appeared in a special issue of *Arethusa* dedicated to examining classical representations in popular culture.[2] Since then, my interest in the relationship between these genres has expanded far beyond one epic and one film, just as my appreciation of the importance of this comparison has grown.

While I do not claim to be the first to consider these parallels, the scholarly attention that has been devoted to connections between the Western genre and the classical past – though somewhat scattered – suggests strongly that something important is going on here which merits further attention. Perhaps credit for initial recognition of the connection between ancient epic and the themes that preoccupy our notions of the Old West should go to Harry Brown, whose 1962 novel *The Stars in Their Courses* is conscientiously constructed as a Western version of Homer's *Iliad* and the surrounding episodes from the Trojan War cycle. The transparent nature of his project is evident not only in clear plot parallels and in the alliterative aspect of the names of characters who serve as counterparts to the Homeric originals,[3] but even in occasional pointed linguistic allusions ("Thus made they funeral for Hallock, breaker of horses").[4] Howard Hawks later developed Brown's novel into the 1966 Western *El Dorado*, although Hawks and screenwriter Leigh Brackett altered the plot considerably, much to Brown's dismay.[5] While largely ignored since, in a 2011 article in *Classical World* Robert Haas directed attention to Brown's work, arguing that using *The Stars in Their Courses* to teach Homeric epics offers a "useful alternate avenue of approach for the student puzzled how to make contact with Homer's world of 2500 years ago or uncertain of its modern relevance."[6]

Along with the loose link between Western film and the classical past Hawks demonstrates through his use of Brown's novel, other Western directors have either implied or expressed a more direct relationship between their work in the Western genre and Greco-Roman antiquity. Homeric references are scattered throughout John Ford's films: in addition to those touched on in later chapters, in his 1939 *Stagecoach*, Doc Boone sarcastically addresses the landlady evicting him with, "Is this the face that wrecked a thousand ships and burned the towerless tops of Ilium? . . . Farewell, fair Helen!"[7] In *The Quiet Man* (1952), the local matchmaker repeatedly (and enthusiastically) describes the tempestuous marriage of the titular hero (John Wayne) as "Homeric," while in his 1957 *The Wings of Eagles*, Ford inserts a joke about the *Odyssey* in a conversation between a director and screenwriter while a volume of that text lies on the table between them.[8] Furthermore, in addition to Sam Peckinpah framing himself as a storyteller in the Homeric tradition as noted in the prologue, both he and Fred Zinnemann have positioned their work in the tradition of the Greek tragedians: in a 1972 *Playboy* interview, Peckinpah responded to criticism of the violence in films like *The Wild Bunch* (1969) by drawing on the idea of catharsis as "a purging of the emotions through pity and fear" stemming back to the plays of Euripides and Sophocles,[9] while Zinnemann also drew on Aristotelian dramatic ideals when he noted of *High Noon* (1952) in his 1992 autobiography that "The construction of the screenplay happens to follow the ancient rules of Greek drama – the three unities of time, space and action."[10] It is worth noting, in addition, that David Milch originally pitched a series about police in Neronian Rome to HBO, but regrouped upon learning that the *Rome* series was already in the works, with *Deadwood* (2004–6) as the result.[11]

Among academics, scholars of many stripes – philosophers, political scientists, literary theorists, English professors, and film critics – have long recognized the Western's connections with the Greco-Roman past. To name a few, André Bazin, John Cawelti, Rita Parks, Peter French, and Robert Pippin have touched on connections between the Western hero and his classical predecessors, along with other confluences between Western themes and character-types and those of Greco-Roman antiquity, while George Fenin and William Everson have pointed to Westerns as a "re-elaboration of the Olympian world."[12] Nancy Warfield has argued for Plato's influence on the works of John Ford; Gerald Mast has positioned Howard Hawks's *Red River* as a descendant of Greek epic; and Roberta Reeder and Glenn Frankel have connected the same film to Greek tragedy.[13] In classical scholarship more specifically, Martin Winkler made the initial foray into this comparison with his 1985 essay "Classical Mythology and the Western Film," but interest picked up considerably following Mary Whitlock Blundell and Kirk Ormand's 1997 article "Western Values, or the Peoples Homer: *Unforgiven* as a Reading of the *Iliad*." Since then, E. Christian Kopff has compared Clint Eastwood's Western (and other) heroes to Aeneas; James Clauss, Erling Holtsmark, and Judith

Fletcher have all examined manifestations of the *katabasis* theme in Westerns; Winkler has looked at the general kinship between Western heroes and Greek ones, as well as arguing for *The Searchers*' connections to both tragedy and Homer's *Iliad*, while as noted above, I have discussed the same film as an *Odyssey*; Geoff Bakewell has looked at Oedipal connections in *Lonestar* (1996); Kostas Myrsiades has looked at *The Gunfighter* (1950) and its connections to Homer; and Carl Rubino has positioned *Shane* (1953) as an *Iliad*.[14]

Although the parallels that have been elucidated between Westerns and classical antiquity are scattered across genres and often focus on comparisons between specific works or the productions of particular authors and directors, the persistent recognition of these connections from a variety of disciplinary viewpoints and generic perspectives surely indicates that there is some fundamental basis for this comparison – a suggestion given support, I would argue, by a tendency for those associated with classically themed films to pop up in Westerns and vice-versa (Table 1). While the majority of the chapters in this book in some ways function as case studies of specific films and how they relate to ancient epic (or epic and tragedy in the final chapter), I am hopeful that taken cumulatively, along with the contextualization provided in the introduction and conclusion, they suggest something larger. Although I began with the premise that one film – John Ford's *The Searchers* – demonstrated important parallels with Homer's *Odyssey*, my expanding research has ultimately led me to understand this relationship more broadly: that is, I contend that America's vision of the struggles required to forge the nation and of the sort of men whose heroic nature was vital to this nation-building process has fundamental parallels with Greek and Roman ideas about the formation of their national identities and the men upon whose heroic feats their own nations were built. Western film and ancient epic – and often ancient drama as well – function as ideal vehicles for expressing these notions, as both draw on narratives from the formative period in their nation's history, encapsulating deeply held beliefs, values, and ideologies while at the same time serving as important mediums for commenting on contemporary social and civil issues. Although many Americans today may not have seen a traditional Western film, its generic fabric both embeds the national character and its generic specifics are in turn so embedded in the national consciousness that they are virtually inseparable. Because of the entrenched nature of these associations, I contend that generalized American audiences necessarily read the presentation of such things as heroism, masculinity, honor, women's roles, confrontation, and conflict in ancient epic

Table 1 Actors who have appeared in both Westerns and classically themed movies

Actor	Western	Ancient World
Marlon Brando	*The Missouri Breaks* (1976)	*Julius Caesar* (1953)
Russell Crowe	*3:10 to Yuma* (2007)	*Gladiator* (2000)
Tony Curtis	*Winchester '73* (1950)	*Spartacus* (1960)
	Kansas Raiders (1950)	
Kirk Douglas	*Gunfight at the OK Corral* (1957)	*Ulysses* (1954)
	A Gunfight (1971)	*Spartacus* (1960)
Morgan Freeman	*Unforgiven* (1992)	*Ben Hur* (2016)
Robert Halmi, Sr.	*Lonesome Dove* (1989)	*The Odyssey* (1997)
Richard Harris	*Unforgiven* (1992)	*Gladiator* (2000)
Charlton Heston	*Big Country* (1958)	*Ben Hur* (1959)
	Will Penny (1967)	*Walt Disney's Hercules* (1997)
	Tombstone (1993)	
John Hurt	*Wild Bill* (1995)	*I, Claudius* (1976)
		Immortals (2011)
		Hercules (2014)
Val Kilmer	*Tombstone* (1993)	*Alexander* (2004)
Logan Lerman	*3:10 to Yuma* (2007)	*Percy Jackson* films (2010, 2013)
Ray McKinnon	*Deadwood* (2004–6)	*O Brother, Where Art Thou?* (2000)
Ian McShane	*Deadwood* (2004–6)	*A.D.* (1985)
		Hercules (2014)
Brad Pitt	*The Assassination of Jesse James by the Coward Robert Ford* (2007)	*Troy* (2004)
Anthony Quinn	*Oxbow Incident* (1943)	*Ulysses* (1954)
	Buffalo Bill (1944)	*Attila* (1954)
	Ride Vaquero! (1953)	
	Man from Del Rio (1956)	
Woody Strode	*Two Rode Together* (1961)	*Androcles and the Lion* (1952)
	Rawhide (two episodes 1961)	*Spartacus* (1960)
	The Man Who Shot Liberty Valance (1962)	*Scipio the African* (1971)
	Once Upon a Time in the West (1968)	

through a "Westerns" lens. By taking a closer look at these generic intersections and examining both correspondences and points of divergence, we can increase not only our appreciation of ancient epic and Western cinema, but improve our understanding of the ways in which material that at first seems unrelated can influence our reception of works from both genres.

GENERIC SIMILARITIES

Western scholar John Cawelti sees the Western as a prime example of what Northrop Frye calls "the *mythos* of romance," one of four basic story forms, this one based on an adventure which most commonly takes the form of a quest. Frye divides the romance into three main stages, drawing on Greek terminology: the *agon*, or conflict; the *pathos*, or death-struggle; and the *anagnorisis*, or recognition of the hero's worth (even if he does not survive).[15] Joseph Campbell has made this basic "quest" pattern a familiar part of the mythological hero's journey, of which Odysseus' perilous and drawn-out homeward voyage after the Trojan War is the prototypical example, while Aeneas' flight from Troy and his expedition to found a new home in Italy is clearly based on the Odyssean model. Western film provides numerous explicit examples of this type of heroic journey: in addition to two that will be examined in later chapters – *Red River* with its dangerous cattle drive and *The Searchers* with its quest to retrieve an abducted niece – films like *Stagecoach*, *Winchester '73* (1950), *Wagon Master* (1950), *The Naked Spur* (1953), *3:10 to Yuma* (1957 and 2007), *True Grit* (1969 and 2010), and *Big Jake* (1971) all center on a perilous search or journey, each culminating in a heroic battle where the hero proves transcendent. Most epics and Westerns can be analyzed as manifestations of the heroic quest, even when the story does not center on a literal journey: both Achilles in the *Iliad* and J. B. Books in *The Shootist* (1976), for instance, face an existential crisis which causes them to question established notions of heroic worth and make peace with their own mortality, struggles which can be read as metaphorical versions of the hero's journey.

While epic and Westerns both fit this larger literary/mythic pattern, it is, admittedly, one that can easily be applied to heroic tales across many genres. I would argue, however, for a much closer relationship between ancient epic and Western film, a kinship that stems from their equivalence in setting and cultural function. Both genres use fictional or fictionalized characters and narratives set in a formative period from the past as a means of exploring national identity, establishing social norms, and justifying persistent ideologies. The works of Homer, many believe, are rooted in a historical conflict between Bronze Age "Greeks" and Trojans; but even if the characters and stories themselves have historical basis, they are heavily distorted and mythologized. Virgil, of course, consciously weaves references to real characters and events into his largely mythological foundation story; but even these historical allusions are prone to the distortion of imperial propaganda or artistic agenda. In an example of this in Western film, *Broken Arrow* (1950) provides a specific 1870 time setting and draws on historical figures like Tom Jeffords, Cochise, and Geronimo, while the hero's introductory voice-over emphasizes that the events of the film happened "exactly as you'll see it" (other than the practical consideration of changing the Apache language to English). Yet despite this assertion, this historically based film was heavily dramatized, with the character of Sonseeahray invented wholesale as a love-interest. Similarly, *Big Jake* utilizes a newsreel-style prologue that overviews developments in America in its 1909 time setting, with references to historical figures from Albert Einstein to President Taft. It ends by acknowledging the birth of moving pictures with *The Great Train Robbery*, and contrasting that "make-believe drama" with the ostensibly "real" crossing of the Rio Bravo by nine men whose attack on the McCandles's ranch initiates the action of the (fictional) narrative. The position of such works at the intersection of myth and history is strategic in that it suggests enough truth to be relevant and significant to the audience, but enough fiction to allow difficult issues to be grappled with and scrutinized from a more comfortable distance.[16]

One of the issues that benefits from this distancing is the question of national identity, which is only truly knowable if we understand from where we came. Greek epic looks back to a time of larger-than-life heroes, like the semi-divine Achilles and Athena's darling, Odysseus. Although the historical Greeks saw men "as men are now" as diminished, this view of their glorious past was crucial to their view of themselves as superior, central, and somehow better than the "barbarians" who surrounded them. The model these heroes provide as speakers of words and doers of deeds both reflected and shaped notions of what men were expected to be, while the portraits of women like Andromache and Penelope did the same for feminine ideals. Virgil's portrait of Rome's roots in the mythological past not only helped promote Augustus' regime, but also positioned the Empire itself as destined, its people as divinely favored; at the same time, Aeneas' *pietas* showcased the trait thought to best define Roman male identity, while women like Dido and Lavinia offered cautionary tales or models for women's behavior. Likewise, the Western's place on the frontier of civilization encapsulates the American view of their essential independence, self-sufficiency, and uniqueness of character, while its heroes furnish a paradigm of rugged masculinity, and its schoolmarms and saloon girls provide important information about women's virtue. Jim Kitses ranks the Western alongside jazz and baseball, saying that the genre "represents a distillation of quintessential aspects of national character and sensibility."[17] The genre's associations with what it means to be an American are strikingly suggested in John Ford's choice of words when introducing himself to the Director's Guild in 1950 before speaking against a loyalty oath (and thus against a blacklist) in the McCarthy-era witch-hunts: "My name's John Ford. I make Westerns." Since Westerns were not very popular at this time and many of Ford's early achievements were in other genres,[18] this was certainly a calculated move, which both in syntax and in associations positioned Ford as a simple, quintessential American.

HEROIC MANHOOD

The fictionalized histories these works construct thus in many ways embody – and help to shape – their respective societies' national self-image, crucial to which are notions of manhood. The Greco-Roman world was intensely patriarchal, and while we have certainly made large strides in this area, our own roots in patriarchal systems are likewise firmly embedded. Both genres, therefore, demonstrate an intense concern with defining masculinity, and as a corollary, showcasing appropriate feminine roles, which are inevitably positioned as secondary or peripheral.

In both epic and Western, the hero provides the model of idealized masculinity. These men are warriors with superhuman skills: in epic, this is quite literal, as Achilles and Aeneas both have goddess-mothers, and they along with Odysseus frequently have divine support in battle. While Western heroes' godlike prowess is less literal, their abilities are framed as incredible – Jimmy Ringo (*The Gunfighter*), for instance, is so fast on the draw that others repeatedly marvel that he only has two hands – and they regularly overcome seemingly impossible odds: in *Stagecoach*, having weighed the odds, a newspaperman drafts an article about the upcoming showdown that includes the Ringo Kid's death, with other casualties TBD; Ringo triumphs, of course, dispatching all three of the dangerous Plummer brothers, and doing so with only three bullets. The godlike nature of these heroes is also frequently emphasized by their near-invincibility: Big Jake McCandles's standard response to the frequent refrain "I thought you were dead!" is an unperturbed, "Not hardly," while numerous

Western heroes – Shane (*Shane*), Ethan Edwards (*The Searchers*), and Josey Wales (*The Outlaw Josey Wales*, 1976), to name a few – carry on relatively undaunted with wounds that would kill lesser men.

Epic and Western warriors are also often set apart by their special weaponry, attire, and attributes: both Winkler and Blundell and Ormand have noted the special relationship of heroes in both genres to their weapons.[19] From Achilles' Pelian ash spear and Odysseus' bow to Steve's engraved pistol bequeathed to the Virginian (*The Virginian*, 1929), Matthew Garth's enviable gun (*Red River*), Big Jake McCandles's derringer "Betsy," Robert E. Lee Clayton's Creedmore (*The Missouri Breaks*, 1976), and Ned Logan's Spencer rifle (*Unforgiven*, 1992), weapons are highly individualized (as Blondie says in *The Good, The Bad, and the Ugly* (1966), "Every gun makes its own tune"), phallic symbols of heroic power and virulent masculinity. In *Winchester '73*, the power of a "special weapon" as a symbol of heroic worth is taken to the extreme, as the titular gun changes hands through competition, theft, gambling, murder, battle, provocation, coercion, and duel.

Costuming, too, takes on heroic significance: the importance of the divine armor of Achilles and Aeneas is clear, but the fringed buckskin of Shane, Clint Eastwood's Mexican poncho in the "Dollars trilogy" (1964–66), the out-of-place hats of Mississippi (*El Dorado*) and Raylan Givens (*Justified*, 2010–15), and even the spirit stick of Ethan Edwards, the blues harp of Harmonica (*Once Upon a Time in the West*, 1968), and the sheriff's badges of Wyatt Earp (*My Darling Clementine*, 1946), Will Kane (*High Noon*), John T. Chance (*Rio Bravo*, 1959), and Seth Bullock (*Deadwood*) all mark their bearers out as special. These trappings, too, are frequently fetishized, for instance through arming scenes where ancient warriors don their gear, which is described in lavish detail, or where cowboys strap on spurs, buckle their holsters, and situate their hats just so.[20] As John Cawelti notes of the Western hero's regalia, but as is equally applicable to ancient armor, these accouterments are both utilitarian and highly artificial,[21] which not only provides an interesting parallel to the oxymoronic blend of history and fiction in the genre, but also signifies the hero's paradoxical nature as a boundary-crosser who establishes order and paves the way for civilization through an excess of violence.

Along with these visual signifiers, heroes in both genres also have a special relationship to language. The leaders of antiquity were expected to be not just doers of deeds, but also speakers of words: both Odysseus and Aeneas draw on verbal strategies to help them negotiate tricky situations – in *Odyssey* 6, for example, when a naked and battered Odysseus successfully begs help from the young princess Nausikaa and her maids. Achilles in the underworld, too, rejoices upon hearing that his son has distinguished himself not just in battle, but in counsel as well (*Od.* 11.504–40). Western heroes, in contrast, are distinguished by laconism, and when they do speak, they use terse phrases, omitting any element extraneous to understanding. The Ringo Kid, for instance, leaves the subject implied and clips words to the bare minimum, even when giving information vital to the group's safety: "Saw a ranch house burnin' last night." Despite this apparent difference, the hero's relationship to language in both cases functions as a signifier of his superior nature, indicating in epic a man with a balance of strengths and in Westerns one too occupied with matters of import to waste time with words. Moreover, as Anne Carson has shown for Greco-Roman antiquity and Jane Tompkins for Westerns, the idealized male language is in both cases set off by the garrulousness of women, whose prattling nature functions to highlight masculine gravity and self-control[22] – a contrast the characteristically brusque Josey Wales highlights when he asks his sidekick Lone Watie in irritation, "Hell man, can't you get her to shut up?"

In another seeming contradiction, heroes of both epic and Western are invariably men of honor, but measure it with a personal yardstick. Achilles, for instance, suggests an individual reckoning of what constitutes honor when he rejects Agamemnon's more-than-adequate offer of restitution for his offense (*Il.* 9.308–429) and tells the ambassadors who have come to persuade him, "I do not need that kind of honor. My honor comes from Zeus, and it will be mine . . . as long as breath remains in my breast" (*Il.* 9.607–9). Western heroes consistently transgress social mores – the titular hero of *The Virginian* mischievously switches babies at a christening, for instance, and Josey Wales spits on enemies' corpses – but demonstrate strict adherence to other codes of conduct they hold dearer: the Virginian hangs his best friend for cattle rustling, and Wales refuses to surrender with the rest of his comrades. Masculine identity in both genres is also inextricably bound to reputation. Epic heroes are quick to brag of their deeds on the one hand – Odysseus' imprudent boast to the Cyclops comes to mind (*Od.* 9.502–5) – while on the other, risking death is preferable to damaging one's reputation: in the *Iliad*, fear of the latter leads Hector to reject his wife's sensible suggestion of a defensive strategy in favor of more glorious fighting in the front ranks (6.431–46), while in the *Odyssey*, we are reminded of Ajax's loss of face in the dispute over Achilles' armor, to which Odysseus attributes Ajax's death (11.543–51). Western heroes, in contrast, often pretend to be unaffected by concern with their reputation: from Shane to J. B. Books (*The Shootist*) to William Munny (*Unforgiven*), Western heroes refuse to trumpet past exploits and reject exaggerated accounts of their deeds, while frequently the concealment of name in part or entirely (as in *The Virginian*, *Shane*, *A Fistful of Dollars* (1964), *The Good, the Bad and the Ugly*, *Once Upon a Time in the West*, *High Plains Drifter* (1973), *The Shootist*, *Pale Rider* (1985), and *Unforgiven*) suggests ambivalence to reputation, with the implication of an imperviousness to requiring it.

Yet honor and reputation, of course, are flip sides of the same coin, and one instance where they can be clearly seen to come together in both genres is in the insistence on standing one's ground in battle. In classical antiquity, fighting in the forefront brought the greatest glory, and this was even the preferred way to die: when in peril at sea, Odysseus envies his comrades who died at Troy (*Od.* 5.306–12), while Turnus, led away from battle by a divinely manufactured phantom of Aeneas, feels himself so disgraced that he attempts suicide (*Aen.* 10.666–86). Western heroes, too, are compelled by a mixture of public repute and a personal sense of honor to face their foes: the Virginian and Will Kane refuse to leave town to avoid a showdown; Shane pointedly re-enters the saloon he has been warned to stay out of; and the heroes of *The Magnificent Seven* (1960) return to face Calvera even after the townspeople have betrayed them. As the Ringo Kid puts it in John Ford's *Stagecoach*, "there are some things a man just can't run away from." That variations on Ringo's statement have become a standard catchphrase for the Western hero suggests how intimately bound honor is with the concept of ideal manhood so central to works in these genres.[23]

WOMEN

In contrast to the centrality of constructions of masculinity in Westerns and in epic, most scholars view women's roles in these genres, along with their values, concerns, and anxieties, as peripheral. Their marginalized position and superfluousness to the male agenda is suggested by the large number of epic and Western heroes whose women are dead or absent, or who refuse to take on the burden of a marriage in the first place. In the *Iliad*, Achilles is unencumbered by a wife, and Aeneas loses both Creusa and Dido in the course of the *Aeneid*. In Westerns, Tom Dunson (*Red River*), Tom Jeffords, Josey Wales, William Munny, and Walt Longmire (*Longmire*, 2012–) are widowers; Jimmy Ringo, Howard Kemp (*The Naked Spur*), Ethan Edwards, Tom Doniphon (*The Man Who Shot Liberty Valance*, 1962), and Raylan Givens lose their wives or would-be wives, usually to another; and many Western heroes simply remain unconnected – a condition the men of *The Magnificent Seven* assert is par for the course for gunmen like themselves.

Women who do play an important role function primarily as foils that serve to magnify male heroic traits, while their concerns appear to be introduced only to be pushed aside by the masculine agenda, which is thereby validated and given primacy.[24] In both genres, expectations for feminine virtue are often suggested through a woman cast as pure – particularly in regards to sexual abstinence or fidelity, signalled by their indicators, modesty and restraint – who is set in contrast with a woman of ill-repute. Thus the virgin (or faithful wife)/whore (or betraying woman) dichotomy so often found in antiquity and epitomized by the juxtaposition between Penelope and Clytemnestra in Homer's *Odyssey* is paralleled in Westerns by the stock roles of schoolmarm and saloon girl, as seen with the virtuous Clementine Carter and the sympathetic but two-timing Chihuahua in *My Darling Clementine*. An even closer parallel can be seen in *The Naked Spur*, where the hero's girl Mary, who betrayed him while he was away at war, selling his ranch out from under him and running away with another man, is cast as a Clytemnestra figure and juxtaposed with Lina, whose virtue seems questionable at first, but who in the end is revealed as a faithful "Penelope," a woman who stands by the hero and facilitates his honorable action. And while these women may ostensibly serve as the origin of male disputes, the underlying conflict is inevitably grounded in masculine honor or ambition, a dynamic Blundell and Ormand have identified in both the *Iliad* and in *Unforgiven*, where Helen's abduction and the mutilation of Delilah Fitzgerald prompt the action, but the real conflict is anchored in male honor.[25] A similar dynamic is also evident in the conflict over Penelope in the *Odyssey* and Lavinia in the *Aeneid*, as well as in John Elder's determination to seek vengeance on the man who killed his father and stole their family ranch, which he asserts is "the least I can do for [my mother]" – an intention that his mother's confidant Mary scorns as contrary to what she would have wanted (*The Sons of Katie Elder*, 1965).

In other cases, women are positioned as complications or as obstacles to male achievement: Andromache tries to hold Hector back from the front lines in Book 6 of the *Iliad*; Calypso imprisons Odysseus, keeping him from his goal; Dido tempts Aeneas to abandon his quest and settle in Carthage; and time and again, women in Westerns – including Molly Stark Wood in *The Virginian*, Amy Kane in *High Noon*, Marian Starrett in *Shane*, and Sarah Wheeler in *Pale Rider* – plead with their men to avoid violent confrontation.[26] But of course, in accordance with generic expectations, the hero disregards the expressed values and needs of his woman, privileging heroic action instead. In both genres, women who are in the end deemed virtuous are those who contribute, or at least concede, to the heroic male agenda: Andromache accepts Hector's viewpoint; Penelope enables Odysseus' revenge; Creusa's ghost steps aside to make room for another wife who will promote the cause of Rome; both Molly and Amy embrace their men, disregarding their own ultimatums; and Marian, like Andromache, supports her man despite her objections to his intended plan of action. On a related note, both genres contain examples of women who appear headstrong and seem or threaten to act independently – women like Penelope, Clytemnestra, Dido, the Trojan women, and Camilla in epic, and like Tess Millay (*Red River*), Laurie Jorgensen (*The Searchers*), Feathers (*Rio Bravo*), and Jill McBain (*Once Upon a Time in the West*) in Westerns. These women must either take on secondary roles as patient supporters (Penelope, Laurie, and Feathers), become social mediators (Tess), or risk sacrifice (Clytemnestra, Dido, and Camilla) or abandonment (the Trojan women and Jill). As a result, while these women offer both positive and negative role models against which female virtue and behavior can be judged, in many ways their main purpose in both classical epic and in Westerns is to provide a reference point against which ideal masculine behavior can be developed and defined.

INTERROGATING IDEOLOGIES

While the male perspective is regularly validated in the end, the objections to violence and resistance to the male agenda which are so often voiced by women in these genres provide a legitimate dissenting viewpoint that not only provides a satisfying plot complication, but also underscores the complexity of the issues at hand. Indeed, despite the widespread impression of a clear-cut "white hats vs. black hats" or "cowboys vs. Indians" mentality in Westerns, the canonical epics and better Westerns under consideration here are far from morally simplistic, but instead grapple with existential issues such as conflicting value systems, contradictions between law and justice, and confrontation with death. What Robert Pippin has said of directors like Ford, Hawks, and Zinnemann could equally well apply to the epics of Homer and Virgil:

> What *is* true is that their presentations of conflict, hesitations, ambiguity, and crises largely concern characters trying to resolve issues of right, justice, responsibility, honor, and the claims of the public world versus the private, and that these situations are presented in both historical and psychological terms that greatly complicate any neat moral dividing line between characters, any straightforward assessment of events.[27]

In one indication of this, the heroes often come into conflict with authority over issues of justice and right action: Achilles butts heads with Agamemnon, Odysseus incurs the wrath of Poseidon, and Western heroes are cast as righteous outlaws as often as they are lawmen – the Ringo Kid, Jimmy Ringo, John Elder, the men of *The Wild Bunch*, J. B. Books, Josey Wales, and William Munny, for example.

Regardless of which side of the law they stand on, the heroes of epic and Westerns grapple with many of the same issues, especially, as Blundell and Ormand have noted, "the justice of revenge, and the interrelationship of violence, law, and persuasion at the heart of the social order."[28] Heroes of both genres, in response to a slight that touches deeply on issues of identity, succumb to a rage that is equal parts savage and superhuman, and the vengeance they seek is routinely cast as both necessary and excessive. Achilles, of course, is the *ur*-example of this phenomenon, slaughtering and mutilating not only Hector, but countless Trojans without regard for the usual protocols of battle – and as Jonathan Shay points out, in direct contradiction to his previous behavior.[29] Odysseus, likewise, refuses Penelope's suitors' offer of reasonable restitution, even after killing their ringleader (*Od.* 22.45–67), and proceeds to slaughter them to a man, along with the maids who slept with them; and in vengeance for Pallas' death, Aeneas in the end succumbs to the same *furor* (impassioned fury) which has been characterized as the antithesis of Roman male virtue throughout the epic (*Aen.* 12.919–57). Likewise vengeance is a constant theme in the Western genre: Wyatt Earp, the Ringo Kid, Lin McAdam (*Winchester '73*), Will Lockhart (*The Man from Laramie*, 1955), John Elder, Harmonica, the Wild Bunch, the nameless avenger of *High Plains Drifter*, Josey Wales, and William Munny are all gripped by rage at the death of a family member or comrade, and pursue their vengeance insatiably until the offending party pays the ultimate price.

Yet despite the heroic stature of the men who seek this vengeance, the better examples of epic and Western film use this theme to interrogate the justice of this revenge rather than presenting it as unproblematic, and through this critique implicitly call into question the construction of the masculine ideologies embodied by the heroes who pursue it. In the *Odyssey*, for instance, the cyclical nature of revenge is suggested when in response to Odysseus' massacre of the suitors – an act of vengeance for their abuse of his household – their fathers and brothers confront Odysseus and his allies in order to avenge their lost kin. In *El Dorado*, Milt draws attention to the same problem when immediately after Mississippi kills Charlie, he steps up and says, "You killed Charlie 'cause he killed your friend, right? . . . Well it happens Charlie was a good friend of mine." Both genres reject simple coming-to-terms or diplomatic resolution: in these two examples, violence is only averted by a *deus/-a ex machina* device when Athena and Cole Thornton intervene (conveniently putting an end to the violence when the balance is in favor of the heroic protagonist); in most cases, however, the cycle of retribution can only be stopped by extraordinary violence or near-total obliteration, as is well-illustrated by the carnage Achilles effects before killing and mutilating Hector and sacrificing twelve Trojan youths over Patroclus' bier (*Il.* 23.175–7); in the inferno that caps the violence in *The Sons of Katie Elder*; in the bloodbath that ends *The Wild Bunch*; and in the town of Lago transformed into hell-on-earth in *High Plains Drifter*. Too often, it is only after enacting such violent excess that the larger-than-life heroes of these works can come to terms with grievous loss or injury.

IDENTITY ISSUES

In addition to the problematic nature of vengeance, issues of right and wrong are further complicated by the fact that the antagonist is routinely set against the hero as an alter ego. In the *Iliad*, Hector is the bulwark of the Trojans, just as Achilles is among the Greeks, but unlike Achilles, whose divine ancestry makes him almost superhuman, Hector is a resolutely human hero, as is emphasized through his familial ties. His function as Achilles' counterpart is suggested by Hector's assumption of Achilles' original armor, so that when they finally face off, Achilles in his immortal armor is in some respects confronting the human aspects of himself with which he is struggling to come to terms. Odysseus, too, confronts his alter ego in a sense when he faces the suitors. Throughout the epic, the fate of Agamemnon, who returned home from Troy only to be slaughtered at a feast by his wife's lover Aegisthus, has been held up in warning as a potential outcome for Odysseus, whose home is overrun by suitors. Odysseus himself, however, has exhibited behavior not entirely unlike that of Aegisthus and the suitors when he invades the Cyclops Polyphemus' home, appropriates his property, and maims him while he is in his cups. Thus when Odysseus slays Antinoos, who has wooed his own wife, as he sits at a banquet table, Homer implies a similar dynamic between Odysseus and his suitors: like Achilles, he conquers not just an enemy, but one who embodies the negative traits he would deny in himself. Aeneas likewise: his nemesis Turnus has been incited to war by the fury Allecto, subjecting him to the same sort of excess of passion and violent behavior exhibited by Dido, the Trojan mothers, and Amato, and which has throughout the epic been cast as the antithesis of the Roman male virtue of *severitas* (seriousness of purpose, self-control). When he sees that the conquered and supplicant Turnus wears his deceased ward Pallas' belt, Aeneas succumbs to a similar excess of passion and kills him in a fury, again revealing an equivalence of traits in the two men, aspects which Aeneas has tried to suppress in himself.

A similar dynamic is often present in Westerns, indicated by the hero and his adversary's shared traits: not only are they are frequently positioned as the two fastest draws in the West, they are both routinely cast as powerful, unflinching, single-minded, and indomitable. Deborah Thomas, for instance, has noted links between John T. Chance and *Rio Bravo*'s co-antagonists Joe and Nathan Burdette in the "potential for violence" Chance shares with Joe and in the "bottled up" quality he shares with Nathan.[30] The function of the hero and his foe as counterparts is also sometimes reinforced linguistically or implied visually, most typically through parallel shots of the two in the final showdown (Fig. I.1). And as with classical epic, the antagonism between the two has deeper implications, as David Milch suggests in his discussion of the complex hate/respect relationship between Seth Bullock and *Deadwood*'s ruthless saloon-owner and pimp Al Swearengen, when he says, "The violence between Bullock and Swearengen is necessary ... because they are parts of the same soul."[31] For this reason, the most significant conflicts in A-Westerns are not stereotypical battles between "cowboys and Indians," but clashes between white men. In *Wagon Master*, for instance, the initially threatening Navajo welcome the pioneers into their camp, while the real menace is posed from within by the malevolent Clegg brothers. Even more suggestive is the conflict in *The Man from Laramie*,

I.1 Joe (Clint Eastwood) and Ramón Rojo (Gian Maria Volonté) in the final shootout sequence from *A Fistful of Dollars* (1964). Jolly Film, Constantin Film Produktion, Ocean Films.

where the hero pursues vengeance not on the Apaches who killed his brother, but on the white man who sold them the repeating rifles they used in the ambush.

In his analysis of Bullock's relationship with Swearengen, David Milch draws on Sigmund Freud's "narcissism of minor differences," which locates the roots of the most violent antagonisms, such as the ones found in epic and Westerns, in the discomfort provoked by intense similarities.[32] Others may see connections with Carl Jung's notion of the "shadow" figure, onto which the conscious "ego" casts what it considers its own inferior or unacceptable traits. Although it would be anachronistic to apply modern psychological theories to works from antiquity, and I do not intend to do so in any formal sense, the positioning of the adversary as a counterpart of the hero in these genres does suggest in both cases a concern with sorting out issues of identity. Exploration of these identity issues is often complicated in both genres by the presence of a third party, a sympathetic subordinate who exhibits a somewhat softer, weaker – often more "feminine" – nature.[33] This dynamic is clearly seen in the *Iliad* in the person of Patroclus: despite his ferocity on the battlefield, through his concern for the suffering of his fellow Greek warriors (11.806–

48, 15.390–404, 16.20–45) and the recounting of his attempts to comfort the captive war-prize Briseis (19.287–300), Homer emphasizes his softer qualities and juxtaposes them with Achilles' hardness (16.34–5). As with Hector, this role is also suggested sartorially, as Patroclus assumes Achilles' armor in his own face-off with the Trojan warrior.[34] As Blundell and Ormand have suggested, Ned Logan fills a parallel role in *Unforgiven*: though a formidable warrior in his own right, his softness when compared with Munny is suggested when he admits that he no longer has the stomach for killing and quits the mission.[35] This relationship is again emphasized through an exchange: Little Bill confiscates the Spencer rifle when he captures Ned, but having regained it, Munny uses it to dispatch the man who has killed his friend. Deborah Thomas's analysis of *Rio Bravo* suggests that Dude fills a similar role for Chance,[36] and David Milch, likewise, positions Sol Star as a more sympathetic counterpart to Seth Bullock: "I think Star completes Bullock in a curious way, and Bullock completes Star, and in that symbiosis we see [a] kind of marriage."[37]

Scholarly work in both fields supports this interpretation: Cedric Whitman has interpreted Patroclus as Achilles' surrogate, while Nadia Van Brock, followed by Greg Nagy, has shown that Patroclus' function as a facet of Achilles is suggested linguistically when Achilles calls him his *therapon* (*Il.* 16.244) – usually translated as "attendant" or "companion," but which was originally borrowed into Greek from a Hittite word that designated an alter ego.[38] Henry Staten, likewise, makes a case for Achilles and Patroclus as "one self differed," and Mihoko Suzuki sees Patroclus as Achilles' "second self" while also identifying Hector as an alter ego Achilles is keen to deny.[39] In Westerns, Leslie Fiedler has analyzed the triangular relationship between hero, savage, and female as a manifestation of the psychological tensions described by Sigmund Freud in *Civilization and its Discontents*; he thus views the violence that erupts in Westerns as a product of the hero being caught between the freedom and spontaneity represented by the savage and the restrictive domesticity of the female.[40] John Cawelti would expand this analysis to include the triangular relationship between the hero and the two stock female types often found in Westerns: the pure, blond, virginal "schoolmarm," who symbolizes his urge toward order and civilization, and the spontaneous, sensual, and passionate "dark" woman who represents the hero's spontaneous, savage side.[41] Another variation with an all-male triad taps into the more negative "feminine" aspects of the hero's subordinate, transforming him into one who lacks restraint and moral grounding, as became more common in the spaghetti Westerns of the 1960s, most notably in *The Good, the Bad, and the Ugly*'s Tuco. Coming closest to the comparison examined in this book, Martin Winkler has noted parallel tendencies in Westerns and Greek tragedy to pair a hero and an opponent who are "two sides of the same coin" in order to showcase the hero's "dual nature."[42] In upcoming chapters, we will explore variations on this dynamic as they occur in both epic and Westerns.

HEROIC SEPARATION

The hero's intense engagement with vengeance and identity issues – both profoundly personal concerns – are positioned in both genres as part of a larger shift from valuing individual achievement to privileging the community:[43] this is evident in the *Aeneid*, where Aeneas struggles to suppress his personal desires for the sake of the Empire to come, while Western heroes like the Virginian, Tom Jeffords, Will Kane, Shane, Tom Doniphon, Preacher (*Pale Rider*), and Seth Bullock all take on or come to terms with personal sacrifice or loss in the interest of preserving or developing the local or national community. Moreover, both genres take pains to demonstrate that the manly achievement the heroes pursue makes an important contribution to the development of a society predestined to reign supreme and whose people are unequalled. Within the texts as we have them, the divinely favored heroes of Greek epic and their triumph over strong-walled Ilium might merely constitute heroic forerunners of the eighth-century BC Greeks, implying current worth through a glorious heritage, but certainly classical period Greeks were able to retroject meaning onto these tales, drawing parallels with contemporary triumphs over the Persians and inferring cultural superiority from this pattern. Virgil, of course, is more intentional in this, stressing the predestined nature of the Roman Empire and positioning it as the culmination of all that had come before. The Virgilian strategy of positioning Aeneas' takeover of the land from the native Latins as a foregone conclusion and part of a divine strategy has important parallels with the early American notion of Manifest Destiny, the widely held belief that American settlers were destined to expand throughout the continent, the accomplishment of which was therefore positioned as a duty. Based on a like notion of the special virtues and inherent superiority of the American people, this doctrine too became a justification for the oppression or removal of Native Americans. As Western scholars like James Cortese have shown, the mythologized history in the

Western genre in part developed in response to the tenets of this doctrine.[44]

Both genres, however, seem to suggest that although society needs these men and their excessive brand of violence in order to establish law, order, and civilization, it then must exclude them for possessing these very traits. Achilles is killed before Troy is taken; Odysseus must set out from home once again; Aeneas must pave the way for Rome, but will never see it established; and once the job is done, Wyatt Earp, Will Kane, Shane, Will Lockhart, Ethan Edwards, "Joe" (*For a Fistful of Dollars*), Blondie (*The Good, the Bad, and the Ugly*), Harmonica, Will Penny (*Will Penny*, 1967), the stranger of *High Plains Drifter*, Josey Wales, and Preacher all ride away; the Wild Bunch *en masse* and J. B. Books die fighting; and Tom Doniphon is simply forgotten. Peter French has discussed the talion principle, which states that retributive justice should be in kind and degree proportionate to the injury (or more familiarly, "an eye for an eye"), as a movement toward civilization in that it limits excess and replaces personal notions of what constitutes appropriate vengeance – as is exemplified with Achilles' response to Patroclus' death – with rule of law.[45] Both by virtue of their larger-than-life heroic stature and by embodying and enacting the excess of violence a progressive society must circumscribe, these men are necessarily exiled to the past, unable to take part in the very society they enable.

An important secondary strain in many works from both genres, however, is the presence of a protégé who provides an alternate model of heroism – one less rigid and more conciliatory, and who is thus ultimately able to integrate into the community in a way that the more traditional hero cannot. This narrative element frequently takes the form of a coming-of-age story: this is abundantly clear in the *Odyssey*, with its heavy focus on Telemachus' growth from an adolescent to a hero who can stand up with his father against terrible odds to defend the honor the suitors have besmirched, but echoes are also seen in the *Aeneid* as Iulus grows from boy to man. This theme, too, appears time and again in Westerns, as will be examined with Matt's role in *Red River*, Joey's in *Shane*, and Martin's in *The Searchers*, but which we also see through the characters of Chico in *The Magnificent Seven*, Mississippi in *El Dorado*, and Gillom in *The Shootist*, along with many others. Like the quest theme discussed above, the coming-of-age story is not uncommon, nor is it limited to the genres under consideration here; it is, however, distinctive in these two genres in that the concern with the youth's development into a man is always secondary to the story of the hero himself.

Ultimately, then, both genres are not about the autonomy and freedom heroic stature brings, but about the limits with which these heroes must come to terms.[46] Despite his superior qualities and the appearance of near-invincibility, the hero of epic and Western in the end faces his own demise. For some, this simply entails the recognition, often merely implied through their silent exit at the end, that they have through the same heroic action that paved the way for civilization ensured their own obsolescence. For others, it requires a coming-to-terms with mortality. Even before the cathartic encounter with Priam that helps him complete this process, Achilles suggests engagement in it when in the midst of his *aristeia* – a period of frenzied excellence in battle – he rejects the Trojan Lycaon's supplication by counseling him,

> No, friend, you die as well. Why lament it? Patroclus too died, and he was far better than you. Don't you see how beautiful I am, and how huge? My father was a worthy man and my mother a goddess. Yet death and unavoidable fate hang over me as well. (*Il.* 21.106–10)

Similarly, when the Schofield Kid rationalizes his first killing with, "I guess [he] had it comin'," William Munny's comfortless reply – "We all have it coming, Kid" – suggests his participation in this process as well. When in the end, Munny responds to Little Bill's objection that he doesn't deserve to die with a blunt, "Deserve's got nothin' to do with it" before shooting him, Peter French see this as an indication that, in contrast to his earlier admission to Ned that he was "scared of dyin'," Munny has now reached an existential understanding "that death is the annihilation of everyone's life and that life is always 'lived at the edge of death'."[47] In these ways, the heroes of both epic and Western grapple with the life-and-death issues that are the common lot of every human, and through them we too reach greater understanding of our own limitations.

As I hope to have illustrated, the genre of Western film demonstrates an important kinship with the epics of Homer and Virgil both in form – as highly mythologized national foundation narratives – and in function – the shaping of national identity and reinforcement and justification of prevailing cultural ideologies, particularly regarding expectations for gender roles. But in addition to these broader affinities, the values and belief systems these genres work to codify have striking similarities and manifest themselves in characters, plotlines, and narrative details so similar that they have more or less become archetypes of Western civilization more broadly. I am aware that I have not troubled to distinguish between different categories of Westerns, lumping together B- with A-level Westerns; Golden Age films with spaghetti and revisionist Westerns; works made under the constraints of the Motion Picture Production Code and ones produced after its dissolution; and examples of the classic, vengeance, transitional, and professional plot types identified by structuralist Will Wright.[48] But I have done so intentionally, believing that the manifestation of important classical elements in Westerns across subcategories attests to their entrenchment in the genre more broadly. But I do not presume to suggest that the parallels I am delineating here are in any way conscious, nor that these threads are unique to these two genres to the exclusion of others. As Robin Wood has noted,

> a given work of art, or a given artist, does not have a single, finite meaning that can be fixed for all time, but is the point of intersection of a multiplicity of interacting codes, hence capable of surrendering a range of meanings, the choice of which will be determined by the requirements of the situation within which work or artist is perceived.[49]

As a result, narratives about the Old West, particularly as they appear in cinema, have significant connections to the foundational myths of antiquity – stories which are central to epic, but which may also be found in other genres. My intention here is not to say that this way of examining these works is the definitive one, but instead that it is useful, important, and mutually enlightening. I might, however, go so far as to argue that so ingrained in our cultural psyche are the notions of manhood, justice, and honor constructed in Western film that for Americans, stories focused on masculine heroic conflict like those in ancient epic are necessarily filtered through a "Westerns" lens. Thus by shining a light on the points of confluence in these genres, we can better understand how our own reception of these epics is constructed.

NOTES

1 Generally said to begin with John Ford's 1939 *Stagecoach* and continuing through the 1940–50s, but sometimes seen as extending into the early 1960s.

2 Day (2008).

3 For example, Percy and Harriet Randal = Priam and Hecuba; Hallock and Ann Randal = Hector and Andromache; Pax Randal = Paris; Cora Randal = Cassandra; Arch Eastmere = Achilles; Nelse Macleod = Nestor; Alan and Mark Lacy = Agamemnon and Menelaus; Oliver Swindon = Odysseus. Less alliterative but clearly related are Ellen Lacy = Helen; George Swindon = Aegisthus; Jock Menzies = Ajax.

4 Brown (1962: 324).
5 Noted by Hawks in McBride (2013: 170).
6 Haas (2011: 245).
7 Boone here misquotes Christopher Marlowe's *The Tragical History of Dr Faustus*.
8 Noted in Clauss (1999: 2).
9 Qtd. in Murray (1972: 68).
10 Zinnemann (1992: 110).
11 Milch (2006: 11). Milch makes the parallel clear when he says, "I wanted originally to do a show about Rome, because that was the point where the organizing principle of humanity moved from pure force to *in hoc signo vinces*, 'In this sign we conquer.' And when I wound up in Deadwood, I just changed the organizing principle from the cross to gold" (2006: 41).
12 Bazin (1971: 147–8); Cawelti (1971: 55–7); Parks (1982: 14–16); French (1997: 80); Pippin (2009: 226); Fenin and Everson (1973: 6). See also Schein (1955: 310–11).
13 Warfield (1975: 15–20); Mast (1982: 334–6); Reeder (1980b: 61); Frankel (2013: 239). See additional information in the chapters that follow.
14 Kopff (1999: 235–42); Clauss (1999); Holtsmark (2001); Fletcher (2014); Winkler (1996; 2001b; 2004); Day (2008); Bakewell (2002); Myrsiades (2007); Rubino (2014). I would also note that a number of papers at conferences in a variety of disciplines have focused on comparisons between the Western genre and various aspects of classical antiquity, including two panels entitled "Classics and the American Western: Making Film, History, and Myth" at the Classical Association of the Middle West and South annual conference in Tucson, AZ in 2008.
15 Cawelti (1971: 68); Frye (1957: 186–7).
16 See Blundell and Ormand (1997: 537–9).
17 Kitses (2007: 1).
18 See Kitses (2007: 27).
19 Winkler (1985: 519–21); Blundell and Ormand (1997: 537).
20 See again Blundell and Ormand (1997: 537).
21 Cawelti (1971: 45).
22 Carson (1995); Tompkins (1992: 49–67).
23 Kitses laments the tendency for Westerns to be seen now through the narrow view of "the genre as essentially a vehicle for the exploration and validation of masculinity" (2007: 3).
24 See Tompkins (1992: 41) on this tendency in Westerns; Perkell (1981: esp. 370) points out a similar dynamic in the *Aeneid*.
25 Blundell and Ormand (1997: 539–40).
26 See Tompkins (1992: 143–4).
27 Pippin (2010: 99).

28 Blundell and Ormand (1997: 536). Blundell and Ormand do not include Roman epic in their discussion, but their observations apply there as well.
29 Shay (1994: 28–30).
30 Thomas (1996: 84).
31 Milch (2006: 157).
32 Milch (2006: 157).
33 What Jungian analysis refers to as the *anima*.
34 Nagy (1979: 292).
35 Blundell and Ormand (1997: 547).
36 Thomas (1996: 84–6).
37 Milch (2006: 111).
38 Whitman (1958: 199–203); Van Brock (1959: 119); Nagy (1979: 292).
39 Staten (1993: 353–5); Suzuki (1989: 48–9).
40 Noted in Cawelti (1971: 48). See also Schein (1955: 312).
41 Cawelti (1971: 48).
42 Winkler (2001b: 123).
43 For more on this in the Western, see Kitses (2007: 30).
44 Cortese (1976: 122).
45 French (2001: 9); see pp. 4–12 for discussion of Achilles' vengeance.
46 See Warshow (1954: 195–6).
47 French (1997: 87); French here quotes Tompkins (1992: 25).
48 Wright (1975: 32–123).
49 Wood (1996a: 164).

1 *Howard Hawks's* Red River

FILM SUMMARY

Red River is the story of Tom Dunson (John Wayne), who breaks away from a wagon train heading west in 1851 to start a ranch with the help of his crusty old sidekick Groot (Walter Brennan). Shortly after they depart, the wagon train they have left is attacked by Indians, who kill Dunson's girl, Fen (Colleen Gray), whom he had left behind with promises to send for her. A young boy named Matthew Garth (played as a youth by Mickey Kuhn) survives the attack and joins Dunson and Groot, who stake a claim in south Texas, wresting it forcibly from the land baron Don Diego. Fourteen years later, Dunson has the biggest ranch in Texas, but no one in the war-impoverished south can buy his cattle and he's broke. He decides to take 10,000 head of cattle north to Missouri, where people are buying. Matt (now played by Montgomery Clift) helps lead his team, along with a young sharpshooter named Cherry Valance (John Ireland), who leaves the employ of a neighboring cattleman to join the expedition. Groot joins them as cook. The trip is difficult and dangerous, and Dunson is a demanding and obstinate leader. After hearing rumors that the railroad has reached Abilene, Kansas, the men want to change routes to sell the cattle there, since the going would be far safer, but Dunson refuses. One night, Bunk, a cowhand with a sweet tooth, rattles pans while trying to steal some sugar; the noise spooks the cattle, provoking a stampede that kills one man and a number of cattle and destroys a grub wagon. Dunson wants to whip the offender; when the man protests, Matt is compelled to step in to prevent Dunson from killing him. Tensions grow as the men are put on half-rations due to the loss of the grub wagon. Some want to turn back, but Dunson holds them to their contract on threat of death. When three men desert, Dunson sends Cherry after them, while he himself drives the remaining men even harder towards Missouri, despite receiving additional indications that the railroad has reached Abilene. When Cherry returns with the deserters, Dunson wants to hang them. A mutiny results, with Matt taking over and turning toward Abilene, leaving behind Dunson, who vows to kill Matt. When they come upon a wagon train, Matt meets and falls in love with a woman named Tess (Joanne Dru), but duty calls, and he presses on toward Abilene, leaving her behind. On Matt's trail, Dunson too meets up with Tess, who tries to stop him from pursuing Matt by persuasion, by force, and even by offering her body as a bribe. Dunson refuses, but agrees to take her with him. Meanwhile in Abilene, Matt and his men not only find the rumors of the rail line confirmed, but also learn that the price of cattle is high, and they are greeted like heroes. After paying his men, Matt takes the remainder of the money in a check made out to Dunson. The next day, Dunson marches into town; Cherry tries to stop him and is wounded. Matt stands up to Dunson, but refuses to draw, even as Dunson fires at him, grazing his cheek and shooting off his hat. A fistfight ensues, but the scuffle is broken up when Tess charges in firing a pistol, ordering them to stop it because, as she puts it, "anybody with half a mind would know [they] love each other." An amused Dunson tells Matt to marry her, and then promises to add an M to the Red River D brand that identifies his cattle.

INTRODUCTION

Howard Hawks's 1948 film *Red River* was a game-changer. Though John Ford had reinvigorated the genre in 1939 with his Academy Award-winning *Stagecoach*, a film which many regard as the first A-grade Western (and the movie that made John Wayne a star), it was Hawks's film that introduced a new brand of psychological complexity to the genre and ushered in what most consider to be the Golden Age of Westerns in the 1950s. Although this was Hawks's first Western,[1] and though he freely admitted to using Ford as a model in his films, this new formula in turn influenced Ford, the recognized master of the genre, and established Wayne as a serious actor rather than just as a star, both of which are suggested by Ford's famous response to Wayne's performance in this movie: "I never knew the big son of a bitch could act."[2]

Red River was based on Borden Chase's story "The Chisholm Trail," which first appeared as a six-part serial in *The Saturday Evening Post* in December 1946–January 1947 and was later published in novel form as *Blazing Guns on the Chisholm Trail*. Hawks bought the rights for $50,000 in January 1946, even before the story appeared, and hired Chase to write the screenplay. Chase, however, resisted collaboration and balked at any suggested alterations,[3] so Hawks enlisted Charles Schnee to rewrite the completed script, and it was Schnee who, among other things, introduced the character of Fen and changed the Tess character from a prostitute to a cardsharp. Most controversially, since Hawks objected to Chase's ending, in which Dunson's death was imminent, Schnee replaced it with a showdown and reconciliation scene.[4] Chase hated the revised ending, as did Montgomery Clift, who called the showdown a "farce."[5] To add to the trouble, Howard Hughes threatened legal action based on similarities between *Red River*'s ending and that of his 1943 film *The Outlaw*, on which Hawks had worked.[6] A compromise was finally reached whereby somewhere between fifteen and twenty-four seconds were cut from the ending of the theatrical release.[7] In the end, *Red River* was more than a million dollars over budget and over two years old by the time of its release in September 1948.[8] Despite these problems, it was a box-office success, taking in $4.5 million on its initial release and eventually bringing in $10 million worldwide.[9] Critics acclaimed the performance of Wayne, who moved into the *Motion Picture Herald*'s top ten list of stars,[10] and both Chase for his story and Christian Nyby for editing were nominated for Academy Awards. Not only is the film today regularly hailed as one of the best Westerns of all time,[11] perhaps even more importantly, *Red River* had a profound influence on the direction the genre would take: in the 1950s, we begin to see Western heroes with moral ambivalence, men whose internal struggles both signify truths about the individual human condition and set forth hard questions about the foundations of an emerging society. In focusing on the flaws of his hero along with his strengths and by asking him to confront and come to terms with a changing world, Hawks succeeds in creating a film whose existential themes are the stuff of enduring epic inquiry and whose roots reach back to the heroic age of ancient Greece.

THE EPIC TRADITION

While the plot and characterizations of *Red River* do not replicate those of the Greco-Roman epics directly, its resonance with classical themes and works has not gone unnoticed: Molly Haskell, for instance, has proclaimed Hawks "the modern counterpart of Homer," going on to note that in Hawks's body of work, "the pioneer hubris, and brashness and naïveté, of the American converges with the austere, man-centred morality of ancient Greece."[12] Roberta Reeder has noted Tom Dunson's connections to the Greek tragic hero in general, while Life Blumberg has compared him to Sophocles' Ajax and Glenn Frankel calls the bulk of the plot "Oedipus-in-reverse."[13] Clark Branson devotes a short section to how Homer's *Odyssey* fits into his Jungian study of Hawks's work in general;[14] and most usefully, in a chapter on *Red River*, Gerald Mast discusses the parallels between Hawks's film and Homeric epic,[15] arguing that they serve a similar purpose in working to "affirm their [own cultural] values and their purpose by converting history into myth"; that they have in common "a juxtaposition of legend and history, myth and fact, oral tradition and written record"; and that they are both "attempt[s] to tell (or retell) to the culture a story of how that culture developed, what and where it had been, so its members could know what it was and, therefore, what it is."[16] Unlike some of the other directors under consideration here, there is no evidence to suggest that Hawks had any strong connection to classical learning.[17] Yet whatever Hawks's background and conscious intention, the epic resonances in this film make it an important example of the same sort of foundational cultural narrative as the works of Homer and Virgil.

From its very opening, the film situates itself as part of the heroic tradition that stems back to Homer's works. Like the ancient epics, the original pre-release version of the film anchors itself in its own society's historical past when the introductory text crawl connects the film's action to the first drive on the Chisholm Trail, the story of which can be found among "the annals of the great state of Texas."[18] At the same time, Dunson's part in this drive is introduced via the device of a handwritten book entitled *Early Tales of Texas*. Both the handwriting, which points to personal recollection rather than historical inquiry, and the word "tales," with its implication of exaggeration and embellishment, suggest that despite its historical basis, the events of this story, like those of the Homeric epics and the *Aeneid*, are distorted and mythologized.

When preview audiences and the film's backers found the movie too long, several scenes were reduced or eliminated, while the time-consuming device of handwritten pages to assist with transitions between scenes was replaced by Walter Brennan's voice-over narration, saving around seven and a half minutes of screen time.[19] By using Groot as narrator, the theatrical-release version of Hawks's film retains – indeed, arguably intensifies – the implication of personal recollection, so that while the film remains anchored in history,

Groot's old-timer rasp periodically reminds us that the subject matter is liable to exaggeration and distortions of perspective and memory. In the introductory scene, this implication is emphasized by Groot's opening words – "Along about August of 1851. . ." – an imprecision which from the beginning locates this story on the border between history and legend.[20]

This loose relationship between fact and fiction is supported by the choice of shooting location: *Red River*'s production base was near Elgin, Arizona, while the Chisholm Trail runs through Texas, Oklahoma, and Kansas, and rather than the titular Red River, the river crossing scenes were filmed on the San Pedro,[21] rendering the landscape a mythic version of reality as well. And just as the epics of Homer, as products of the oral tradition, conflate artifacts and practices from different periods of history ranging from the Bronze Age in which they were set to the Archaic period when they were written down, so too does *Red River* include anachronisms due to the constraints of its narrative format: for instance, historically, the cattle in *Red River* should have been Longhorns, but their scarcity at the time of filming meant that Hawks had to make do with just a few, putting them in the foreground while filling the background with more readily available Herefords.[22]

More telling than anachronisms, however, are the similar values and ideologies found in ancient epic and in Westerns as they manifest themselves in Hawks's film. *Red River*, for instance, contains echoes of the Greek concept of *xenia*, which term describes the expectations inherent when male peers in Bronze Age Greece enter into a guest–host relationship. This is suggested in the film when, despite their own short rations, Dunson feeds the injured survivor of an earlier failed cattle drive whom they happen upon, and later by the welcome Tess's wagon train offers to Dunson. Similar value-systems in antiquity and in the Old West are also demonstrated through their concern with the progeny whose succession will ensure the continuation of their own achievement and identity. Odysseus' profound concern with his wife's fidelity, as many scholars have recognized, is located in part in the implications it has for the paternity of the son through whom his (proto-) *oikos* (family or household) will be perpetuated. In *Red River*, a similarly critical significance is demonstrated when Dunson, finding himself violently estranged from his surrogate son Matt, offers Tess half of his possessions to provide him with a heir.

Despite the forthrightness of Fen and the tough, spunky attitude of Tess – as well as the reputation of "the Hawksian woman" as strong, free-spirited, and sophisticated[23] – *Red River* also exhibits attitudes toward women that recall those prevalent in antiquity. For instance, Cherry's comment that the only two things more beautiful than a good gun are "a Swiss watch or a woman from anywhere" positions women as objects of the male gaze; their objectification is later reinforced by Buster's rhetorical query when attempting to convey Tess's beauty: "Oh Matt, do you remember that little filly I used to own?" – an equivalence that recalls the themes of Greek lyric poetry, which often positions young beautiful maidens as wild animals to be tamed and broken.[24] This "wildness" and the corresponding need for taming relates to the stereotypical view of women as lacking restraint, and therefore in need of males to control them.[25] Tess's lack of self-control in *Red River* is demonstrated verbally, her chattering so incessant that, at one point, she asks Matt to stop her, which he does by putting his hand over her mouth. And despite her positive role in the final scene, she exits a weeping, blubbering mess. Tess's verbal "leakage" suggests inadequate control over her emotions,[26] and as Jane Tompkins has shown, typifies characterizations of women in Westerns, contributing to the view of them as "other" and as the yardstick against which the ideal qualities of men, whose speech is generally terse and controlled, are measured.[27]

On a related note, as Louis Giannetti has argued for Hawks's corpus in general, in both ancient epic and *Red River*, men's work is central and women are kept at the peripheries.[28] The "separation of the male and female, public and private worlds" that Mast has noted in *Red River* is suggested early on by Fen's exhortation to Dunson to listen with his heart (representing feminine emotion) as well as his head (male rationality), along with her reminder that the sun shines only half the time (associating male with outside) while the rest of the time it is night (when male enters the interior realm of the female).[29] Mast's observations, and even the language he uses in describing the gulf between men and women in *Red River*, strikingly recall the "divided world" of men and women in antiquity, as Marilyn Katz discussed via Book 6 of the *Iliad*, where Hector's vision of cooperation between male and female spheres is ultimately exposed as grounded in the subordination of the female realm to the male rather than a true merging of the two.[30]

A final ideological equivalency *Red River* demonstrates with ancient epic is a similar underlying notion where death is concerned: Mast has noted the shared expectation in these works that the remains of an adversary be respected, part of the Homeric code which is paralleled in Hawks's film by Dunson's insistence on burying and then reading the Bible over men he has killed.[31] In addition, like ancient epic, *Red River* emphasizes the importance of how men die. In antiquity, dying in battle was considered noble, and death by sword was associated with honorable warriors fighting in the forefront; hanging, on the other hand, was seen as a woman's death, most often associated with suicide in response to romantic disaster.[32] Thus when Odysseus orders his son to put the disloyal serving-women to the sword but Telemachus decides to hang them instead, he explains that a "clean death" is too good for these traitors (*Od.* 22.435–45 and 457–64). A like valuation is suggested in *Red River* by the fact that it is not Dunson's decision to execute the deserters that tips the balance toward mutiny, but his order that they be hanged, effectively adding insult to injury by associating them with criminals.

In addition to these similarities in value-systems and beliefs, *Red River* recalls the epics of antiquity in the characterization of its protagonist: Hawks clearly presents Tom Dunson as a hero of epic proportions, a "force of nature," as Glenn Frankel puts it.[33] The opening interchange between Dunson and the wagon master who challenges his decision to break off on his own establishes Dunson's heroic traits with brisk efficiency. In this scene, Dunson is revealed as a man of honor when he says, "I signed nothing. If I had, I'd stay"; he is characterized as brave when he brushes off warnings that hostile Indians are about; he is portrayed as savvy, since he alone has noticed that the land to the south is, as he says, "good land, good grass for beef"; he is cast as superior in skill when the leader objects that he is "too good a gun" to let him leave; and he is depicted as supremely confident when he responds that he is "too good a gun for you to argue with." Groot completes this heroic characterization first by casting Dunson as stubborn and willful when he warns the wagon master, "He's a mighty set man when his mind's made up," and then by attesting to his superior strength when he advises "mind he don't stomp on you [on] the way out."

The heroic stature of the protagonist is conveyed not only through these narrative details, but through casting as well. Although John Wayne was not widely respected as an actor before *Red River*, Howard Hawks clearly recognized the potential of his on-screen persona: as he later said of Wayne,

> He has more power than any other man on the screen. The only problem with Wayne is who [*sic*] do you get to play with him? If you get somebody who's not pretty strong, why he blows them right off the screen. He doesn't do it purposely – that's just what happens.[34]

Hawks's utilization of Wayne's on-screen power contributed greatly to the heroic impression Dunson's character makes, and indeed, the combination of Dunson's stubborn indomitability and Wayne's powerful screen presence was so effective that not only did these characteristics become trademarks of Wayne's on-screen characters from this film forward,[35] but audiences even today consider these to be traits of Wayne himself rather than part of his screen persona. As the paradigmatic Western hero, Wayne's Tom Dunson set the bar for Western protagonists to come, but at the same time the heroic qualities he demonstrates show striking connections with the epic heroes of antiquity.

THE *ILIAD*

Although Dunson displays the classic traits of the Western hero in general – traits which can be broadly compared to those of the epic hero – there is also much about Dunson's initial characterization that is particularly Achillean. In Achilles' frenzy as he re-enters battle to confront Hector in the *Iliad*, Homer emphasizes his simultaneously super- and subhuman nature by comparing him to elements like fire and metal on the one hand (i.e. 22.25–32, 134–5) and to predatory animals on the other (i.e. 22.139–44, 189–93). A similar description appears in Chase's original story, where Dunson is described from the outset as a "bull of a man" with eyes like bullets,[36] metaphors that are reiterated throughout the narrative. Although film generally relies on visual cues rather than metaphors such as these, casting here is significant: as Deborah Thomas has shown, John Wayne's characters are often associated or associate themselves with "imagery of metal and stone."[37] Although in *Red River* this is mostly implicit, the initial sketch of Dunson provided by the exchange with the wagon master (much expanded from that in the original tale) discussed above is broadly reminiscent of Achilles' brand of heroism: not only is Dunson more powerful and more perceptive than others, like Achilles he is a skilled fighter who exhibits an air of near-invincibility along with unwavering self-confidence and stubborn inflexibility.

In both the original story and in the film, Dunson's heroic nature becomes gradually more Achillean as the plot progresses, as is seen when each man takes a stance that imperils his comrades: Achilles not only withdraws from battle, but persuades the gods to favor the Trojans to teach Agamemnon a lesson, and Dunson refuses to alter their dangerous route even as evidence accumulates that Abilene is a safer and equally lucrative option. Both men, too, manage to intensify the animosity against them through their rigid inflexibility and unforgiving dispositions. When Achilles obstinately refuses to return to battle even after Agamemnon has backed down and offered more than adequate reparations, it only serves to harden the Greek forces against him (9.696–711). Similarly, when Dunson threatens to whip the already ashamed and remorseful Bunk as punishment for triggering a destructive stampede, he achieves the opposite of what he intends: Bunk is spiritually reunited with the group, and it is Dunson himself who becomes more alienated.[38] Soon, moreover, Dunson manifests a lethal rage, which, like Achilles' famous wrath, is provoked by a slight to his sense of honor and results in profound estrangement from his comrades.[39] In both cases, the hero's isolation results from a crisis of authority, though *Red River* in some ways inverts the situation found in Homer: that is, while Achilles himself withdraws after coming into conflict with a superior whose leadership has become tyrannical, Dunson is forcibly excluded when his own leadership slips into the realm of dangerous and unreasonable tyranny. In both epic and film, however, the result of this conflict is that the focal hero is stripped of honor and identity as he is radically separated from society. Dunson's isolation is emphasized by the camera, which in the scene when Matt leaves him behind "remains as motionless as Dunson and works toward his back, emphasizing the man's stooped figure, his separateness, particularly when the men ride off together, leaving him alone, a solitary figure in a vast framed space."[40]

Despite his spearheading of the mutiny, Matt serves as a Patroclus figure in that, in both cases, the hero is thrown into a crisis by the loss of his closest companion. In the *Iliad*, Achilles responds to news of Patroclus' death with intense grief, which he channels into an existential rage at his companion's killer, the Trojan Hector. In *Red River*, Dunson loses Matt not through death, but through what he sees as betrayal, so that the rage Dunson feels at Matt's loss is directed at Matt himself: thus in some ways, Matt serves as both Patroclus and Hector to Dunson's Achilles. As noted in the introduction, in the *Iliad*, a complex identification is established between Achilles, Patroclus, and Hector, where Patroclus represents the softer, more feminine side of Achilles and Hector represents his more human side: where Achilles is hard and unyielding, disregarding the suffering of his comrades in order to safeguard his honor, Patroclus is compassionate and distraught at seeing the suffering of his fellow Greeks, even begging Achilles to send him back into battle. In this scene Homer has Achilles utilize a "reverse simile" that compares Patroclus to a young girl tugging on his mother's skirt (16.7–11), further suggesting his softer, more feminine nature. Hector, on the other hand, functions as an alter ego for Achilles, as is suggested by their analogous positions as the strongest and most formidable warriors among their people. But while, like Achilles, Hector is stubborn and strong-willed, he is also a very human and sympathetic hero – the "man" to Achilles' "lion," as Achilles puts it before their final showdown (22.262–7), a telling characterization which reflects not only Achilles' simultaneous super- and subhuman nature, but also his scorn of the human weakness Hector embodies and which he abhors in himself. This complex triangular relationship between Achilles, Patroclus, and Hector is symbolically suggested through Achilles' armor, which he first lent to Patroclus, and which Hector wears in facing Achilles, so that Achilles, now in the immortal armor bestowed by his goddess-mother Thetis, in effect is facing the human version of himself that he wishes to suppress.

Red River contains a similar dynamic, but condensed into two men. Like Patroclus, Matt is positioned as a more compassionate version of the hero both through dialogue and plot. For instance, not long after Groot in the voice-over version says of Dunson that "Tom had changed: he'd always been a hard man: now he was harder,"[41] Cherry tells Matt that his heart is "soft – too soft" – a description scornfully reiterated by Dunson following Matt's mutiny, and again in the final showdown.[42] The mutiny itself is motivated by Matt's desire to spare more lives, as his earlier wounding of Bunk Kennelly was designed to save his life by preventing Dunson from killing him. Like Patroclus, Matt is concerned for the lives of his comrades, which he privileges over the stubborn stance of his dearest companion to whom he is ostensibly subject. And just as Patroclus is positioned as the feminine side of Achilles' nature, Matt's association with the feminine is suggested in several ways: on their first meeting, Dunson has just lost his cows – uncoincidentally at the very time he has lost Fen – and Matt provides a replacement – both the cow that will be necessary for producing a larger herd, and himself as a symbolic stand-in for Fen.[43] The fact that Dunson later gives to Matt his mother's snake bracelet, initially given to Fen as a love-token, supports his feminine function as a replacement for the woman Tom has lost.[44]

Despite their more sympathetic, gentler natures, Patroclus and Matt are not only given (secondary) heroic stature, but revealed as counterparts to the heroes themselves. In the *Iliad*, this is suggested by Patroclus' assumption of Achilles' armor; in *Red River*, Hawks implies an equivalence between Matt and Dunson even from the beginning of the cattle drive when the famous 180-degree panoramic shot of the cattle and men as they await the signal to depart initiates from Dunson's point of view, but ends with a view of Dunson from Matt's perspective, a device which suggests that the "two physical points-of-view . . . are really a single spiritual point-of-view."[45] The alter ego qualities of these companions are further suggested when they are mistaken for their betters: Patroclus gives spirit to the Greeks and provokes fear in the Trojans by assuming Achilles' armor (thus giving the impression that Achilles himself has rejoined the fray); in *Red River*, Groot jumps at Matt's approach in fear that he is the pursuing Dunson, and later, despite their dissimilarity in looks and stature – the slightly built Clift was some six inches shorter than the burly Wayne[46] – Buster aims a gun as Matt approaches him in the fog, taking him for Dunson. Tess reinforces this when she despairs of convincing Matt to run from Dunson's threat because "You're too much like him." In both epic and film, it is in part this identification and equivalence that make the hero's loss of his companion so devastating and provokes the rage which leads him to an inevitable showdown with the man whom he holds responsible – though in *Red River*, unlike the *Iliad*, that man and the companion he has lost are one and the same.

In Hawks's film, Matt functions as a Hector figure not just because he becomes Dunson's primary adversary, but also because, like Hector, he serves as a reminder of the hero's humanity and the mortal condition to which even great men are subject. As with the armor that positions Hector as a reflection of Achilles, Matt's function as a mirror of Dunson is also suggested through costuming, as Matt faces Dunson wearing a fringed buckskin shirt similar to the one Dunson himself sported as a young man (Fig. 1.1a–b). Like Hector to Achilles, Matt is a near-match for Dunson, but has shown himself to be sympathetically human when compared to Dunson's intractable super- yet subhuman nature. And in both works, the contrast between the two men is highlighted in the lead-up to the climactic showdown scene by the terrible tension we feel in the approach of the invincible and pitiless warrior as the more vulnerable, fearful opponent awaits the confrontation. In the *Iliad*, Hector stands alone outside the city walls, debating his options as Achilles approaches like a point of light moving in coldly and relentlessly, an unstoppable force of nature. The scene in *Red River* has much the same feel: Matt stands apart awaiting the approach of Dunson, who moves in like a cyborg assassin, barely pausing at Cherry's challenge and hardly flinching even when a bullet pierces his side. The tension in this scene is underscored both by Hawks's camera, which advances along with Dunson, and by the "insistent, rhythmic pulse" of the film's score.[47] The show-

1.1a and b At left, Matthew Garth (Montgomery Clift); at right, Tom Dunson (John Wayne). *Red River* (1948). Monterey Productions.

down in both cases, moreover, reinforces the connection between the men through wounding. In the *Iliad*, Achilles stands above the dying Hector, who prophesies Achilles' death (22.358–60) in a clear parallel to Patroclus' death scene, when Hector likewise stood over him as he predicted Hector's own impending demise (16.851–4), with the dying man in both cases wearing Achilles' mortal armor. Similarly in *Red River*, the bullet from Dunson's gun which grazes Matt's cheek results in a wound that echoes a scar on Dunson's own face.

Significantly, in both cases this confrontation is followed by an unexpected and emotional intervention which helps the primary hero come to terms with an earlier loss: in the case of Achilles, the Trojan king Priam's emotional petition as he humbles himself before his enemy and begs for his son's body allows Achilles to grieve for his lost companion Patroclus and mourn his father Peleus' inevitable grief over Achilles' own imminent death; for Dunson, Tess's intervention and the prospect of his adoptive son finding the happiness that eluded him helps Dunson put the loss of his own girl years earlier behind him.[48] This symbolism is suggested both musically – when Dunson questions Tess about her relationship with Matt, Fen's theme music is playing in the background[49] – and, again, sartorially: Tess's

1.2a and b At left, Tom Dunson (John Wayne) and Fen (Colleen Gray); at right, Nadine Groot (Walter Brennan) and Tess Millay (Joanne Dru). *Red River* (1948). Monterey Productions.

dress in this scene is of the same cut and a similar pattern to the dress Fen wore as Dunson bid her farewell for the last time (Fig. 1.2a–b). Ultimately, then, both works are less concerned with bringing the task at hand to completion – the *Iliad* does not depict the conclusion of the war, and the successful conclusion of the cattle drive does not bring *Red River* to a close – than they are with bringing closure to the protagonist's existential angst. As such, the Golden Age Western hero that Hawks ushers in with Tom Dunson is a clear heir to the complex superhuman yet all-too-human nature that characterizes the first hero of Western literature.

THE *ODYSSEY*

In addition to its *Iliadic* qualities, *Red River* also demonstrates kinship with Homer's *Odyssey*. As noted above, Clark Branson briefly explores this relationship in his Jungian study of Hawks's corpus, while Gerald Mast, in his discussion of the parallels between Homeric epic and Hawks's film, finds that "*Red River* finds its closest epic affinity with *The Odyssey* . . . the long and arduous journey that tests the strength of the leader and the travelers from outside and inside."[50] While Mast's short exploration is both useful and insightful, the Odyssean qualities of the journey on which Dunson embarks in *Red River* are pervasive enough and their implications significant enough to merit a more thorough exploration.

To begin, the long and dangerous journey on which the hero embarks in both cases has an end goal of preserving the home he has worked to establish. In both tales, the hero is profoundly concerned with the preservation of the wealth that secures his survival and establishes his very identity in these emerging societies. In the case of Odysseus, he must defend his home from the suitors who would deplete his wealth through egregious disregard of propriety, as they eat and drink their way through his stores and woo his wife. For Dunson, he must get his cattle to market, defending them from the border gangs who would steal them for their own profit and kill him and his men in the process. But while the wealth each man is defending is profoundly important and the journey he takes to preserve or defend it central, the real subject of these works is the internal struggles of the hero himself and the tensions that emerge as he negotiates relationships with his allies. Homer implies this with the first word of the *Odyssey*'s proem – *aner*, or the man himself – suggesting that this epic, like the *Iliad*, is as much about self as it is about society.

Although Dunson's lethal rage and superhuman persona connect him to Homer's Achilles, in his moral ambiguity he also recalls the wily and sometimes ethically questionable Odysseus. Odysseus, of course, is known as a master of tricks and disguise. It was he, after all, who devised the stratagem of the wooden horse that helped put an end to the ten-year war against the Trojans. Then he not only returns home in the guise of a beggar, fooling the members of his own household, arguably including his wife, but as Helen recounts in Book 4, he even managed to sneak into Troy at the end of the war by disguising himself on that occasion as well (240–64); and he fabricates at least three elaborate fictional life-stories in the *Odyssey* as a means of safeguarding his true identity (the so-called Cretan lies).[51] Admittedly, it is because of deceptions like these that Odysseus manages to survive and flourish, and in many ways he models the sort of information management that anthropologists tell us has for thousands of years been vital to the honor, status, and very survival of the family in the Mediterranean culture basin.[52]

Yet while in some ways the charge of "moral ambiguity" seems to be externally imposed by modern Western societies with profoundly different value-systems from those in operation in Bronze Age Greece, there are indications that, even in antiquity, traits such as these resulted in Odysseus' honor being called into question. For instance, in the *Iliad*, Achilles tells Odysseus, "Zeus-born son of Laertes, much-scheming Odysseus, . . . hateful to me as the gates of Hades is that man who would conceal one thing in his mind, but say another" – a seeming indictment of the man to his face.[53] In later times, Odysseus' ambiguous traits led to his identification as the son of Sisyphus, the notorious "sinner" whose punishment in the afterlife served as a warning to those who would challenge the gods, and to his depiction in Classical period tragedy as callous and unscrupulous.[54] And while Odysseus' subterfuges in the *Odyssey* might arguably be seen as clever strategies against his enemies or necessary precautions to safeguard his interests, more difficult to explain away is his own men's suspicion that he is hoarding gold and silver for himself, a mistrust that leads them to open the bag of winds, thwarting their homecoming (10.34–49). Thus, while much of what appears to us as vice in Odysseus might result from cultural bias, there is a clear suggestion that even in antiquity, and within the *Odyssey* itself, his brand of heroism was not above question or reproach.

Those who have seen *Red River* cannot have missed a similar anti-heroic quality in Tom Dunson, whose tyrannical leadership leads to a mutiny, following which he menacingly vows to kill his adoptive son. A closer look, however, reveals that the connections with Odysseus run deeper than just a broad brand of moral ambiguity. Both men, for instance, demonstrate a similar hypocrisy. Odysseus despises the suitors for invading his home and consuming his wealth in flagrant disregard of the principles of *xenia*, but he shows a similar disrespect for his "host" when he enters Polyphemus' cave uninvited and helps himself to his cheese in his absence. Likewise, Dunson seizes Don Diego's land for himself, killing a man in the process, and later brands his neighbors' cattle with his own mark; yet when men fleeing his tyranny supply themselves with food and ammunition from the grub wagon, he is quick to label them thieves and wants to hang them for their crime. Both men also put their own self-interests above their men's safety and well-being. Although Homer emphasizes his hero's concern with bringing his men home safely in the *Odyssey*'s proem, in Book 9 Odysseus first insists over his companions' prudent protests on waiting for Polyphemus to return in the hopes of receiving guest-gifts, and later twice trumpets his victory to the blinded Cyclops, disregarding his shipmates' vehement objections that it will endanger all their lives by revealing their position. In *Red River*, although Dunson also exhibits concern for his men, he drives them relentlessly despite lack of food and sleep, and he is willing to sacrifice some of their lives in order to achieve his goal his way by keeping to the more dangerous course toward Missouri rather than taking the safer route to Abilene.

The ultimately self-interested nature of both men leads their companions to question their motives and decisions at several key points. In addition to the mistrust of him that Odysseus' shipmates all demonstrate in the bag of the winds episode, his kinsman and second-in-command Eurylochus twice questions his leadership: he first challenges Odysseus' command that the men join him at Circe's house, calling Odysseus *thrasus* (rash) and reminding the others that at the cave of the Cyclops, their companions had "perished because of his recklessness" (10.436–7); and later, he objects to Odysseus' orders to pass by the island of Thrinakia, calling him *sketlios* (hard-hearted or cruel: 12.279). In the former instance, Eurylochus' statement of Odysseus' earlier mistake, despite its basis in truth, provokes a violent anger in Odysseus, and he is only prevented from drawing his sword and striking off Eurylochus' head by the rest of the men, who manage to dissuade him (10.438–45). Similarly, Dunson's failings as a leader cause his men to question him: Matt tells him that he is to blame for a deadly confrontation with three of his men, and Teeler tells him he is "crazy . . . [or] skin close to it"; even the loyal Groot twice rues Dunson's decision to leave Fen behind, and on more than one occasion tells him pointedly, "You were wrong, Mr. Dunson." And like Odysseus, Dunson reacts violently when his men object to his decisions: when Bunk, for instance, refuses to be whipped for inadvertently provoking a stampede, Matt steps in and prevents Dunson killing him by winging the otherwise doomed Bunk himself. When Dunson's tyranny goes so far that he threatens to execute the men who have crossed him, Matt leads a full-scale mutiny. In this way, despite their characterizations as natural leaders, both Odysseus and Dunson demonstrate serious shortcomings in managing their men.

The significance of the strained relationship between the hero and his men is suggested by the theme of heroic restraint. In both works, the lack of such restraint in the heroes' companions threatens to endanger the expeditions' larger goals. In the *Odyssey*, this is demonstrated repeatedly: by the temptations of the Lotus-Eaters in Book 9, by the pleasures of Circe's island in Book 10, and in the end, fatally, by the gnawing hunger that leads his men to slaughter the Cattle of the Sun while Odysseus sleeps in Book 12. In *Red River*, a similar fatal lack of restraint is demonstrated through the character of Bunk, whose sugar-stealing leads to the stampede that diminishes their herd, kills Dan Lattimer, and compromises the integrity of their mission with the loss of the grub wagon.[55] That this incident is intended to suggest a larger principle is signaled even before this tragic turn when Groot in disgust says of Bunk's weakness that a "sweet-tooth is 'most as bad as having a whiskey tongue or liking a woman." Despite his judgmental attitude, Groot himself has already demonstrated his own lack of restraint when he lost half-interest in his "store teeth" in a poker game; in addition, as we have seen, his persistent chattering runs counter to Western codes of masculine heroic conduct, as their Indian wagon driver Quo implies when he advises him to "Keep face closed."

While pains are taken in both cases to demonstrate lack of restraint as a potentially fatal moral failing, in each work the hero himself is implicated in this flaw. Odysseus' lack of restraint leads him to remain in the Cyclops' cave, despite every indication that the inhabitant is not a member of the civilized community; to taunt the Cyclops despite the fact that it will advertise their position and thus endanger their lives; and to linger on Circe's island, delaying his return home for an entire year. In each of these cases, his companions provide the voice of reason, begging Odysseus to depart before the cave's inhabitant returns, objecting to his need to boast of his victory, and urging him to resume their journey. Dunson, too, shows a lack of restraint, both in his violent behavior and by overindulging in the whiskey that Groot has earlier characterized as a dangerous vice. And as with Odysseus, his men themselves object to his indulgence in this habit: Matt by intentionally kicking over his whiskey bottle; Groot by pointedly pouring an excess of whiskey on Dunson's leg wound to cause him pain as he tends it; and Teeler by connecting it, and his lack of sleep, to the tyrannical behavior that leads to his downfall. At the same time, Matt provides a counter-example: when Teeler threatens the deposed Dunson, Matt comes close to killing him for it, but holds himself back, which Mast sees as suggesting "the character's careful balancing of unchecked emotion with conscious self-control, of head ruling heart."[56]

By demonstrating that the hero is complicit in the sorts of behaviors he himself condemns in his companions, these works suggest that the journeys these heroes are on are in one sense interior ones: through his failings, each of these epic heroes is revealed to be on an all-too-human quest to sort out his place in the world and to understand his mortality in relation to his heroism. This conundrum is symbolically illustrated by a coincidental yet striking parallel that serves to intensify Dunson's Odyssean nature: in *Red River*, the gunshot wound to

Dunson's leg is reopened when he "hook[s] it on a horn," a powerful reminder of the wound Odysseus received as a youth from the tusk of a boar, and which he later uses as a means of verifying his identity. For both heroes, then, their physiques themselves bear a visible symbol of their human limitations.

Another indication that the narrative in both the *Odyssey* and *Red River* is about larger existential and identity issues is the central role of the hero's relationship with his son figure, which takes the form of a coming-of-age story. In both cases, however, the primary focus of the coming-of-age story is not the change in and implications for the youth, but the importance of this relationship for the father. In the first four books of the *Odyssey*, often referred to as the *Telemachia*, the action centers on Odysseus' son Telemachus as he, prompted by Athena, sets about finding information on the whereabouts of his absent father, a mini-quest which kick-starts the process of becoming a man. *Red River*, too, establishes the father–son relationship as crucial to the tale from the outset when the introductory text-crawl[57] makes the father–son story appositive to "the story of the Red River D" – implying that in the world of the Old West, the relationship between male progeny and the transfer of property, status, and masculine identity functions in a manner similar to the one at play in ancient Greece. Although in *Red River*, Matt is not Dunson's biological son as is the case with Odysseus and Telemachus, he is from the start characterized as akin to Dunson in spirit and ability. When he first approaches Dunson and Groot after escaping the Indian attack, the young Matt demonstrates grit and spunk when he warns Dunson, "Don't ever try to take [my gun] away from me again," prompting Dunson to tell Groot approvingly, "He'll do."[58] Dunson then becomes a mentor to Matt, instructing him on how to beat another man to the draw in a showdown by watching his eyes, and then telling Matt that in order to add his M to the Red River D brand, he will "have to earn it."[59] Thus, it rapidly becomes apparent that Matt is being groomed as a successor to the childless Dunson. Matt's suitability to assume this heroic role is demonstrated when a grown-up Matt returns to the ranch after the war; not only are the two paralleled through mannerisms – for instance, both men habitually rub their noses – but Matt even beats Dunson to the draw in a friendly match-up.

At the same time, in both works, the relationship between father and son is not without tension. In the *Odyssey*, this tension remains a mere undercurrent: although Telemachus questions his paternity in Book 1, his reservations are aimed toward his mother, and his legitimacy becomes a non-issue by the time he meets his father in Book

16; later, Telemachus prematurely steps on his father's "turf" when he nearly succeeds in stringing Odysseus' bow, but he backs down obligingly at his father's signal. More significantly, Telemachus acts contrary to his father's orders when he hangs the betraying maidservants rather than putting them to the sword, but this neither goes against the spirit of Odysseus' directive nor constitutes a threat to his father's goals. In *Red River*, in contrast, the father–son tensions do reach a tipping point. As with Telemachus, we see Matt gradually moving toward independence by asserting himself and differentiating himself from his parent. When Dunson gestures to Matt, then still a boy, to step back as a confrontation with Don Diego's man becomes tense, the young man shakes his head and holds his ground. A more serious move toward independence comes on the cattle drive when, although begrudgingly acquiescing to Dunson's command, Matt makes clear, "Don't try and tell me what to think. I'll take your orders about work, but not about what to think," kicking over Dunson's whiskey bottle to punctuate his thought.

And unlike the case of Telemachus, Matt's independence becomes a serious threat to his father when he openly challenges Dunson and then goes so far as to wrest authority from him in a humiliating public display. Afterwards, anxieties surrounding the issue of succession turn lethal, with Dunson telling Matt point blank, "I'm going to kill you . . . Every time you turn around, expect to see me. 'Cause one time you'll turn around and I'll be there. I'm gonna kill you Matt." But even after this rift, the father–son relationship and their spiritual kinship continue to be highlighted. In Dunson's initial interview with Tess, he twice begins to tell her that "Nothing [she] can say or do" can stop him from killing Matt; sandwiched between these statements is Tess's report that when she asked Matt to take her with him, he responded that "nothing [she] could do or say could make him change his mind," underscoring their similarly stubborn dispositions and like dedication to the masculine agenda. Even more explicitly, before the final showdown, Tess tells Matt, "I was going to ask you to run, but no. . ., you're too much like him." In addition, Matt has from the first been positioned as utterly loyal to Dunson – Valance, for instance, tests him early on with, "I suppose if I tangled with [Dunson] I'd have to take you on too" – and despite the serious rift between them and Dunson's hostility, in the end, when Matt asks that the check for the profit on the cattle be made out to Dunson, it is clear that Matt, like Telemachus, has been working in his father's interests all along, and indeed has saved him from his worst enemy – which in this case is himself.

Significantly, Matt's usurpation of the cattle drive enables him to obtain the sort of practical, worldly experience he needs to come fully into his manhood and step into Dunson's shoes, much as the *Telemachia* does for Telemachus in the *Odyssey*. In the first four books of Homer's epic, Telemachus gains practice in public speaking, seafaring, and diplomacy, experiences that prepare him to stand beside his father when he finally appears and prove himself a hero in his own right. In much the same way, Matt's participation in leadership, battle, and negotiation after he wrests control of the cattle drive from Dunson prepare him for the reunion with his father that allows both of them to put aside the paternalistic relationship of Matt's youth and interact on a more equal, adult level. In this reading Cherry Valance can be seen as analogous to the *Odyssey*'s Peisistratus – an age-mate and peer who is "lent out" by a neighboring elder to accompany the young man on what will become for him a journey to complete his transition to manhood and rediscover his father. In both cases, however, the young man's maturation, while crucial to the story, is not central: rather, it is the older man and his struggle to secure his home, his honor, his identity, and his legacy that remains the main focus of the narrative.

Another facet of the larger life, death, and identity issues with which both of these epics grapple is the hero's relationship with a woman. In the short glimpse we get of her at the film's outset, Dunson's girl Fen is quickly characterized as a Penelope figure of sorts. Homer's Penelope is primarily known for her fidelity, which she demonstrates by remaining true to Odysseus during his twenty-year absence. Fen's loyalty and fidelity are suggested by her clear devotion, by her eagerness to accompany Dunson on his perilous quest to strike out on his own, and by her promise to come to him whenever he sends for her, despite her anguished disappointment when he refuses to take her. Additionally, she is, like Dunson himself, strong, stubborn, and forthright in her insistence that he let her join him and in her assertion that his decision to leave her behind is "wrong." Their shared qualities and Fen's bold self-assurance work together to suggest that their relationship is one that is relatively balanced and harmonious. As Sarah Bolmarcich has shown, the relationship between Odysseus and Penelope is characterized by a similar quality the Greeks referred to as *homophrosyne*.[60] This is perhaps best indicated by the wariness which characterizes them both: Odysseus owes his survival to his caution in approaching his home in disguise in order to assess the situation, while Penelope is described more than fifty times in the *Odyssey* as *periphron*[61] – a difficult word to translate, but meaning something like "thinking all around." Both partners, too, are likened to each other when they successfully solicit gifts, Odysseus from the Phaeacians, and Penelope from the suitors – an act for which she receives the disguised Odysseus' amused but tacit approval (18.281–3). While the similarities between these couples are general, they are reinforced by two striking details: first, as Dunson takes his leave, Fen says her knees feel "like they've knives in them," a statement reminiscent of Penelope's famous weak-kneed reception of Odysseus when she finally fully accepts him as her husband ("her knees were loosened": 23.205). Secondly, before he goes, Dunson gives Fen his mother's bracelet as a token of their love; it is this bracelet that Dunson later finds on an Indian he has killed, which signifies to him that Fen is dead. Although it works somewhat in reverse, this bracelet functions in a similar way to the brooch that Penelope gave to Odysseus before he left for the war, and which Odysseus in disguise describes for Penelope in Book 19 in response to her request that he give some proof that he has met her husband (215–31). In both cases, a love-token with symbolic significance serves as an identifying device between lovers at a critical juncture.

Despite Fen's death, she lives on as a symbol for Dunson. Her presence is revived by the introduction of Tess, who becomes for Matt what Fen was for Dunson. Like Fen, Tess is spunky and headstrong; like Fen, Tess is left behind when her man leaves in pursuit of his masculine goals; and like Fen, Tess is loyal – in her case, willing to sacrifice even the integrity of her body to keep Matt safe. Tess also recalls Fen in her near-fatal wounding in an Indian attack; in her appeal to Dunson to take her with him, as Fen had before;[62] and most explicitly, when Dunson finds her wearing the same bracelet he had once given to Fen as he took his leave, and which Matt has now given to Tess as he left her behind. Finally, Dunson, completing Tess's thought about how she felt when Matt left, says, "you felt like you had knives sticking in you," echoing Fen's description of her feelings when Dunson left her many years before, and again evoking their epic predecessor. An additional connection with Penelope is suggested when Tess and Matt, in their initial romantic encounter in the rain, exchange tales throughout the night, much as Penelope and Odysseus do at their reunion.

Both Penelope and Tess also play a crucial role in the resolution of the violent battle that serves as a climax in each work. In the *Odyssey*, many scholars see Penelope as actively and knowingly helping the disguised Odysseus to exact revenge on the suitors: by setting up the bow contest, she provides him with both the weapon and the opportunity to confront the suitors using a platform on which he alone has succeeded in the past.[63] Likewise, it is Tess who provides a way out of the impasse that threatens the lives of Dunson and Matt and prompts a reconciliation. As such, she might initially be seen as a sort of *dea ex machina* in the spirit of Athena at the end of the *Odyssey*, another situation that cannot otherwise be resolved without loss of pride or life on one side or the other.[64] On closer examination, however, her role is more Penelopean: not only does she provide Dunson and Matt with the opportunity for resolution, she in effect "exposes" their true identities, revealing the underlying father–son love that their hostility and aggression attempt to mask, in much the same way as Penelope exposes Odysseus' identity with her bed-trick in Book 23 of the *Odyssey*. Indeed, Tess's assessment that Dunson has been "pretending [he was] going to kill him" strikes Hubert Cohen as an indication that Dunson has been perpetuating an elaborate deception,[65] again associating him with Homer's Odysseus. If so, Dunson's motivation for this "deception" is clearly his besmirched honor, a possibility that brings to mind once more anthropological notions about honor in the Mediterranean culture basin and the common acceptable use of deception to preserve it.

In these ways, alongside his kinship with Achilles, Hawks's hero demonstrates close connections with Homer's Odysseus. Rather than seeing this as problematic or contradictory, however, I would argue that it helps to support the notion that an important kinship exists between the genre of Greek epic and the Golden Age films of the American West. Connections with Virgil's *Aeneid*, moreover, show that these parallels can be extended to Latin epic as well.

THE *AENEID*

While scholars like Branson and Mast have argued for broad connections between *Red River* and Homer's epics and the *Odyssey* in particular, to my knowledge Hawks's film's relationship to Virgil's *Aeneid* has been overlooked almost entirely. Some of these parallels result from Virgil's strategy of using Homer's works as an explicit model: he set out at Augustus' behest to make an epic for Rome that would fill a equivalent cultural role to that of Homer's epics in Greece. In so doing, Virgil clearly designed the first half of his work, in which the Trojans are seeking their new home, as an *Odyssey*, and the second half, in which Aeneas and his men clash with the natives, as an *Iliad*. As a result, some of the observations I have made about connections between Homer's works and Hawks's film will apply to

Virgil's narrative as well, especially where he draws on Homer explicitly. Yet Virgil's epic is far from derivative, and *Red River* also relates to the *Aeneid* in ways that are purely Roman.

As noted in the introduction, as an epic the *Aeneid* is largely concerned with the struggles and sacrifices that are inherent to nation-building, specifically the founding and establishment of a nation by a people devastated by war. After their defeat by the Greeks, the Trojans' homes are destroyed and they are stripped of their land and property. In response, they set off on a long, perilous journey to found a new home and build new lives. In *Red River*, a people already in the process of building a new nation are devastated by war: their homes are lost, their cattle scattered, and their land stolen. Unable to sell his cattle among such devastation, Dunson sets out on a long, treacherous journey to sell them up north in order to preserve the ranch he has worked so hard to establish. In both works, then, the land takes on a symbolic significance. In the *Aeneid*, Virgil highlights the importance of the land and the Trojans' predestined right to it from the beginning by describing his hero in the proem as "the first to come from the shores/ of Troy, exiled by Fate, to Italy and the Lavinian coast" (1.2–4). Within the narrative, Aeneas and his followers are directed toward the land that will become Rome in Book 3 by a Delian prophecy:

> Much-enduring sons of Dardanus, the soil which first bore you from your ancestral origin will embrace you again in its fertile bosom. Seek your ancient mother. There, the house of Aeneas, both his children's children and those born from them, will rule over all the land. (94–8)

Italy, then, is positioned not only as theirs by right as their ancestral homeland, but also as a place over which they are destined to reign by divine decree, regardless of the fact that it is currently occupied. In Western films, the white settlers' right to the land is taken as a given, despite the presence of Native Americans. Manifest Destiny – the notion that white Americans were destined to expand their territory all the way to the Western edge of the continent – provides a generic parallel to the Trojans' divine right to the land emphasized in Virgil. As in the *Aeneid*, the symbolic significance of the land in *Red River* is demonstrated from the beginning, when the words of the film's opening credits are drawn as mesa-like formations, suggesting an intimate connection between land, identity, and the story at hand. In both cases, too, the usurpation of the land is conveniently positioned as a moral imperative: in the *Aeneid*, Aeneas acts on the orders of the gods and at the behest of Fate itself. In *Red River*, when Dunson wrests the land from Don Diego, as Robert Sklar observes, "morality and utility are invoked" with Groot's objection to Don Diego's ownership: "That's too much land for one man. Why, it ain't decent! Here's all this land aching to be used and never has been! I tell you, it ain't decent."[66] The cattle drive, too, is positioned as part of a larger, more important goal, as Teeler reminds Dunson when he tells him, "This herd don't belong to you. It belongs to every poor hopin' and prayin' cattleman in the whole wide state."

The concern with empire and the building of a nation in both these epics leads to an intensified concern with issues of succession and the importance of the paternal line. As we have seen with *Red River* and the *Odyssey*, in the *Aeneid*, too, there is a coming-of-age in Ascanius, who in the course of the epic grows from a boy to a man, ultimately maturing into the sort of warrior and leader worthy of succeeding his father. While here, focus on the father–son relationship is not central, issues of succession are, as is indicated by prophecies that repeatedly remind us of Ascanius' future founding of Alba Longa and his place in the long line of kings who will be Aeneas' descendants, men who will eventually found not just Rome itself, but the great Roman Empire – all the way down to the emperor Augustus. In *Red River*, we not only follow Matt's development from a boy into the sort of man who is able to rival and even overtake Dunson, but we also see a particular concern with succession issues, first indicated by Dunson's stipulation that Matt must prove himself worthy before his initial can be added to the Red River D brand. This is made more explicit in his later conversation with Tess after Matt's mutiny, when Dunson reveals just how much his anger and disappointment are anchored in succession anxiety: asked why he wanted a son, he explains, "Because I'd built something, built it with my own hands, and I can't live forever. I can't live to see it grow. I thought I had a son. But I haven't. And I want one." Dunson's comments, and his following offer to give Tess half of what he owns if she will bear him an heir, signify the vital role legacy plays here, much as it does in Virgil's work: while in both cases the father's work is important, it comes to nothing if it does not grow into something bigger after he has gone. For this reason, the true conclusion of the film is not the end of the cattle drive, nor the reconciliation between the two men, nor Matt's obtaining of the marital happiness that eluded Dunson, but the resolution of this issue with Dunson's decision to add Matt's M to the Red River D brand.

Another theme *Red River* has in common with the *Aeneid* is that the profound importance of nation-building and of the male lines of succession which support this effort are emphasized by the sacrifices inherent in pursuing this agenda – in both cases emblematized by the sacrifice of women.[67] In Book 2 of the *Aeneid*, Aeneas recounts how he lost his first wife Creusa in the fall of Troy: as they prepare to flee, Aeneas takes his crippled father upon his shoulders and leads his son by the hand, directing Creusa to follow "some distance behind." In the confusion and danger that follow, he takes no thought for her, nor does he notice that she has disappeared until he reaches safety. When he goes back to find her, he encounters only her ghost, who tells him that her death was willed by the gods and that a new wife is destined for him when he reaches Hesperia (2.707–91). In Book 4, Aeneas engages in a torrid affair with Dido, the beautiful queen of Carthage; but once Mercury reminds him of his divinely ordained duty, Aeneas turns his back on her abruptly, receiving with a stony demeanor her distraught pleas and pointed references to her imminent death, which is in fact achieved soon thereafter by suicide. Then in Book 5, when the weary Trojan women despair and are prompted by Iris to set fire to the ships, they are abandoned along with the weak as a hindrance to the mission (613–771). Thus, in the *Aeneid*, the abandonment of women is systematically employed to emphasize the priority of the masculine agenda and the unfortunate, but necessary, sacrifices that masculine enterprises entail.

Although less persistently emphasized, this narrative strategy is evident in *Red River* as well. Dunson's decision to leave Fen behind leaves her vulnerable and indirectly results in her death. Like Aeneas' failure to consider Creusa at the critical moment in his anxiety for self, father, and son – the paternal line – Dunson's shunting Fen to the side in favor of single-minded focus on his masculine goal is positioned as an error by Groot, who twice comments (or starts to), "We shoulda took her along." In Fen's vehement attempts to sway him and Dunson's stubborn refusal even to engage in discussion, their interaction before her death also recalls Aeneas' encounter with Dido: in both cases, the hero, firm and inflexible, leaves over the objections of a passionate woman, whose abandonment leads to her death. Women in both works are thus positioned as obstacles to the effective accomplishment of masculine duty and legacy-building, in a sense devaluing women's roles in this process and the feminine more generally. Yet this systematic sacrifice of women in the *Aeneid* also works to suggest that in single-mindedly pursuing political and military goals, the hero in many respects compromises his humanity,[68] so that although Virgil works to promote the project of establishing Rome and all its glories, he refuses to ignore what is lost in the process. As Roberta Reeder has noted, *Red River* does something similar: by rejecting Fen, Dunson "has rejected the emotional, human side of himself,"[69] after which he becomes increasingly brutal and unreasonable, suggesting that here, too, the relentless pursuit of masculine goals often comes at the expense of humanity itself.[70]

Virgil's acknowledgment of some of the problems the nation-building project entails is, in the view of some scholars, part of a conscious but subtle attempt to complicate the ostensibly pro-imperial propaganda piece Augustus anticipated when he commissioned this work. While the overarching thrust of Virgil's work promotes the glories of Rome and the *Pax Romana* (Roman peace) by positioning it as the divinely ordained end of a heroic project worthy of epic remembrance, many recent scholars discern subtle efforts to challenge this unambiguously glorious picture. For instance, the famous "Parade of Heroes" in Book 6 of the *Aeneid* sets forth the future of Rome, starting with Aeneas and culminating in the glorious reign of Augustus (752–887). Yet many have noted an undercurrent of criticism in this passage: Scott Davis, for instance, has discerned a "subtle condemnation of the Augustan reign cloaked in sycophantic praise," and reads this passage as a warning that the imperial regime could signal a return to hated tyranny.[71] Others have noted that Aeneas' exit after this episode is not through the gate of horn reserved for "true shades," but through the gate of ivory – the one designated for "false dreams" (6.893–8) – so that in effect Virgil tarnishes the Golden Age quality of the portrait he has just painted.

Some film critics see a similar coding in Hawks's film, which at first glance seems, like most Westerns, ideologically vacuous: Kyle Crichton suggests as much in his 1948 review ("Nobody can yell 'propaganda' at a motion picture full of cows, horses, gun play, brave women and daring men"); Peter Bogdanovich called Hawks's films in general "Neither socially conscious nor self-consciously artistic"; and André Bazin praised the film for not "distracting our attention with some social thesis."[72] As Robert Sklar has argued, however, this appearance is deceiving: it is instead

> a film about the territorial expansion of one society by the usurpation of land from others, and the consequences arising therefrom – in the relations between men and women, in the relations between men and other men, in the social compact that binds people together for a common purpose.[73]

On one level, then, *Red River* is another heroic tale of the Old West, chronicling the quest of brave men as they strive to build civilization out of wilderness, while on another, it is a complicated examination of issues of ownership and empire. Like the *Aeneid*, *Red River* is an epic that pretends to be one thing but, to a discerning eye, is quite another.

CONCLUSION

While specific characterizations and plot trajectories in *Red River* do not replicate those of a particular ancient epic exactly, strong affinities can be found between Hawks's film and each of them, connections which are pervasive enough to illustrate that the generic kinship between Westerns and ancient epic that we examined in the introduction runs deep. This kinship results both from their similar positions at the so-called "frontiers" of their respective societies and from the fact that, though widely separated in time and space, Westerns are a direct heir to the heroic tradition as it was established by these seminal literary works of Western civilization. As we continue our exploration in subsequent chapters, we shall see that many of the themes touched on here are replicated time and again in some of the most critically acclaimed Western films of the Golden Age, works that have achieved canonical status, like the epics of Homer and Virgil, precisely because they struck such a deep resounding chord with audiences who identified with their themes and ideological undercurrents.

NOTES

1 Hawks had previously worked on two Westerns, but left both due to artistic disagreements (Mast 1982: 5, 7).
2 Qtd. in McBride (2013: 146).
3 McCarthy (1997: 408). Hawks's views on the difficulties he had with Chase are recounted in McBride (2013: 150–1). Chase's perspective, of course, is somewhat different.
4 Eyman (2014: 171). McCarthy (1997: 411–12) recounts the very different shootout/reconciliation ending as it appeared in Schnee's original shooting script.
5 McCarthy (1997: 424); Eyman (2014: 175).
6 See note 1 above. According to Mast (1982: 343–4), Hawks himself wrote the scene in Hughes's film. Hawks's perspective on how the dispute came about and his own perspective on it are recounted in McBride (2013: 61–2).
7 Sources disagree (e.g. McCarthy 1997: 441; Eyman 2014: 177–8). The excised sections include Dunson's repeated verbal challenges to Matt to draw; his scornful reiterated description of Matt as "soft"; and pro-

gressively closer shots focused on Matt's eyes (see Mast 1982: 343). Although an agreement was reached and the film was released on schedule, legal and financial problems surrounding the film's production persisted for several years (see McCarthy 1997: 438–45).

8 Eyman (2014: 171–7). Although Hawks lays blame on "the man who made out the budget" for neglecting to account for travel and the transport of cattle (McBride 2013: 152), he himself was known for going over schedule and budget with some regularity.

9 Hughes (2008: 23).

10 Hughes (2008: 24).

11 In 1988 the British Film Institute voted *Red River* the fifth best Western of all time, after *High Noon*, *The Searchers*, *Stagecoach*, and *Shane* (Hughes 2008: 25).

12 Haskell (1980: 474–5). Haskell so describes Hawks at Ford's expense: "it is not Ford but Hawks who is the modern counterpart of Homer, or perhaps Herodotus, a teller of tales describing what men *are* through what they *do*."

13 Reeder (1980b: 61); Blumberg (2006); Frankel (2013: 239).

14 Branson (1987: 34–6). Although my analysis of this film in relation to Homer's *Iliad* has some relation to Jungian psychological theory, I would not dispute McCarthy's assessment of Branson's book as "one of the most astonishingly esoteric critical books ever published" (1997: 14).

15 Mast (1982: 334–6).

16 Mast (1982: 334).

17 Mast, however, considers it likely in consideration of his educational background that Hawks read the ancient epics at some point in his life (1982: 336). Indirect classical influence is demonstrated in Hawks's film *El Dorado*, which was based on Harry Brown's novel *The Stars in Their Courses*, a reworking of the *Iliad* as a Western – a story Hawks himself described as "sort of a Greek tragedy" (qtd. in Mast 1982: 336); and by *Red River*'s conscious reliance on the 1935 film *Mutiny on the Bounty*, which Mast characterizes as "a much more obvious direct descendant of Homer's *Odyssey*" (1982: 336).

18 A page from the book providing a narrative transition at the end of the drive reinforces this historical anchoring: "And history was written that day in Abilene, August 14, 1865, a day that marked completion of the first drive on the Chisholm Trail."

19 See Mast (1982: 338–41). The problem of the existence of two versions of the film is a confusing one: Mast (1982: 337–46) provides the most extensive (and useful) discussion of the issue I have found. Mast considers the "book" version the authoritative one (1982: 340–6), while other critics, such as John Belton and Peter Bogdanovich (noted in McCarthy 1997: 441) prefer the voice-over version. Sources disagree on whether Hawks himself had a preference. As my attention to both

implies, I consider both versions equally valid subjects for discussion in the comparison at hand, in much the same way that the Homeric epics existed in multiple equally valid versions, being changed over time, or expanded or condensed or given varying emphases depending on the audience and venue, before it was crystallized in written form. See also Winkler (2009: 28–34), who analogizes scrutinizing variant versions of film to analyzing different manuscripts of classical texts, using *Red River* as an example.

20 The voice-over version transfers the information the book version gave in the text crawl to the handwritten book entitled *Early Tales of Texas*; the information originally given in the handwritten book is then transferred to the voice-over narrative Groot provides.
21 See McCarthy (1997: 417); Hughes (2008: 21).
22 McCarthy (1997: 423).
23 McCarthy (1997: 12); McBride (2013: 1). Others (e.g. Wood 1996a: 166; Kitses 2007: 30) have noted that the Hawksian woman's positive aspects are problematic in that they position her as an honorary male. Hawks betrayed a similar attitude in himself when he complimented screenwriter Leigh Brackett by attributing her skill to the fact that she wrote "like a man" (noted in Wollen 1996: 3–4). Molly Haskell further notes that Hawks's male stars (like Wayne) appeared over and over again, "being allowed to grow old," while his female stars (with the exception of Lauren Bacall) appeared only once "carrying the implication that having once served, a woman had had her day and, like the aftermath of a love affair, was now 'used'" (1974: 39; see also 1980: 485) – an attitude reminiscent of Greek attitudes toward women's sexual peak in contrast to men's (see Carson 1990: 145–8).
24 i.e., Anacreon 417.
25 See Carson (1990).
26 Mast (1982: 324–5) and Tompkins (1992: 60–1) discuss Tess's loquacity in a similar vein.
27 Tompkins (1992: 55–7). See also introduction.
28 Giannetti (1981: 197).
29 Mast (1982: 304).
30 Katz (1981: 35–7).
31 Mast (1982: 335). I might note that the code only includes white men and Mexicans; fallen Native Americans receive no such respect.
32 Loraux (1987: 7–17).
33 Frankel (2013: 239).
34 Qtd. in Goodwin and Wise (1973: 21).
35 Mast (1982: 302).
36 Chase (1946a: 9).
37 Thomas (1996: 75–6).
38 Noted by Mast (1982: 317).

39 Mast has also made this observation: "[I]f *The Iliad* sings of the unbending, single-minded anger of Achilles, *Red River* sings of the unbending, angry single-mindedness of Dunson" (1982: 336).
40 Mast (1982: 321).
41 The corresponding transition in the book version says that the "hard work became harder and Dunson became a tyrant."
42 As noted above, I consider both book and voice-over versions of this film equally valid subjects for examination, but in discussing the ending, I follow the pre-release book version, since the excised sections were the result of a legal tussle and were overseen not by Hawks, but by Christian Nyby, as Hughes's threatened injunction came just one week before the film was set to open and on the very day Hawks was scheduled to leave for Germany to work on another film (Mast 1982: 344–5). As Mast argues, the scene in its original form shows that Dunson's approach is "deliberate, rational, and controlled"; his orders to draw reinforce the code of honor Dunson has exhibited throughout; the reference to Matt's softness reiterates one of the central themes of the film; and the progressive close-ups of Matt's eyes harken back to the lesson Dunson gave Matt when he was a boy. The shortened ending, on the other hand, eliminates these nuances and has Dunson approaching Matt "shooting like a wild man" (Mast 1982: 343).
43 Mast (1982: 302); Sklar (1996: 157). Sklar observes that this is even more emphasized in Chase's original script, for instance when Cherry tells Matt he is "as tender as a mother and child" (1996: 158), recalling Achilles' comparison of Patroclus to a girl tugging her mother's skirt.
44 Mast (1982: 306). Wood (1996a: 170) also discusses Matt as "a potential alternative to the woman."
45 Mast (1982: 313).
46 Eyman (2014: 174).
47 Mast (1982: 327).
48 Cohen sees the conversation in Tess's tent as "cathartic" for Dunson (2010: 90); I would view this interaction as a step in the process, but see the more important intervention happening at the end.
49 O'Brien (1996: 189).
50 Mast (1982: 337).
51 To Athena in disguise (13.256–86); to the loyal swineherd Eumaeus (14.199–359); and to his wife Penelope (19.165–202, 221–48).
52 See Du Boulay (1994: 172–3 and 188–200) for a discussion of the uses of deception in modern rural Greece; Winkler (1990: 133–7) briefly discusses the application of the work of modern anthropologists on this topic to the *Odyssey* in particular.
53 9.307–13. While Odysseus is not explicitly cast as deceptive in the *Iliad*, his characterization as smooth-tongued and his employment in both diplomatic and covert missions is not incompatible with his portrayal in the later poem.

54 As in Sophocles' *Ajax* and *Philoctetes*, the plays of Euripides in general, and later Latin works such as Horace's *Satires* II.v. For more on Odysseus' increasingly negative portrayal in the fifth century, see Stanford (1963: 90–101).
55 In Chase's story, the corresponding stampede (the original story contains not one but three stampedes) is triggered when Bunk's saddle strap breaks and his rifle slides out and discharges. As Mast notes, "Hawks converts this pure accident into a moral action" (1982: 316).
56 Mast (1982: 320).
57 Or, in the voice-over version, the handwritten book which replaces the text-crawl.
58 A similar dynamic was evident between the actors who played these characters: Wayne was skeptical that Clift, a rising Broadway star who had to learn how to ride a horse (McCarthy 1997: 413–14), was right for the part, but after shooting a couple of scenes, he admitted to Hawks, "You're right. He can hold his own. . ." (Eyman 2014: 174). See also Stevens (2006: 125).
59 The motif of the Red River D brand does not appear in Chase's original story; its introduction in the film intensifies issues of succession. Hawks's view of its importance is suggested by the fact that he is said to have given all the principal players in the film a personalized belt buckle sporting the Red River D brand. In a gesture of friendship, Hawks and Wayne later exchanged buckles (McCarthy 1997: 418).
60 Bolmarcich (2001).
61 e.g. 1.329 and 19.53, 59, 89 and 103. See Heitman (2005: 109).
62 Mast (1982: 323–4).
63 See e.g. Fitzgerald (1963: 503); Winkler (1990).
64 As with the ending of the *Odyssey*, this conclusion has been highly controversial. It bothered not only Chase and Clift, as noted above, but many critics as well: Peter John Dyer calls it "the effeminate clowning of a sham showdown" (1972: 92) and Richard Corliss disparages Tess's role as "the *dea ex machina* whose clumsy contrivances will tidy up a more complex dilemma" (1996: 188). Others, including Robin Wood (1967: 11), John Belton (1972: 102), and Jacques Rivette (1972: 70), see the ending in a more positive light. Hawks himself called the ending "rather corny" (qtd. in McCarthy 1997: 424), but like Belton, argued for its merits based on characterization: "with the characters that I had and their relationship, that was the only ending you could possibly use. Anybody who says it different isn't a student of characters" (qtd. in McBride 2013: 154). Chase's original ending, in which Dunson dies from a wound inflicted by Valance, is more Iliadic, with the hero excluded from the society whose advancement he has helped to bring about.
65 Cohen (2010: 90–1). In my view, if Dunson is perpetuating a deception here, it is primarily a self-deception.

66 Sklar (1996: 159).
67 See Nugent (1999); Keith (2000: 111–19).
68 See e.g. Perkell (1981); Skulsky (1985).
69 Reeder (1980a: 57).
70 Reeder (1980b: 62) sees an opposition here: "In the *Aeneid* there is no ambiguity about the role an emotional relationship may play in the epic hero's life. He must deny such a relationship if he is finally to achieve his task ... In *Red River*, however, the opposite is true. One of the main themes of the film is that the feminine principle is necessary to the accomplishment of the epic task."
71 Davis (2005).
72 Bogdanovich (1962: 5); Bazin (1971: 154).
73 Sklar (1996: 153).

2 *Fred Zinnemann's* High Noon

FILM SUMMARY

High Noon opens with the marriage of Will Kane (Gary Cooper) and Amy Foster (Grace Kelly). Kane has been serving as marshal of Hadleyville, but following the ceremony, he officially relinquishes his badge, as he and Amy plan to move to another town where Kane will tend a store rather than carry a gun. As they prepare to leave, however, word comes that Frank Miller (Ian MacDonald) has been paroled and is scheduled to arrive on the noon train; Miller's old gang is already waiting at the station. When he was convicted, Miller had sworn to return and kill Kane, who had arrested him. Kane's instinct is to postpone his departure and stay to protect the town, since the man who is to replace him as marshal is not scheduled to arrive until the next day, but his friends convince him to make use of the little more than an hour he has before the train arrives and follow through with his plans.

The newlyweds hit the road, but they don't get far before Kane reconsiders and turns around over Amy's protestations. Back in town, Kane explains the situation to Amy as he reassumes his badge, intending to recruit special deputies to help him in the anticipated showdown with Miller. Amy pleads with him to avoid the confrontation, but although he recognizes the religious grounding of her opposition to violence, he remains resolute – even when she offers him the ultimatum that if he won't leave with her, she'll be on the next train without him. As she takes her leave, Kane encounters Judge Percy Mettrick (Otto Kruger), who sentenced Miller, and who is now packing to leave town, advising Kane to do the same. Just then, Kane's regular deputy Harvey "Harv" Pell (Lloyd Bridges) appears and tries to manipulate Kane into backing him as the new marshal;

when Kane refuses, believing he isn't ready for the job, Harv accuses him of speaking against his petition for the position to the city fathers out of jealousy over his relationship with Kane's ex, Helen Ramírez (Katy Jurado) and turns in his badge. When Helen hears this, she breaks it off with Harv and arranges to sell her share of the local store in preparation for leaving town. Kane, meanwhile, attempts to solicit special deputies, but time and again he is rejected by the men he thought he could count on: patrons at the local saloon, his friend Sam Fuller (Harry Morgan), churchgoers led by the mayor Jonas Henderson (Thomas Mitchell), and even the man who preceded him as marshal, Martin Howe (Lon Chaney, Jr.). Back at the hotel, Amy speaks to Helen in the hopes that she can intercede, and learning that she no longer has influence, the two come to an understanding. Meanwhile, a disheartened Kane contemplates fleeing, but his resolve returns when Harv Pell pushes him to do so with gleeful and self-interested enthusiasm.

As noon approaches, Kane finds himself alone. Amy, accompanied by Helen, has boarded the train Miller came in on, determined to leave town rather than wait and see if she's "a wife or a widow," and the one man who had volunteered to stand up with Kane, when he hears of the odds, calls it "suicide" and backs out. Kane makes out his will before marching forward grimly to meet Miller and his gang. When the first shots ring out, however, Amy has an abrupt change of heart: jumping from the train, she runs back to town. Kane manages to kill two of Miller's companions, and Amy shoots the third in the back. Miller then grabs Amy, using her as a shield to confront Kane, but she manages to wrench herself away, and Kane is able to get in the shots that bring Miller down. As the townspeople swarm forth into the previously deserted streets, a disillusioned Kane takes off his badge and throws it into the dust before he and Amy mount a carriage and ride away wordlessly.

INTRODUCTION

For many Americans, Fred Zinnemann's 1952 film *High Noon* is, as Don Graham puts it, "*the* Western movie."[1] The film was a critical and commercial success: it not only earned $3.4 million on its first release, but garnered seven Academy Award and seven Golden Globe nominations, both including Best Picture, with four wins each. It was named Best Film and Zinnemann Best Director by the New York Film Critics Circle, and Carl Foreman won the Writers Guild of America award for Best Written American Drama. And though his career had started to decline, his successful appearance in *High Noon* pushed Gary Cooper for the first time to the top of the box-office popularity chart in 1953.[2]

Yet the film has not been without its detractors – far from it. Film critic Robert Warshow was among the many Western purists who censured *High Noon* as "displaying a vulgar anti-populism" as part of a "social drama" in violation of the true Western form.[3] George Fenin and William Everson saw *High Noon* as over-rated, calling its script "inauthentic" and its direction "over-studied."[4] And Robin Wood has called it a film that "reeks of contrivance," bemoaning its lack of "inner logic" and "organic development."[5] Howard Hawks and John Wayne, moreover, were so appalled by the idea of a Western hero who asked for help rather than getting the job done himself that they made the 1959 *Rio Bravo* as a pointed response to Zinnemann's film, which Wayne called "the most un-American thing I've ever seen in my whole life."[6]

And despite his numerous awards and accolades – including a Lifetime Achievement Award from the Directors Guild of America in 1970 – Zinnemann's work more broadly has also been a target, particularly of the French *auteurist* critics who came to venerate Hawks in the 1950s and their followers. American *auteur* theorist and film critic Andrew Sarris, for instance, condemned Zinnemann in unambiguous terms, saying that, "At its best, his direction is inoffensive; at its worst, it is downright dull."[7] Structuralist critics like John Cawelti and Will Wright along with scholars of genre studies like Jim Kitses and Philip French often replicate this tendency, focusing on directors embraced by the *auteurists* – a partiality J. E. Smyth suggests stems from an underlying bias toward native-born directors:[8] to be sure, as an Austrian-born Jew who trained in Paris, Zinnemann is far from the red-blooded American male ideal the Western genre venerates. Zinnemann, however, brushed his critics aside, expressing disdain for Hawks as "a man so obsessed with 'professional' heroes that he remade the same film again and again" and scoffing at *auteur* theory as "little more than a gimmick."[9]

An additional complication when discussing this film is that unlike most works whose fictionalized and distanced setting in the heroic past makes them "safe . . . context[s] in which to test, question, and reaffirm the values" of contemporary society,[10] *High Noon*'s clear social commentary has made it particularly susceptible to specific political readings. Harry Schein, for instance, has argued that *High Noon* works as an explanation of US foreign policy during the Cold War, with Kane representing America, Frank Miller and his gang representing the international Communist threat, Amy symbolizing pacifist movements within the US, and the townspeople representing other nations who refuse to stand beside the United States in Korea in order to preserve world peace.[11] Others see the film as a comment on the contemporary House Un-American Activities Committee (HUAC) investigations, where Miller and his gang, representing McCarthy and his supporters, threaten the innocent Kane, who is abandoned by a community too afraid to stand up for what is right.[12] Screenwriter Carl Foreman, who was blacklisted and fled the US in 1953 in the wake of his appearance as an "unfriendly" witness at HUAC hearings into alleged communist activities,[13] did not comment at the time, but later said that he intended the film as a metaphor for what was going on in Hollywood.[14] Still others have suggested a more personal interpretation, seeing parallels between Kane and Zinnemann: Stephen Prince, for instance, connects Zinnemann's situation as an Austrian Jew to Kane's position, in that each man is "deserted and made a scapegoat by his community and by people he believed were his friends," while Smyth implies a similar parallel based on the place Zinnemann, as a European-born Jewish director of a Western, occupied as a genre "outsider."[15]

Zinnemann himself seemed baffled at the notion that the film was a commentary on the Cold War,[16] and though he expressed respect for Foreman's views, he emphasized that at the time, he himself did not in his "wildest dreams" consider it an allegory of any sort,[17] arguing instead for the film's broader, more universal meaning:[18]

> This for me was not a political film. This was read into it because a lot of people shared Carl Foreman's concept without really thinking beyond it. I don't think that the film survived because of its political value. It survived simply because I tried to deal with basic questions of human conduct.[19]

Phillip Drummond's suggestion that audiences in 1952 were more or less oblivious to its political implications[20] supports Zinnemann's perspective, as does Don Graham's belief that later audiences too were unlikely to read into the film specific allegorical meanings without being nudged.[21]

Still, as Zinnemann himself has acknowledged, the film "seems to mean different things to different people,"[22] a fact well illustrated by the political uses to which it has been put. It is the Hollywood movie most often shown at the White House over the past fifty years, including screenings by Dwight D. Eisenhower, Bill Clinton, and George W. Bush,[23] while US presidents from Lyndon Johnson to George W. Bush to Barack Obama have been compared to its hero

Will Kane.[24] Ronald Reagan himself drew upon Kane's situation as a comparison with the lonely position of being a Republican in Democratic territory.[25] Although its employment by those on both sides of the political spectrum may seem surprising, Peter Biskind has argued that if we didn't have Foreman's explicit statement about the film's meaning, it would be hard to distinguish this film from one on the political right; indeed, at least one commentator, partly influenced by the casting of the right-wing Cooper, read the film as a call to stand up to communism.[26] Joanna Rapf suggests that for more recent audiences, it is neither a right- nor a left-wing film, but "one that is aimed at a broad-based coalition against the center."[27] Nor have its usages been restricted to America: its imagery was (successfully) utilized in propaganda for Poland's national elections in 1989.[28]

While the meaning Foreman offered is often taken as definitive, the many different interpretations that have been given and the vast number of political uses to which the film has been put suggest to me that, like classical mythology, it is a story that is useful because it is applicable to a broad range of human experiences. Not long before his death in 1997, Zinnemann said, "If you ask me today what do I think, I would say it is about self-respect. Three years ago I would have said it's about conscience. Ten years ago I would have said the characters' destiny,"[29] suggesting a fluidity of meaning that characterizes so many enduring works. Thus in a more general sense, like Greek and Roman epic, *High Noon* is "political in the way that the genre is political, for it is about leadership [and] community,"[30] and as such, the film resonates with universal themes and concerns in addition to the more precise allegorical meanings often assigned to it.

Regardless of how the film is read and of criticisms that have been directed toward it, it would be difficult to dispute that *High Noon* has entered the canon of paradigmatic American Westerns: in 1988 members of the British Film Institute voted the film "best western ever made,"[31] and in 1989 the National Film Preservation Board selected it as one of twenty-five films to be included in the National Film Registry in its inaugural year. It has inspired remakes and sequels;[32] homages appear in the opening sequences of Peckinpah's *Once Upon a Time in the West* and Burt Kennedy's 1973 *The Train Robbers*;[33] and it has spawned numerous offshoots, both critical, like *Rio Bravo*, and reverential, like both the 1957 *3:10 to Yuma*, which uses time to create tension and focuses on a hero abandoned by his allies, and Clint Eastwood's 1973 *High Plains Drifter*, in which a mysterious avenger punishes a town for its cowardly desertion of its marshal.[34] And though most young people today likely have not seen *High*

Noon, its thorough integration into our cultural vocabulary is well illustrated by an episode of the recent FX series *Justified* where the villain, disappointed that his partner has not killed Marshal Givens, complains, "I thought you were going to go all *High Noon* on him!"[35]

Because of its central place in the genre and in the American consciousness, if the Western in general is to be considered a cultural counterpart to Greek and Roman epic as this book contends, this is a film that cannot be ignored. But at the same time, it does not fit easily into this comparison. Will Kane's affinities with Greek and Roman epic heroes are not immediately apparent – he does not exhibit Achilles' famous rage, Odysseus' wariness, or Aeneas' *pietas* (devotion to gods, country, and forefathers) – but he does embody characteristics found in each of them. And while its mythic-historic anchoring, as we shall see, is unusual for a Western, the film's plot and central concerns intersect significantly with those of the ancient epics. As I hope the analysis of *Red River* in the previous chapter has begun to suggest, the many meaningful connections between this film and all three canonical epics from Greco-Roman antiquity demonstrate perhaps better than an obvious parallel with just one of them that while Western filmmakers do not simply recycle ancient material by consciously inserting specific character-types and plotlines, the similar position each genre occupies in its respective cultural imagination and their common concern with establishing cultural ideologies – in particular with defining what it is that makes a man – position Western cinema as the epic genre for modern America.[36]

THE EPIC TRADITION

As with Hawks, there is little to connect Zinnemann himself directly with the Greco-Roman past, although his statement that *High Noon*'s screenplay "happens to follow the ancient rules of Greek drama – the three unities of time, space and action," along with his praise for directors of his day for following "the two-thousand-year-old rule that a drama, in order to create real emotional relief, has to have a balance of terror and pity"[37] suggest at least an indirect familiarity with Aristotle's *Poetics*. Nor has the film's relationship to antiquity been adequately explored: although the ending has prompted Stephen Tatum to label the film "a distinguished Western version of Greek tragedy" and Martin Winkler has briefly noted some affinities between Kane and Greek tragic protagonists,[38] to my knowledge there has been no sustained examination of its relationship to ancient works. And perhaps in part due to its eschewing of great vistas and grand timeframes, *High Noon*'s "epic" qualities seem to have been ignored almost entirely. To be sure, many of the broad connections this film has with epic are not transparent; unlike *Red River*, for instance, this film exhibits no evident concern with notions of hospitality, progeny, burial, or legacy.

Even its position as mythologized history is far more tentative than with most Westerns: it does not offer a specific date or a real location to imply historicity, nor does it refer to historical figures from the Old West or center on a historical event. In fact, the same elements most Westerns use as an historical anchor *High Noon* uses to create a mythic quality. The vague time and place setting offer the impression that this could be any Western town at some imprecise time in the frontier era, a vagueness supported by the small number of external references, which Philip Drummond has observed "confer a weak sense of diegetic reality, and . . . open up a passing sense of a world 'out there.'"[39] Also unlike most Westerns, the historical anchoring that does occur in this film is almost entirely aesthetic: that is, Zinnemann was aiming for a documentary style, and he and his cameraman Floyd Crosby deliberately set out to make it "look like a newsreel of the period, if newsreels had existed around 1870, which of course they didn't."[40] To this end, Zinnemann and Crosby studied the photography of the Civil War era, particularly the work of Lincoln's cameraman Mathew Brady, and attempted to replicate the flatness, the coarse grain, and the white sky, shunning filters and soft focus.[41] Producer Stanley Kramer reportedly tried to fire Crosby for this, but Zinnemann defended him, arguing for the look as more historically accurate and authentic.[42] In addition, the film's intense focus on time – not only with repeated images of ticking clocks, but also its apparent unraveling in "real" time – in some ways lends the sense of realness that the temporal and geographical setting evades. Yet despite the impression of the film's action taking place in real time, careful observation shows that time sometimes stands still or even runs in reverse, so that time, too, is a mixture of real and unreal that parallels the mythic-historical anchoring.[43]

More than most Westerns, then, *High Noon* offers a sense of realness divorced from a particular time and place, the importance of which is suggested by the single reference to actual (not insignificantly, Greek) history: while packing – specifically, while folding an American flag – Judge Mettrick cynically predicts the town's reaction to Miller's return by recalling an incident in fifth-century BC Greece when the citizens of Athens welcomed back with open arms a brutal tyrant they had earlier deposed and banished, and then stood by while he executed members of the government. Mettrick follows this with a reference to a similar thing happening "about eight years ago" in the fictional town of Indian Falls. While the fictional nature of Indian Falls and Hadleyville gives the Western setting of *High Noon* a mythic quality, the reference to real ancient history effectively suggests that the film's events hold a larger lesson, one applicable in any time or place. This brand of mythic-historic contextualization, while unusual, implies a pattern of human behavior that works both to reinforce and to counter the specific political applications discussed above – suggesting that none of them are correct but, at the same time, they all are.

Closer scrutiny also shows that despite initial appearances, *High Noon* is unusual in its treatment of gender. At first glance, the casting of Gary Cooper seems to situate the film in the heroic Western tradition, since, to many, Cooper embodies the particular brand of heroism and masculinity this genre promotes. His criticism of *High Noon* notwithstanding, Robert Warshow used Cooper in his lead role in the 1929 film *The Virginian* as a model for his definition of the Western hero.[44] Louis Giannetti and Steven Tatum have also noted his status as the paradigmatic Western hero, with Tatum calling him "the embodiment of the ideal American male."[45] And Philip Drummond calls him "a global cinematic icon associated with a powerfully solid and undemonstrative form of masculine performance."[46] Yet not only had Cooper's box-office appeal dropped in the later 1940s, but he was past fifty when *High Noon* was filmed, and his age showed: his face was lined, and he was suffering from arthritis, a bleeding ulcer, and a bad hip. As a result, he was gaunt, stooped, and walked a bit stiffly.[47] In addition, some critics saw the role itself as running counter to the established ideal of what a Western hero should be. Howard Hawks, for instance, scorned the character for "[running] around and trying to get help and no one would give him any," calling it "rather a silly thing for a man to do."[48] J. E. Smyth has noted somewhat less critically that unlike "the contained, impregnable bastion of the Western hero" embodied by John Wayne, Cooper's portrayal here shows that "the hero's physical borders have a permeability" – he sweats, he winces, he breaks down in despair – "usually reserved for the projection of women in Cold War Westerns."[49]

In other ways, however, Kane fits the heroic bill. He is tall with rugged good looks; his deep, commanding voice is used sparingly, with the typical laconism of Western heroes ("I've got to. That's the whole thing"); and despite his trepidation, he is largely drawn as a man of honor, courage, and resolve. As Don Graham notes, the fact that, in the end, he is willing to die to satisfy his own notions of what is right is a commitment that firmly links him to the established heroic tradition, while Smyth ultimately concludes that Cooper's character "reformulated the image of the Western hero as one who didn't have to project a hyper-violent, impregnable façade in order to articulate his American individualism and masculinity."[50] As a result of these contradictions, both within the movie and in a broader sense, Cooper's character works to question and reconfigure the "generic codes that underwrite accepted epic values and behavior," illustrating the reinvention that Blundell and Ormand identify as lying at "the heart of the Western epic."[51]

But questioning and reconfiguration aside, in order to be identified as a Western or epic hero, a man must ultimately provide a model for idealized masculinity, and in this, Kane undoubtedly succeeds. Despite what has gone before, the film culminates in a heroic battle, aggrandized as in epic by the arming scenes (Fig. 2.1) and tense anticipation that precede it, in which the hero's violent masculine superiority is confirmed through his triumph. So definitive is the model Cooper provides that even fifty years later in the

2.1 Jack Colby (Lee Van Cleef) and Jim Pierce (Robert Wilke) arm for battle in *High Noon* (1952). Stanley Kramer Productions.

critically acclaimed HBO series *The Sopranos*, Tony Soprano sees Cooper's character from this film – "Gary Cooper: now there was an American. The strong, silent type. He did what he had to do. He faced down the Miller gang when none of those other assholes in town would lift a finger to help him" – as an archetype for idealized masculinity.[52]

Like Kane, the female characters here are not typical, not least in their prominence. Many have noted that the insertion of two fully developed female characters is one of the most significant changes Foreman made to the short story on which the vengeance plot of *High Noon* is loosely based, John Cunningham's "The Tin Star," in which the only female character mentioned is the late wife of the sheriff (there called Doane).[53] But while Amy Fowler Kane and Helen Ramírez have unusually large roles for female characters in Westerns, at a glance they seem to conform to the familiar dichotomy of white, virginal wife vs. dark, sexually experienced mistress. This familiar division was reinforced by casting – Zinnemann called the largely unknown Grace Kelly "a lucky piece of casting" because "she gave the illusion of this totally pure image of the virginal feminine ideal of those days,"[54] while Katy Jurado was a Hollywood newcomer but an established Mexican film actress who specialized in roles as a dangerous seductress – and by costuming – Alan Marcus notes the way Zinnemann contrasted the women's costumes, with "the virginal woman all in white, but closeted. Her chest is bound, her sexuality suppressed, contained. As opposed to Ramirez [*sic*], who was voluptuous, sexy and dressed half the time in a negligee" (Fig. 2.2).[55] Yet others have noted that the film's conformity to these stereotypes is only apparent: both Amy and Helen are strong, mature, articulate, and principled women. Indeed, in the shooting script, Amy describes herself as "a feminist."[56] These striking advances in the portrayal of female characters have led scholars like Don Graham, Joanna Rapf, Gwendolyn Foster, and J. E. Smyth to see them as active players and transgressive agents who subvert traditional notions of Western masculinity.[57]

But while in many ways I can agree that the strong and independent Helen and the active and self-determining Amy represent a revolution in the depiction of women in Westerns, they ultimately serve to reinforce rather than undermine generic expectations about gender. That is, Amy's arguments and threats to leave her man throughout most of the film are a subversion of expectations that in the end serve to make her turnabout more dramatic. As Rapf says,

2.2 Helen Ramírez (Katy Jurado) and Amy Fowler Kane (Grace Kelly) in *High Noon* (1952). Stanley Kramer Productions.

> We can see this resolution as the familiar Hollywood cliche of the woman finally recognizing that her man is most important in her life and that right or wrong he comes first even if it means giving up her ideals whereas *he* must never be put in a position where he must give up his.[58]

But although Rapf introduces this view in order to refute it, in the end this message is the takeaway. As we find in ancient epic, the virtuous woman is the one whose actions and intentions ultimately work to support the masculine heroic agenda, and if she does occasionally offer an alternative to male heroic action, it appears to be introduced in order to be swept away and discounted. For all his animosity toward the film, John Wayne's assertion later in life that women and their concerns had no place in the "real" Old West[59] is here born out: Amy's idealistic anti-violence stance may sound good in the abstract, but when push comes to shove, feminized notions of pacifism go out the window.

These sorts of unusual treatments of context and gender, along with the social drama *High Noon* includes, have led many to question whether it is a Western at all: even those less critical than Warshow suggest that despite its setting, it gets its "content from elsewhere,"[60] while Zinnemann himself has repeatedly insisted that it is "not a Western, as far as I'm concerned; it just happens to be set in the Old West."[61] But while the film does seem to subvert many of the usual generic expectations, closer examination reveals that not just in geographical setting and iconography, but in mythic-historical anchoring, in the self-questioning nature of the hero, and in the gendered models that emerge by the film's end, it ultimately conforms to the Western framework as we have seen it applied elsewhere and fits into the larger epic context as well. It is my hope that by drawing out its particular resonances with Homer's poems and the *Aeneid*, not only will *High Noon*'s close relationship to ancient epic be revealed, but it will at the same time be firmly redeemed for the Western genre.

THE *ILIAD*

Despite the surface dissimilarity in plot and motivation, there are a number of connections between *High Noon* and Homer's *Iliad* that suggest more than a passing affinity. The most immediately apparent basis for comparison here is that both works focus on a hero who is fundamentally estranged from the community and whose disillusionment with the status quo ultimately forces him to question traditional values and ideologies. In the *Iliad*, Achilles' separation from Greek warrior society is immediate, taking place in Book 1; it is self-imposed, as he removes himself from battle after an insult to his honor; and it results primarily from a conflict with just one man, the great king Agamemnon. Will Kane's estrangement in *High Noon*, on the other hand, is more gradual, taking place over the course of the film as he is abandoned one by one by the men he thought he could count on; it is not initially self-imposed, as it is the community members who refuse to fight with him rather than vice versa; and it results from the divergent viewpoints of the hero and the townspeople more generally, rather than being focused on the hero's disagreement with one particular individual. These discrepancies contribute to characterizations of the heroes that are very different in spirit. While the primary emotion the audience connects with Achilles is rage – an association emphasized from the first word of the epic's proem[62] – Will Kane's character is shaped more by a grim determination bred from feelings of abandonment, despair, and even loneliness, emotions emphasized in the famous crane shot, when the camera pulls up and away from an apprehensive Kane setting out alone in the deserted streets to meet Miller's gang (Fig. 2.3). In both cases, however, the heroes initially have an untarnished faith in the justice of the social

2.3 Will Kane (Gary Cooper) in *High Noon* (1952). Stanley Kramer Productions.

system as they know it, and both men become radically isolated as the men who should provide the backbone of this system fail them.

In both cases, too, the hero's estrangement forces him to reconsider the values for which he fights and the reasons behind the battle. After his degradation at Agamemnon's hands, Achilles begins to question the ethic compelling Greek warriors to fight for the glory that offered a semblance of immortality to all-too-mortal men. When Agamemnon takes away his war-prize Briseis and thus deprives him of his proper honor, Achilles complains:

> I did not come here to fight because of the warriors
> Of Troy, since there are no grounds for me at all. . ..
> But for you, O shameless one, we followed you here so that you might rejoice
> as we win honor for Menelaus and for you, dogface,
> from the Trojans. You do not take heed of these things or care about them at all;
> and now you even threaten to rob me of my prize,
> for which I toiled greatly, and which the sons of the Achaeans gave me. (1.152–62)

In Achilles' view, it is one thing to be fighting in the interest of fellow Greeks when there is glory to be gained, but when those men are ungrateful and exploitative, honor falls by the wayside and it becomes a different matter entirely. So too does Will Kane become disillusioned with his initial reasons for standing up to Miller and his gang once the men of the town refuse to stand beside him: as Don Graham puts it, "To die for a town worth dying for is one thing; to die for a bunch of backbiting hypocrites is something else."[63] In this way, the community in *High Noon* fulfills a parallel role to that of Agamemnon in the *Iliad*. In each case the hero, who functions on a physically and spiritually superior level, works for an entity with which or with whom he becomes disillusioned when that entity is exposed as hypocritical and contemptible.[64] Both men ultimately engage in battle only after finding a higher, and more personal, purpose. For Achilles, it is the visceral need for revenge he feels after Hector slays his companion Patroclus, while Kane ultimately must be willing to fight for himself, not only for his own safety and peace of mind, but also to live up to his own expectations of manhood and to satisfy his own sense of what is right.

Furthermore, attempts in *High Noon* to repair or prevent the rift between the hero and the larger community mirror similar movements in Homer's epic. In Book 9 of the *Iliad* – the so-called "Embassy to Achilles" – Agamemnon sends Odysseus, Phoenix, and Ajax to offer Achilles an apology and restitution on his behalf. By choosing these three men, Agamemnon approaches Achilles from intellectual, emotional, and physical angles, as Odysseus is the most cunning of the Greeks, Phoenix is a father-figure of sorts to Achilles, and Ajax is second only to Achilles in physical prowess and ability in battle. Agamemnon's ploy fails, however, as Achilles stubbornly rejects his offer and refuses to return to battle. Achilles' refusal intensifies his estrangement from the Greek troops in general, as Diomedes suggests when, upon hearing Achilles' response, he says, "[Achilles] is haughty enough already; now you have incited him even further into arrogance. But let's forget about him. Let him either go or stay" (9.699–702).

In *High Noon*, we have a sort of reverse embassy, in which Kane approaches various members of the community individually. As in the *Iliad*, each man represents something important both in the community and to Kane himself: Judge Mettrick represents justice; his friend Sam Fuller symbolizes friendship and loyalty; Mayor Jonas Henderson stands for progress and community; and his predecessor as marshal Martin Howe, in addition to representing law and order, has been a mentor and father-figure to Kane. Yet each of these men refuses to help, and in doing so, subverts the very principles he is supposed to embody. Rather than standing for justice, Judge Mettrick demonstrates self-interested pragmatism and expresses a cynical lack of faith in the community. Instead of loyalty, Fuller reveals the worst kind of cowardice, compelling his distressed and reluctant wife to lie and say that he isn't home rather than facing Kane himself. Henderson should be ready to defend the progress and cohesion of the community, but is most concerned for how gunplay in the streets will affect the town's economic well-being.

Finally, although we expect Howe to be a champion of law, order, and justice, instead he suggests apathy. Although he uses his arthritis as an excuse, Howe implies that his real reason for refusing to join Kane is disillusionment when he says of their profession,

> It's a great life. You risk your skin catchin' killers and the juries turn 'em loose so they can come back and shoot at you again. If you're honest, you're poor your whole life. And in the end, you wind up dyin' all alone on some dirty street. For what? For nothin'. For a tin star.[65]

Like the embassy to Achilles, these interactions only serve to widen the rift between Kane and the community at large by distancing him from men he had counted as friends. Thus while the movement of these two embassies on the surface is in opposite directions, both function as a means of demonstrating the completeness of the heroes' estrangement from the various segments of the community with whom they used to identify.

Another point of comparison is that in both works, the hero comes into conflict with the person closest to him over the issue of whether or not to re-enter the fight. In the *Iliad*, Patroclus pleads with Achilles to return to battle out of pity for the dying Greeks (16.21–45), while in *High Noon*, Kane's wife Amy begs him *not* to engage with Miller due to her aversion to violence and her fear of losing him. While Patroclus' and Amy's arguments at first glance seem, again, to be in opposition to one another, both are based on ethical considerations which conflict with the hero's position and which compel the audience to reconsider the integrity of his stance: Patroclus' distressed pleas on behalf of his imperiled comrades make Achilles' stubborn defense of his honor seem selfish and petty, while the religious basis of Amy's horror of violence and its origins in the violent deaths of her father and brother bring the morality of Kane's intentions into question and position him as insensitive to his wife's past trauma.

In addition, both of these companions enter the battle themselves, and in ways that run counter to the wishes and expectations of the heroes. While Patroclus' initial re-entry into battle is with Achilles' consent, Achilles has ordered him to push the Trojans away from the Greek ships, but then back off (16.87–96). Patroclus instead not only approaches the Trojan city walls, but dares to fight with the greatest Trojan warrior Hector, a decision that costs him his life. As a woman and a Quaker, Amy's engagement in battle runs counter to all expectations. Like Patroclus, she oversteps the limits of expected behavior, and as a result, her life is endangered when she is taken hostage by Miller. Unlike Patroclus, however, she survives when she pushes Miller away and Kane manages to shoot him.

In both works, moreover, the hero ultimately engages in the confrontation with the enemy only after undergoing a sort of sea change. In the *Iliad*, Achilles' anger over Agamemnon's slight is more or less forgotten, replaced with a purer, more existential grief and rage when he learns of Patroclus' death. In *High Noon*, the motivation behind Kane's determination to confront Miller shifts from idealistic notions of community solidarity to more visceral instincts toward self-preservation and more deeply ingrained and individualized notions of manhood and integrity. In the end, then, the protagonist in each of these works is compelled to scrutinize and reassess social codes and ideologies he once took as given. Thus in *High Noon* as in epic, as Blundell and Ormand put it, "the real hero is not the one who simply states and defends the accepted rules of society . . . but the one who reaffirms those rules only after questioning and redefining them in his own terms."[66]

Another point of convergence in the *Iliad* and *High Noon* is the psychological identification suggested between the hero, a companion, and his opponent. In the *Iliad*, as we have seen, Homer sets up a triangular relationship between Achilles, Hector, and Patroclus that in some ways anticipates the work of Carl Jung, in that both Patroclus and Hector are identified as different facets of Achilles' persona, with Patroclus representing his more sensitive feminine side (what Jung termed the *anima*) and Hector his darker, "shadow" characteristics – that is, Hector embodies the traits which Achilles is reluctant to acknowledge in himself. This identification is symbolized visually, first when Patroclus dons Achilles' armor in Book 16 and morphs into a fierce and (nearly) unstoppable Achilles-like force in battle, and then when Hector in turn, having killed Patroclus, assumes this same armor in Book 22 and wears it in the showdown with Achilles, forcing Achilles, in effect, to come face to face with his second self.

So too in *High Noon* is Will Kane subtly paralleled with both an ally and an enemy.[67] Although, in some ways, Amy fills a Patroclean role – and indeed clearly represents the feminine balance to Kane/ Cooper's masculinity – Kane's deputy, Harv Pell, also serves as a softer, though more negative, foil for Kane: while both are lawmen and both have been involved with the same woman, Helen Ramírez, Harv's impetuousness, selfishness, and immaturity are constantly highlighted to emphasize Kane's better qualities.[68] Unlike Kane, who is willing to fight for the community despite the risk to himself and the threat to his marriage, Harv refuses to fight Miller unless he is rewarded by being named Kane's successor, a position for which the city fathers apparently think he is unsuited; he *is* willing to fight Kane, however, in order to get his way. The contrast between the two men is made explicit when Helen tells Harv, "You are a good-looking boy. You have big broad shoulders. But [Kane] is a man. It takes more than big broad shoulders to make a man, Harvey, and you have a long way to go."

Kane is also identified with his nemesis Frank Miller long before Miller's arrival. As Richard Slotkin notes, the hero's name combines a hint of "'will' as the drive to power with a homonym of the Bible's first murderer," associating Kane with the sort of villainy Miller embodies.[69] His propensity for violence is suggested when, overhearing the saloonkeeper betting against him, Kane punches him, an action for which he is immediately criticized – censure he himself accepts as valid. Furthermore, he is positioned as an "outlaw" at the impromptu town meeting at the church when one man reminds the crowd that he is no longer marshal and then implies that Kane is motivated by "personal trouble" rather than by desire to safeguard law, order, and public safety. The mayor himself defines Kane's stance as anti-progressive and against the town's interests, and in the end the townsfolk decline to support him either in body or in spirit, making him, in effect, a vigilante of sorts. In addition, despite the clear overall characterization of Kane as protagonist and Miller as the "bad guy," symbolic color associations are reversed, with the hero wearing mostly black with a black hat, while we find that the villain, when he arrives, is dressed in light colors, a detail which problematizes black-and-white categorizations metaphorically speaking as well. The "triangular" relationship between Kane, Harv Pell, and Miller is then further attested when we learn that Miller, too, has a history with Helen Ramírez. In symbolic terms that unfortunately are not altogether dated, Kane's past with Helen, a "dark" Mexican woman with a questionable reputation (as Mr. Weaver implies when he explains, "my wife thought. . .," but diplomatically stops himself mid-sentence) and his subsequent turn to Amy, a "pure" virginal white woman of the Quaker faith – a juxtaposition emphasized through more traditional color-coding (see figure 2.2) – signifies Kane's earlier potential to have been "like" Miller, and his ultimate "instinct for goodness," the quality which in the end distinguishes the two men, otherwise so alike.[70] In both epic and film, then, the final showdown on some levels represents the hero's struggle to come to terms with his darker side.

Furthermore, in *High Noon* we do not see the hero in action until the final scenes of the film, just as in the *Iliad* Achilles' prowess is known only through his reputation, and he does not actually take the field until Book 21. In both cases, the final showdown represents the hero's move toward assuming a fully realized heroic identity both physically and psychologically. And in both cases, this heroic identity cannot be achieved "until the purpose of fighting has shifted to something more than a quarrel over a woman."[71] Just as the Trojan War was initially instigated by the abduction of Helen, and Achilles' disagreement with Agamemnon centered on the rights to the war-prize Briseis, so too, it is implied, is Miller's grudge with Kane at least in part located in Kane's relationship with Miller's former girlfriend, also named Helen. Ultimately, however, both heroes move away from motives of public honor where the quarrel over women is located, and, as suggested above, enter the fight for more personal reasons: Achilles is motivated by grief and revenge, and Kane both by concern with self-preservation – he knows that he now has little time to run, and that if he does, he'll always be looking over his shoulder – and by his need to conform to unspoken notions regarding what it takes to be a man.[72]

When the two heroes finally meet their foes, both show indisputable superiority in battle: Achilles is described as a godlike force, and as we have seen, is repeatedly likened to elements like fire and metal; so fearsome is he that all the Trojans run for the cover of the city walls and Hector himself loses courage and takes flight (21.606–11 and 22.136–66, 188–201). While Kane's prowess is not characterized as quite so superhuman, he does courageously take on, and ultimately defeat, four men almost single-handedly in a sequence reminiscent of the *aristeia* common in classical epic. But despite their skill, both men are assisted by a *dea ex machina* of sorts: in the *Iliad*, Athena first deceives Hector to encourage him to stand firm and later spirits Achilles' spear back to him after a missed shot (22.226–47, 273–7); in *High Noon*, Kane is unexpectedly assisted by his wife Amy, who rushes back to town at the last minute and manages to shoot one of the villains in the back, an action contrary to both her Quaker principles and the very code of the West.

In the end, the triumph of the hero over his opponent in both epic and film works to restore the correct balance of power through the defeat of a man who upholds injustice:[73] Hector fights on behalf of Paris, who transgressed societal notions of propriety by cuckolding Achilles' comrade Menelaus, while Frank Miller himself is a convicted criminal and the embodiment of the Western villain. Nonetheless, in both cases, the heroes themselves cannot truly re-enter the society they have helped to preserve: as Achilles' goddess-mother Thetis has told us in the *Iliad*, Achilles will not return home, but his death will follow hard on that of Hector (18.94–6). Kane, too, is ultimately excluded from the society he risks his life to save, both psychologically, as is suggested when he hurls his badge into the dust, and physically, as his rapid departure with his wife indicates. As Blundell and Ormand observe, this "image of the hero as an outsider who must leave town, who cannot be part of the society he redeems or destroys, is a standard trope of both Western and epic closure."[74] On a more positive note, however, both men do succeed in coming to terms with death. As we have seen, Achilles' conflict with Hector represents a struggle against his own mortal limitations, and the process of accepting this is complete when, in Book 24, his cathartic interaction with Priam allows him to put his anger aside, releasing Hector's body and accepting not just Patroclus' death, but also his own. So too at the end of *High Noon*, Kane looks his own death in the eye, writing out his last will and testament in an implicit recognition of his human impermanence. In both works, then, the hero's existential crisis and its resolution through acceptance of the mortal condition is a significant part of the heroic trajectory.

Ironically, despite these close affinities with Homer's Achilles, Will Kane is a very human hero, and as such, he also demonstrates similarities worth exploring with Achilles' foe, the sympathetic Hector. Like Hector, Kane fights a battle that is not entirely his own: Hector fights in reluctant defense of his brother Paris' abduction of Helen, while Kane, who technically is no longer marshal, defends a town too craven to defend itself. Like Hector, who is deserted by his comrades and left alone to face Achilles – an abandonment felt all the more acutely when Athena first offers solidarity and support in the form of Hector's brother Deiphobus and then abruptly disappears – Kane too is abandoned by those he thought he could rely on, a situation whose completeness is also highlighted by a last-minute desertion, that of Herb, the one comrade who had promised to fight alongside him. Like Hector, who hesitates, first trying to think of a way out and then fleeing around the walls of Troy three times before finding the courage to stand firm and face his foe, Kane too first considers fleeing and later succumbs briefly to grief and despair, slumping over his desk with his head in his arms. As such, despite a prevailing resemblance to Achilles, Kane also works as a Hector figure through the sheer force of his humanity.

In addition, the gender dynamic that emerges in *High Noon* reflects to a large extent that found in the *Iliad*, a parallel best shown through Hector's interactions. Although the Homeric poems in general exhibit a less rigid dichotomization of gendered activities, roles, and attributes than that found in the "divided world" occupied by the ancient Greeks of the classical period, the *Iliad* does set up a strategic opposition in Book 6, where the feminine world of the city, now devoid of all its warriors, is contrasted with the masculine sphere of the battlefield.[75] When Hector enters the city, he encounters three women in succession, Hecuba, Helen, and Andromache, each of whom serves as an example of a different role for women – the mother, the seductress, and the good wife. While *High Noon* offers no maternal model, Helen Ramírez is a close parallel to the role of her ancient namesake. As with Homer's Helen, ambiguity about her past behavior and present associations surrounds Helen Ramírez, casting doubt on her virtue. Like Homer's Helen, who left Menelaus for Paris, married Deiphobus after his brother Paris' death, and later returned to her first husband Menelaus, Helen Ramírez has "multiple historical allegiances":[76] she is a widow who has engaged in affairs with three men, two of whom are mortal enemies and two of whom are colleagues. And like Homer's Helen, who "subjugates warriors instead of being subject to them,"[77] Helen Ramírez "insists on her own control of her physical relation to men."[78] Helen's destructive potential in each case, moreover, is highlighted through her dominance over one of these men: as one of my students observed, in the *Iliad* the impetuous and superficial Paris is feminized by his relationship with Helen, while in *High Noon* Harv Pell is similarly characterized.

Likewise in both works, the Helen characters' dangerous associations work to highlight the virtuous qualities of the wives Andromache and Amy, who, though they too both pose a threat, are ultimately cast as virtuous. Like Amy, Andromache tries to entice the hero to pull back from the more perilous aspects of battle: contrary to expectations for women, she offers him advice on military strategy, suggesting he take up a more defensive position on the rampart where he will still be able to act as Troy's defender, but which course would require that he give up his quest for the *kleos* (glory) by which masculinity and heroism were measured.[79] Hector, of course, rejects Andromache's appeal, placing his public standing and the desire in his own heart for glory above all other considerations (6.431–46). Similarly, in *High Noon* Amy represents a domesticating force, voicing a passionate and rational opposition to violence of any sort, which Foster describes as a "rupture of the discourse of warmongering and blind patriotism,"[80] much as Andromache's advice to Hector constituted a challenge to accepted codes of male combat by presenting a sensible strategic alternative. But like Hector, Kane stubbornly refuses to reconsider. That his stance is based on societal notions of manhood and honor is suggested by the film's theme song:

> If I'm a man I must be brave
> And I must face that deadly killer
> Or lie a coward, a craven coward
> Or lie a coward in my grave. . . .
> Although you're grieving'
> I can't be leavin'
> Until I shoot Frank Miller dead.[81]

The ideology of manhood implied here is strikingly similar to that found in the Homeric world in that both societies explicitly disregard women's needs and desires in pursuit of manly achievement – a dynamic Amy refuses to ignore, responding to Kane's sympathetic, "Sure I know how you feel," with a defiant, "But you're doing it just the same!" As Jane Tompkins argues, it is almost as if the feminine viewpoint "is introduced in order to be swept aside, crushed, or dramatically invalidated,"[82] and it is through this opposition that the male world of violent heroism – and indeed manhood itself – is defined. In epic as in the Western, "far from being peripheral, women's discourse, or some sign of it, is a necessary and enabling condition."[83] In both genres, not only does male honor take precedence over feminine needs and values, but in both cases the male perspective is validated when the woman concedes to his position – in Andromache's case, by her submissive deferral to Hector's decision, and in Amy's, by her more dramatic last-minute renunciation of her non-violent stance in order to stand by her husband rather than leaving him as she had initially threatened.[84] In both cases then, attention to women's concerns primarily functions as a sort of straw man, introduced in order that the alternate male perspective be more fully endorsed through their defeat.

While *High Noon*'s connections to the *Iliad*, therefore, are not perfectly neat and straightforward, they are pervasive, and begin to build a case for this film's relationship with ancient epic despite criticism which would exclude it from the Western genre altogether, a relationship which examination of the film's connection to the *Odyssey* will help to strengthen.

THE *ODYSSEY*

Unlike *Red River*, with its focus on a physical journey and a protagonist with distinct anti-heroic qualities, *High Noon* does not at first suggest any obvious connection with Homer's *Odyssey*, but as with the *Iliad*, an interesting kinship emerges on closer inspection. To begin, Will Kane shows some basic situational similarities and character traits in common with Odysseus. Both men are estranged from traditional religion: Odysseus is cursed by Poseidon, who delays his return home in revenge for Odysseus' blinding of his son Polyphemus (1.68–75), while Kane, as the parson points out bitterly, neither attends church regularly, nor did he "see fit" to be married there. Both men are human heroes whose superiority is grounded in strategy as much as in physical prowess, a kinship illustrated by their similar means of escaping from a "closed room" scenario: in Book 9, Odysseus and his men escape the Cyclops' cave clinging to the bellies of sheep, while Kane escapes a burning barn clinging to the side of a horse. Indeed, a photo caption describing Kane in Louis Giannetti's *Masters of the American Cinema* as "a mere mortal, not a superman, [who] must use cunning and stealth to outwit three killers"[85] could just as well apply to Odysseus, who is known for his cunning and trickery and whose humanness – unlike Achilles and Aeneas, he has no divine parent – is emphasized in the epic by his refusal of Calypso's offer of immortality (5.201–24). Both men also suffer a devastating loss of companions: Odysseus loses all his shipmates to various hazards on the journey home, while Kane gradually finds that he is abandoned by those he thought he could rely on in his hour of need. In both works too, the heroes move toward a showdown with those who demonstrate an egregious disregard for the sanctity of the home or community – Odysseus must fight the suitors who have been abusing his household and wooing his wife, and Kane must confront those who would make the town unfit once again for women and children. And in the end, each faces the foe bravely despite overwhelming odds against him.

In both works, too, the hero's leadership and integrity is called into question at crucial points. As we have seen, not only does Eurylochus challenge Odysseus' decisions twice, but his companions as a group both berate him for boasting to the Cyclops and suspect him of hoarding gold and silver for himself. Likewise, not only does Kane's deputy Harvey Pell accuse him of secretly blocking his appointment as successor to the position of town marshal, the hotel clerk – played by the uncredited Howland Chamberlain – freely admits that he himself does not like Kane and implicates the town more broadly when he says, "there's plenty people around here think he's got a comeuppance coming."

Both the *Odyssey* and *High Noon* also emphasize the issue of heroic restraint and the danger that accompanies a lack of it. Odysseus' return home is first imperiled when his men succumb to the pleasures of the Lotus and are unable to tear themselves away (9.83–102), and then again when they are unable to resist the lure of Circe's song and are transformed into pigs (10.224–43); in the end, Odysseus' remaining companions are doomed when they eat Helios' forbidden cattle despite grave warnings (12.339–419). In contrast, although he too occasionally succumbs to a lack of restraint – as with his boasting to the Cyclops and his lingering in Circe's bed – Odysseus himself does exhibit heroic restraint at critical times, such as when he returns home in disguise rather than rushing in unwarily as Agamemnon before him had done, with fatal consequences. In *High Noon*, the lack of restraint shown by Frank Miller's brother Ben (Sheb Wooley), particularly for liquor, but also for revenge and sex, is emphasized throughout the film and criticized repeatedly even by own his comrade Pierce (Robert Wilke).[86] Harvey Pell also demonstrates a lack of self-control, taking solace in liquor when he is upset. He is also easily angered, taking offense at the smallest provocation and initiating a fight when Kane refuses to leave town. For his part, Kane, like Odysseus, occasionally gives in to impulse, as when he punches the saloonkeeper who puts the odds against him; this slip is presented as uncharacteristic, however, surprising all who witness it, and in the bulk of the film he is a model of self-containment. His ability to restrain his impulse, for instance, is suggested when he raises his hand to slap a back-talking youth named Johnny (the uncredited Ralph Reed), but stops himself, grabbing his arms good-naturedly instead. And in both works, lack of restraint in their enemies contributes to the heroes' triumphs over them: Odysseus and his men succeed in putting out Polyphemus' eye because his excessive indulgence in Maron's wine has incapacitated him, while Kane is alerted to his opponents' position in the final showdown when Ben breaks a shop window to steal a woman's bonnet (so he can "be ready").[87]

While the two works thus show some affinities in theme, plot, and characterization, perhaps most significant in this comparison is the role of women, who in both the *Odyssey* and *High Noon* occupy unusually prominent positions. In both cases, the wife is not only cast as a valued partner for the hero, but as a like-minded counterpart as well. Sarah Bolmarcich has shown that in the *Odyssey*, Homer projects the *homophrosyne* (like-mindedness) usually reserved for close male companions onto the relationship of Odysseus and Penelope by emphasizing their shared traits of cunning (she successfully solicits gifts from the suitors: 18.250–303), deceit (she puts off the suitors' entreaties through her shroud-trick: 19.138–51), and restraint (she does not fall rashly into her husband's arms, but waits to confirm his identity: 23.88–110). In *High Noon*, Amy is as stubborn and assertive as Kane in their initial argument, but their similarity is driven home when Kane finds Amy at the hotel and they embrace each other, each assuming the other has had a change of heart, and then shrink away in mutual disappointment when they realize their mistake.

The importance of the wife as a partner and female counterpart in both works highlights the crisis posed to the hero's manhood by the potential for betrayal she exhibits when she considers her own interests or principles over his. In the *Odyssey*, the question of whether or not Penelope will remain faithful to Odysseus or whether she will give herself away to one of her suitors creates a sense of urgency; this tension is replicated in *High Noon* by the ticking clock, which, from the time Kane returns to town over his wife's objections, moves, seemingly in real time, ever closer to "high noon" as we wonder whether or not Amy will follow through with her threat to leave her husband if he insists on confronting Miller. In both cases, the wife's loyalty is thrown into greater doubt by an implied comparison with another woman who is positioned as dangerous in her ability to cast men aside. In the *Odyssey*, Clytemnestra, who cuckolded and killed her husband Agamemnon, is repeatedly held up as a negative model, an implication of the threat that Penelope poses simply through the fact that she is a woman. In *High Noon*, Helen Ramírez, the dark, sensual, exotic woman who can shift her allegiance from one man to another and who is independent enough to pick up and leave town when the situation no longer suits her, is juxtaposed with the light, virginal Amy, who nonetheless threatens in a similar way when, following through on her threat, she befriends Helen and they ride to the station together. And throughout the film, the question of Amy's loyalty is highlighted by the repetition of *High Noon*'s famous theme song, with its insistent refrain:

> Do not forsake me, oh my darlin'
> You made that promise when we wed
> Do not forsake me oh, my darlin'. . .
> Wait along, wait along.

As these lyrics suggest, the film, like the *Odyssey*, is presented from an exclusively male perspective while the woman's interiority is minimized or discounted, and the woman's role – despite Amy's firm assertion that she will not wait to learn the outcome of a battle she opposes – is cast as primarily one of waiting patiently for men to complete their manly activities.

In the end, the wives of both heroes not only prove to be loyal, but turn out to be key allies in their victories: in the *Odyssey*, Penelope's arrangement of the bow contest in Book 21 enables Odysseus to demonstrate his prowess while supplying him with both the weapon and the opportunity to exact his vengeance, while in *High Noon*, as noted above, Amy, who has heretofore been steady in her Quaker values and her stance against violence, takes up a gun herself and shoots one of Kane's opponents in the back, helping to even the odds considerably. In each case, the woman's virtue – and what constitutes virtue for women – is vividly demonstrated when her attitudes and actions ultimately align with those of her husband in a climax that is made all the more dramatic by the serious doubts about her allegiance that have been emphasized throughout.

Thus, *High Noon* has much in common with the *Odyssey* as well. Although both are works that afford women unusual prominence, both exhibit an intense concern with making women's chastity and virtue a function of their relationship to male goals and values. In both cases, the hero explicitly disregards the woman's needs and desires in pursuit of manly achievement, so that in the end the presentation of women serves primarily as a vehicle for exploring male identity.[88]

THE *AENEID*

In a chapter entitled "Arms and the Man: Clint Eastwood as Hero and Filmmaker," E. Christian Kopff has called *High Noon*'s ending, in which, after saving society from an enemy whose *furor* (madness) threatens it, Kane drops his badge in the dust and leaves the craven community behind, "in a way quite Virgilian."[89] Kopff hits on an important connection in this passing reference, but in my view the affinity between these two works deserves a more thorough examination. We have seen that Virgil's work and Westerns are both profoundly concerned with the ideals and sacrifices inherent in nation-building, a theme well illustrated in *Red River*. *High Noon* provides another good example, in that like Aeneas, who works throughout the *Aeneid* to establish a new homeland destined for greatness, Kane is partly motivated throughout *High Noon* by his determination to preserve the community he has helped to build. His work in the past has transformed Hadleyville from a place where "a decent woman couldn't walk down the streets in broad daylight" and where "it wasn't a fit place to bring up a child," as one churchgoer puts it, into a progressive, safe, and civilized community, and Kane is initially pulled back in part by his dedication to what he calls "my town" and a determination not to let that work be undone.[90] The importance of community-building in *High Noon* is highlighted in the church scene, which is placed at the film's center both thematically and in terms of running time (opening credits excluded). Stephen Prince sees the "explicitly philosophical debates about the nature of law and historical progress" in this scene as typical for the genre. As Prince notes, although Henderson's arguments, particularly when viewed through the lens of the Western genre, come across as "callous and opportunistic," the scene draws on and reinforces the concern with the march of civilization at the genre's heart.[91] In the same sense, then, that *High Noon*'s concern with nation-building likens it to the *Aeneid*, it also argues for its place within the Western genre despite the attempts to exclude it noted above.

And although other considerations enter into his decision to stay, the key role played by Kane's profound sense of duty to preserve the community is suggested by his refusal to accept that his obligations to the town ended when he turned in his badge. Although Amy argues for a clean separation between his job as marshal and his new role as a private citizen, Kane's weary insistence that "I'm the same man with or without [the badge]" positions his role in promoting law, order, and civilization as an inseparable part of his heroic identity, and is a trait that likens him strongly to Virgil's Aeneas. While R. Alden Smith has made a similar observation about Western heroes more generally – "[L]ike the noble cowboy of a rugged western, Aeneas is a man of duty"[92] – Kane's kinship with Aeneas in this area is particularly strong: as with Aeneas, Kane's sense of duty to the community is framed as a burden, one which he bears with a resigned sense of *gravitas* (seriousness of purpose) in the interest of a higher goal and at the instigation of a higher power. With Aeneas this is unambiguous: he pursues his quest on the direct orders of the gods, who have told him that his destiny is to found what will become a great empire, but the weight he feels as a result is emphasized from the start. In Book 1 alone, he groans (93) and sighs (371); he puts on a brave face for his men, but inside he is sick with distress and his heart is anguished (208–9); he lays awake contemplating his many cares (305); he bemoans his past suffering (459–60, 597); he frames his coming work as a burden (330); and he envies those whose nation-building efforts are already coming to fruition (437). Kane's dedication to his cause, in contrast, comes from within: he repeatedly tells those who urge him to leave that he has "got to stay," and when Harv Pell asks him why he won't get out, Kane is unable to elucidate his reasoning and answers simply, "I don't know." By locating Kane's convictions in his heroic intuition, the film suggests that he, too, is responding to a higher purpose, one that is universal and instinctive.[93] But although his heroic action is not externally compelled, he too sets about it with a resigned weariness emphasized by Cooper's aged, care-worn countenance and stiff, arthritic gait. He tells Amy that she is "crazy" if she thinks he likes what he has to do, and he admits to Harv that he is tired and scared. As noon draws near, he slumps over his desk moaning softly, and in the end goes to meet his fate not with steely-eyed determination and an air of invincibility, but sweating, fearful, and apprehensive. The overall impression Zinnemann gives is of "the pain [Kane] bears as the standard-bearer of 'justice' within a patriarchal society."[94] For both men, then, the heroic task of building or preserving civilization is framed as one thrust upon them, and as a burden that weighs on them heavily.

For both men too, the heroic task entails subjugating their personal desires to the needs of the community, and in both cases this sacrifice is highlighted when their private inclinations temporarily distract them from their goals. In Book 4, Aeneas lingers in Carthage, content to idle in the comfort of a ready-made city and what seems to be a happy marriage with the beautiful queen Dido, until the gods reprimand him for his neglect and order him back to his mission (4.265–78). Kane, too, is tempted to take the easy road, initially leaving town with his new wife in order to avoid the confrontation with Miller, but after struggling with his conscience, he turns the wagon around. Kane's conflict between his personal desires and his obligation to the community is emphasized, once again, by the film's theme song, which asks, "Oh to be torn 'twixt love and duty/ Supposin' I lose my fair-haired beauty?" Like Aeneas, Kane's personal desires are at odds with what his heroic duty requires, and in both cases this conflict takes the form of a struggle between a romantic relationship and an obligation to build up or preserve civilization. But for both men, their commitment to the community quickly takes precedence over the women who symbolically serve as obstacles that threaten to derail them from their duty.

The heroic choice each man makes, moreover, throws him into violent conflict with the woman he loves. For both Dido and Amy, the hero's return to duty represents a betrayal of the vows and commitments he has made to her. Dido calls Aeneas "perfidious," his betrayal *nefas* (a sin, or impious act), and asks, "Does neither our love give you pause, nor your right hand pledged, nor the cruel death awaiting Dido?" (4.305–8). Amy also appeals to their marital commitment: "We were married just a few minutes ago. We've got our whole lives ahead of us. Doesn't that mean anything to you?" And just as Dido's implication of her imminent suicide signifies the permanence of the choice Aeneas is making, Amy's ultimatum that "No, I won't be here when it's over . . . I mean it, if you won't go with me now, I'll be on that train when it leaves" shows that Will, too, chooses heroic duty even at the cost of his marriage. But while both women view the men's intentions as a matter of choice, Aeneas and Kane frame it otherwise. Aeneas swears that the gods have commanded him, and asserts, "Not by my own will do I seek Italy" (4.361). More typical of the laconic Westerner, after making clear that he does not like what he has to do ("If you think I like this, you're crazy!"), Kane implies his lack of choice in the matter with a simple, "I've got to stay." Both women, too, are similar in their stubborn persistence: Dido sends pleas for time through her sister Anna, and rebuffed again, she raves and rails against Aeneas and curses his line (4.416–73, 533–53, 586–629). For her part, Amy stands firm in her stance, following through on her threat by purchasing a ticket, but holding out hope that Kane will have a change of heart, even interceding with his former mistress on the chance that she is what is keeping him there.

At this point, however, the works diverge: while Dido carries through with her suicide, Amy jumps off the train when she hears the first shots, runs back to town, and even takes up arms alongside her man in direct contradiction of her stated moral and religious convictions. But while the rift between Dido and Aeneas is therefore permanent and that between Amy and Will is repaired, the role of women is in both cases located in a similar value-system: neither work offers a permanent place for a strong, independent woman, but rather both imply that the natural order of things is for the woman to subjugate her needs, values, and desires wholly to the man. Women like Dido who do not conform to this value-system are symbolically sacrificed. In *High Noon*, Kane, too, was willing to sacrifice his relationship with Amy when she was unwilling to submit to his agenda and wait patiently for him to complete his task. Only when she abandons her own needs and principles and adopts his way of thinking is there room for the female in a progressive, forward-moving society.

The implications of Amy's change of heart are strengthened when we come at the gendered framework from another angle that takes into consideration Helen Ramírez, who can be seen as an alternative Dido figure. Both Dido and Helen have uprooted themselves and settled in a foreign land where they are surrounded by hostile communities, but nonetheless each has managed to gain an unusual amount of success for a woman in her society – Dido is now queen of Carthage, and Helen is a successful businesswoman whose economic power puts her in a position of authority over several men. Each woman engages in a passionate affair with the hero and is bitter when he leaves her, in part to pursue a more appropriate marriage with a less independent woman whom society deems more virtuous – Aeneas is destined to take the silent, passive maiden Lavinia as his bride, and Kane weds the blonde, virginal, and morally upright Amy. The presence of Helen, therefore, helps to shape expectations for women's roles as a contrast to Amy in much the same way that Dido does with Lavinia, supporting a gendered framework that in both cases defines feminine virtue through the subjugation of women's needs to the patriarchal program.

Finally, *High Noon* resembles the *Aeneid* in its questioning attitude toward foundational myths. As we have seen, Virgil uses his epic both to promote and to interrogate national mythologies: though he uses the trappings of epic – the definitive genre for shaping national identities – to elevate Augustus and his regime by supplying a divine lineage and positioning the Roman Empire as predestined, at the same time he subtly undercuts the prevailing message, offering warnings about a return to tyranny and cutting the legs out from under the grand vision he takes pains to build. In many ways, Zinnemann does something similar with *High Noon*, but far less subtly: by building his social drama on a Western framework – and featuring a star who embodies idealized Western masculinity – he draws on established notions of national identity in order to break them down. As we have seen with Judge Mettrick's reference to parallel events from ancient Greece, Zinnemann "demystifies the American exceptionalism inherent in American formulations of the frontier by claiming that the story and the conflict could have happened in another time and place."[95] The more transparent nature of Zinnemann's attempt to critique the present by de-mythologizing the past has surely contributed to the censure many critics have directed at the film, not least because this critique of American heritage and the threat it poses to national self-image comes from a "foreign outsider,"[96] but also perhaps because it cuts too close to home: that is, rather than using traditional Western distancing techniques of projecting negative qualities onto groups or individuals that represent the "other" – outlaws, Indians, or Easterners – Zinnemann and Foreman place them squarely onto the white middle class.[97] Like the *Aeneid*, *High Noon* chips away at the mythologies that underlie national identity all the more effectively by situating its critique in the framework of the genre most closely associated with promoting them.

Yet despite this de-mythologizing thread and the threat it poses to foundational notions of national identity, both works have been remarkable for the contradictory interpretations applied to them and the conflicting uses to which they have been put. Virgil's work was written at Augustus' behest, and it contains a sufficient amount of regime-promoting propaganda that Augustus chose to preserve and promote it even in direct contradiction to Virgil's stated wishes on his deathbed. Numerous scholars over the centuries, too, have read the epic as a straightforward patriotic elevation of Rome and all its glories. But other scholars have read subtle critique into the work, seeing cautionary messages and challenges to foundational myths embedded within it. Like the *Aeneid*, *High Noon* has been susceptible to readings that initially seem contradictory: politicians on both the right and the left have been able to identify with Kane and apply his situation to their own circumstances and to their own advantage. *High Noon*'s inception, interestingly, can also be traced to an impetus not unlike Virgil's. When a representative of the United Nations who was scouting possibilities for a film about the UN approached Stanley Kramer's production company, Carl Foreman, who was working on another film for Kramer at the time, was intrigued and "began to consider an oblique approach to the subject through the vehicle of the western," and it was his outline that contained the "bare bones" of the eventual film.[98] These works, therefore, have similarities in impetus and in interpretation: both were created by a prompt for a political propaganda piece, and much as Virgil's work has been read as a support and as a critique of imperial policy, US leaders on both sides of the aisle have read Zinnemann's film as an allegory for their own predicaments and as a validation of their own brand of leadership.

CONCLUSION

Despite Judge Mettrick's reference to Athenian history and Zinnemann's own nods to Aristotelian dramatic ideals, I do not view the connections I am making between *High Noon* and ancient epic as conscious or explicit. At the same time, just as the themes and imagery of *High Noon* have entered into the American collective imagination, so too do many of the characters, stories, and concerns from classical epic mythology form the undercurrents of our cultural knowledge even for those without first-hand experience of them, and in one way or another, these strands not infrequently seep into modern creations. This sort of occasional unconscious insertion of themes, character-types, and narratives into ostensibly original works is powerfully demonstrated in the story of this film's inception: after Carl Foreman produced the above-mentioned outline containing the basic framework of the final film in 1948, the story struck his agent E. Henry Lewis as familiar, and eventually its roots in John Cunningham's 1947 short story "The Tin Star" were tracked down. Foreman admitted that he may have read the story and been guilty of "unconscious plagiarism," and eventually bought the rights from Cunningham,[99] who receives writing credit even though the film in its final form is radically different from the original story.[100] Leslie Fiedler has also criticized the film for its "unacknowledged plagiarism" of Owen Wister's *The Virginian*:[101] and indeed, the argument between newlyweds Kane and Amy in *High Noon* over his intention to face Miller is strikingly similar to the scene in the film where Gary Cooper's character argues with his fiancée Molly about his own upcoming confrontation with Trampas.

Just as elements of these other Westerns may have unintentionally slipped into the fabric of *High Noon*, so too might we consider that some of the most gripping narratives, the most moving themes, and the most affecting characters from the large body of myth from classical epic have slipped unnoticed into our cultural consciousness and infiltrated narratives of the Old West. It is not my intention, however, to argue for this: instead, I am interested in showing that the parallel positions of epic and Western in describing formative periods of history and working both to shape and reflect patriarchally driven cultural ideologies result in striking connections that can be mutually informative. At the same time, these fundamental generic similarities may also mean that Western film lends itself more readily to the adoption of the epic and mythological elements in our subconscious repertoire.

Both classical epic and the Western genre are a "mishmash of history and myth, fiction and contemporary values" which work to define "the ideology of heroism"[102] and of manhood itself.[103] As with *Red River*, the particular echoes of various ancient epic themes and characters that emerge and recede, intertwining and resounding throughout *High Noon* help to illustrate that, standing as they do on the frontier of civilization in their respective cultures, both ancient epic and Western film concern themselves with common problems and anxieties and promote similar heroic qualities that are neither simplistic nor unproblematic, but complex enough to contend with the difficulties inherent in the precarious situations associated with the process of nation-building.

NOTES

1 Graham (1979: 51).
2 Drummond (1997: 24); Hughes (2008: 41).
3 Warshow (1954: 199–200).
4 Fenin and Everson (1973: 335).
5 Wood (1996b: 88).
6 Hughes (2008: 42).
7 Sarris (1968: 169). Nolletti (1999: 5), Marcus (2000: 49), and Smyth (2014: 6) defend Zinnemann as, in Marcus's words, "a consummate auteur."
8 Smyth (2014: 98).
9 Noted in Smyth (2014: 5) and Nolletti (1999: 13), respectively.
10 Blundell and Ormand (1997: 538).
11 Schein (1955: 316). See also Slotkin (1998: 395); Drummond (1997: 72).
12 Graham (1979: 53–4); Slotkin (1998: 395); Belton (1994: 247); McGee (2007: 114).
13 Drummond (1997: 19, 37). Though Zinnemann supported Foreman, producer Stanley Kramer did not, and Foreman lost his Associate Producer credit on the film as a result. Gary Cooper, ironically, was a staunch conservative and anti-communist. Nonetheless, he remained loyal and supportive to Foreman until he eventually "bowed to threats . . . concerning his future employment prospects" (Drummond 1997: 37–8). See also Belton (1994: 247); Hughes (2008: 42); Smyth (2014: 120).
14 Rapf (1990: 75).
15 Prince (1999: 84); Smyth (2014: 98).

16 Zinnemann (1992: 96).
17 Marcus (2000: 53).
18 See Zinnemann (1992: 96); Nolletti (1999: 15); Prince (1999: 83–5).
19 Qtd. in Marcus (2000: 52). See also Zinnemann (1986: 13); Stevens (2006: 414).
20 Drummond (1997: 38).
21 Graham (1979: 54).
22 Zinnemann (1992: 96).
23 Beale (2003); Hoberman (2004).
24 Hoberman (2004); Cohen (2013).
25 Clip available at youtube.com/watch?v=PQFAYy5Ocfg.
26 Biskind (2001: 48); Neve (1992: 185).
27 Rapf (1990: 77).
28 Zinnemann (1992: 110); Prince (1999: 79).
29 Qtd. in Marcus (2000: 52).
30 Graham (1979: 59).
31 Hughes (2008: 41).
32 *High Noon* (TBS, 2000) and *High Noon, Part II: The Return of Will Kane* (CBS, 1980). See Hughes (2008: 41).
33 Hughes (2008: 41).
34 Hughes (2008: 41). For more on the film's influence, see Graham (1979: 60–1); Drummond (1997: 63–5); Hughes (2008: 41–2).
35 Season 1, episode 3. This expression is repeated in Season 2, episode 6.
36 Blundell and Ormand (1997: 536).
37 Zinnemann (1992: 110) and qtd. in Nolletti (1999: 13). See also Drummond (1997: 39, 46).
38 Tatum (1987: 74); Winkler (2001b: 122).
39 Drummond (1997: 58).
40 Zinnemann (1992: 101). Zinnemann repeatedly cites documentary filmmaker Robert Flaherty (*Nanook of the North*, 1921) as his biggest professional and personal influence (Zinnemann 1986: 12–13; 1992: 24–5; Stevens 2006: 413; Smyth 2014: 103).
41 Giannetti (1981: 371–2); Zinnemann (1986: 66; 1992: 101); Drummond (1997: 35); Marcus (2000: 50); Stevens (2006: 419–20); Smyth (2014: 103).
42 Smyth (2014: 104).
43 For more on time in *High Noon*, see Combs (1986); Drummond (1997: 58).
44 Noted in Tatum (1987: 60).
45 Giannetti (1981: 370); Tatum (1987: 60).
46 Drummond (1997: 20–1).
47 See Zinnemann (1992: 100); Drummond (1997: 36); Hughes (2008: 36). Both Zinnemann and Hughes see Cooper's ailments as beneficial to his performance.
48 Qtd. in Bogdanovich (1962: 34); see also McBride (2013: 163).

49 Smyth (2014: 116–17).
50 Graham (1979: 54); Smyth (2014: 117).
51 Blundell and Ormand (1997: 534).
52 Season 4, episode 3.
53 Graham (1980: 245); Drummond (1997: 52); Smyth (2014: 111).
54 Qtd. in Marcus (2000: 55).
55 Marcus (2000: 55).
56 Noted in Graham (1980: 251); Rapf (1990: 79); Drummond (1997: 54); Smyth (2014: 111).
57 Graham (1980: 244–7); Rapf (1990: 77–8); Foster (1999: 94–6); Smyth (2014: 111–12). See also Giannetti (1981: 370).
58 Rapf (1990: 78).
59 Smyth (2014: 113).
60 Drummond (1997: 66).
61 Zinnemann (1986: 67); Stevens (2006: 420).
62 "Rage: sing, goddess, the deadly rage of Achilles, son of Peleus..." (1.1–2).
63 Graham (1979: 54).
64 See Graham (1979: 54–5).
65 In Cunningham's short story, Doane himself gives essentially the same speech to Toby, but with very different implications, as he suggests it is a job worth doing anyway (1947: 11).
66 Blundell and Ormand (1997: 534–5). Drummond's analysis of themes prevalent in the work of *High Noon*'s scriptwriter Carl Foreman reinforces the applicability of this comparison to Zinnemann's film in particular by using language remarkably similar to Blundell and Ormand's: "[Foreman's] films are studies of men marked by identities which isolate them and cause them to re-examine and to re-interpret their understanding of their masculinity" (1997: 19).
67 Graham also looks at triangular relationships in this film, seeing a number of them centered on the figure of Helen (1980: 246).
68 Drummond has similarly noted Pell's function as Kane's "other" (1997: 50). Pell's more negative id-like qualities in contrast to the softer, more sympathetic nature of Patroclus and *Red River*'s Matthew Garth in some ways anticipates the direction this triangulation will take in the spaghetti Westerns of the 1960s (see introduction).
69 Slotkin (1998: 393–4).
70 Slotkin (1998: 394).
71 Blundell and Ormand (1997: 546).
72 Slotkin (1998: 392–3). Slotkin also mentions professional and social components of his decision, which factors will be discussed below.
73 See Blundell and Ormand (1997: 539).
74 Blundell and Ormand (1997: 550).
75 Katz (1981: 19–20).
76 Drummond (1997: 60).

77 Katz (1981: 26).
78 Drummond (1997: 50).
79 Katz (1981: 32–3).
80 Foster (1999: 96).
81 While the film's theme song was performed by Tex Ritter, versions of this song by Frankie Laine (Columbia), Ritter (Capitol), and Bill Hayes (MGM) were released in the summer of 1952 even before the film's official release at the end of July (Drummond 1997: 40).
82 Tompkins (1992: 41). See also Tompkins (1992: 143–4).
83 Tompkins (1992: 41).
84 See Tompkins (1992: 143–4).
85 Giannetti (1981: 361, fig. 15.4).
86 See Drummond (1997: 56).
87 Drummond (1997: 56).
88 See Tompkins (1992: 41–4).
89 Kopff (1999: 241–2).
90 See Slotkin (1998: 393).
91 Prince (1999: 89).
92 Smith (2003: 434).
93 For more on Western heroes' underlying motives and their inexpressibility, see Warshow (1954: 194).
94 Foster (1999: 100).
95 Smyth (2014: 113).
96 Smyth (2014: 104).
97 Cortese (1976: 127).
98 Drummond (1997: 30–1).
99 Drummond (1997: 30–1, 37).
100 For instance, the female characters Amy and Helen are absent from the short story; the townspeople do not play a role as a source of conflict; and instead of the antagonism of Kane's deputy Harvey Pell, we have a more supportive second-in-command, there called Toby, who at first declines to take over for the retiring marshal, there called Doane, though he is willing to see him through the showdown. The story ends with Toby stepping into the fight when he thinks Doane has been killed, and then Doane sacrificing his life by taking a bullet meant for the injured Toby, who subsequently assumes Doane's mantle. Many, like Howard Hughes, see the relationship between story and film to be so negligible that Cunningham's writing credit is undeserved (2008: 36).
101 Fiedler (1975: 259–60).
102 Blundell and Ormand (1997: 539).
103 See Slotkin (1998: 393).

3 *George Stevens's* Shane

FILM SUMMARY

Shane opens with Alad Ladd as the title character emerging from the mountains above a sparse Western settlement. As he is passing through the homestead Joe (Van Heflin) and Marian (Jean Arthur) Starrett share with their young son Joey (Brandon De Wilde), the Ryker gang, a group of cattlemen hostile to the local settlers, appear and accuse Starrett of squatting on their grazing land. Trouble is averted when Shane unexpectedly aligns himself with Joe, and the gang rides off without incident. Shane is invited to dinner and soon agrees to stay on with the Starretts as a hired hand. He rapidly becomes a hero-figure to young Joey and a valued friend to Joe, while meaningful looks are exchanged between him and Marian.

Later, having gone into town to buy work clothes, Shane stoically endures the taunts Chris Calloway (Ben Johnson), one of Ryker's followers, directs at him when he stops into the saloon to buy a soda for young Joey. Back at home, Shane walks in on a meeting of the settlers Joe has called in response to a neighboring homesteader's decision to leave as a result of Ryker's intimidation. Joe convinces the others to stick together as a group, and they plan to ride into town together the next day to shop for the upcoming Fourth of July celebration. When they do, Shane re-enters the saloon as a tacit challenge to Calloway, who has warned him to stay out. A fight ensues, and when Shane knocks Calloway out, the leader of the cattlemen Rufus Ryker (Emile Meyer) offers him a job, which he refuses. This provokes the rest of Ryker's men and at first Shane takes them on single-handedly; soon, however, Joe joins in, and despite being outnumbered, they more than hold their own until the fight is broken up by Sam Grafton (Paul McVey), the saloon's owner.

Tensions mount following this incident, and Ryker sends for the notorious gunslinger Jack Wilson ([Walter] Jack Palance). After the Independence Day festivities, Ryker and his men visit the Starretts and offer to take Joe himself into their fold. When Joe refuses, Ryker departs quietly, but instructs Wilson to do whatever it takes to discourage the settlers. Soon after, Wilson provokes a confrontation with the hot-headed homesteader Stonewall Torrey (Elisha Cook, Jr.) and guns him down in the street. At the funeral, Joe urges the discouraged settlers to stick it out, but some are determined to follow the lead of Fred Lewis (Edgar Buchanan), who has packed his wagon, intending to flee the valley after the funeral is over. When a fire started by Ryker is spotted at the abandoned Lewis homestead, this malicious act bonds the settlers together, and they all agree to stay and fight on. That night, Ryker sends for Joe, and Joe prepares to face him over Marian's tearful protestations. When Shane learns from Calloway, who has had a change of heart, that Joe is walking into a trap, he straps on his original buckskin attire and fights Joe, knocking him out to prevent him from meeting Ryker. After a meaningful farewell with Marian, Shane rides off toward town followed by Joey. At the saloon, Shane and Wilson face off, and Wilson is killed, along with Ryker. Joey, looking on, sees a hidden gunman and shouts a warning to Shane, who kills that man as well. Afterwards, Shane bids a tearful Joey goodbye, explaining that a man can't change who he is; he then rides off into the mountains whence he came as Joey calls after him to "come back."

INTRODUCTION

In many ways, George Stevens's 1953 film *Shane* occupies a position in American cinematic history not unlike that of *High Noon*. Both films were commercial successes and received numerous awards. *Shane* was one of the most financially successful Westerns ever,[1] and like *High Noon*, it was nominated for an Academy Award for Best Picture. While neither film won, this was an unusual honor: although Westerns were abundant in the 1940–50s, they were rarely taken seriously, and in these decades only three received Oscar nominations for Best Picture.[2] *Shane* also received Academy Award nominations for Best Director for Stevens, Best Writing for A. B. Guthrie Jr.'s screenplay, and Best Supporting Actor for both Brandon DeWilde and Jack Palance, while Loyal Griggs won for Best Color Cinematography. Stevens was nominated for the Directors Guild of America's Outstanding Directorial Achievement in Motion Pictures award, got second place for Best Director from the New York Film Critics Circle, and won Best Director from the National Board of Review. Guthrie and Jack Sher were nominated for Best Written American Drama by the Writers Guild of America, and there were BAFTA Award nominations for Best Film from any source and Best Foreign Actor for Van Heflin.

Despite this critical acclaim, as with *High Noon*, Stevens's film and its director had strong detractors. Robert Warshow, who had criticized *High Noon* for its "social drama," disparaged *Shane* for its "aestheticizing tendency" and Stevens for trying to "freeze the Western myth once and for all." Andrew Sarris and André Bazin, too, saw *Shane* as too self-consciously at work on the creation of myth.[3] Others viewed the presentation from young Joey's perspective as a cheap way of absolving the film from charges of idealization and immaturity.[4] Although the point-of-view mostly replicates that of Jack Schaefer's 1949 novel on which the film's narrative is based,[5] it is perhaps devices like this that have led critics like V. F. Perkins to disparage Stevens (alongside Zinnemann and William Wyler) as a director who "victimises his audience as unscrupulously as anyone."[6] The stark differences in opinion on this film are illustrated in opposing takes on the scene where Torrey's dog paws at his master's coffin as it is lowered into the ground: Howard Hughes calls this "a simple, moving moment that is enormously effective," while Bob Baker characterizes it as a "sucker shot."[7]

Yet like *High Noon*, *Shane* has undoubtedly entered the Western canon. It was admitted to the National Film Registry in 1993 and consistently appears on lists of Best Westerns of all time – as of this writing, IMDb ranks it fifth, and it is number three on the 2014 American Film Institute's top 10 list.[8] Like *High Noon*, it has also achieved iconic status in the American imagination and spawned many offshoots. Howard Hughes notes that Clint Eastwood's "man with no name" screen persona was shaped by Ladd's character,[9] and his 1985 *Pale Rider* is widely recognized as a virtual remake of Stevens's film. A 1966 TV series based on the film and starring David Carradine lasted just one season, but works that contain homages cover a broad range, from *The Good, the Bad, and the Ugly* and *The Shootist* to Mel Brooks's *Blazing Saddles* (1974), Eastwood's *Gran Torino* (2008), and even four episodes of the 1966–68 TV series *Batman*.[10] And even if they can't place its origins, most Americans today recognize the mournful cry "Shane! Come back!" as a touchstone of cultural literacy. But whereas *High Noon* has been heavily linked to contemporary politics, *Shane*'s mythic dimensions are its most persistent association, while its stunning Jackson Hole, Wyoming setting and broad vistas seem designed to lend it an epic scope.[11] Because this film consciously draws on mythic character-types and narrative threads and positions itself as an epic Western film, it makes a natural comparison with the epics of antiquity, which too draw on mythic tales and their heroes.

THE EPIC TRADITION

Like *Red River* and *High Noon*, *Shane* has no apparent direct connection to the epics of antiquity, but it is interesting to note that Jack Schaefer, the author of the novel on which this film is based, was principally interested in classics and creative writing while an undergraduate at Oberlin College.[12] Although he later changed direction, Gerald Haslam has called Schaefer's prose "a style that often borders on the oral tradition," and Schaefer, too, has described himself as one who "likes to believe that he is bumbling along in the ancient tradition of tale-tellers."[13] Schaefer likened *Shane* in particular to a Greek drama,[14] a comparison also made by critics of the film version. Peter French, for instance, has called attempts like Shane's to shun one's heroic identity "a version of a Greek tragic fault, a failure to 'know thyself'," while seeing Ryker as an example of a Western villain about whom we might ask the same questions we would ask with respect to Oedipus' fate.[15] Erling Holtsmark has examined the ending of the film as a *katabasis*, and like French connects Shane's coming-to-terms with his identity to the Delphic injunction toward self-knowledge.[16] Most usefully for our purposes, Carl Rubino has devoted a 2014 article to looking at *Shane*'s relationship to the *Iliad*. Here again, it seems, we have a film that exhibits important connections with the myths of antiquity that result from common ideological concerns and a similar position in the forging of national identity rather than from conscious intent.

As in previous chapters, we begin with the film's mythic-historical anchoring. While the town itself is unnamed in both film and Schaefer's novel, in the written work Shane's recent path is traced by the news he brings from Cheyenne, Dodge City, and elsewhere, and he eventually offers that his parents came from Mississippi and settled in Arkansas;[17] in the film, all this is left a great mystery, just as the date – which the novel gives as 1889 from its opening sentence – is left vague. This elusiveness contributes to the mythic quality for which the film is known (and sometimes disparaged). Yet Bob Baker notes that "the aspect [of *Shane*] which most impressed contemporary reviewers was the realism, the part of the film which seeks to retrieve a historical reality from the genre's tangle of myth, wish-fantasy and show business," noting the realistic nature of the Starrett homestead, the scrubbiness of the huddle of buildings they call a town, and details such as Joe browsing a Sears, Roebuck & Co. catalog and Marian contemplating a glass jar in wonder.[18] Stevens himself notes that he attempted to be "extremely authentic" down to details such as costuming: "Our women are frumpy and bedraggled-looking rather than glamorous, and our men wear beavers, not Stetsons."[19] In addition to these touches of realism, oblique references anchor the film to a particular period in frontier history: indications of North/South tensions place it not long after the Civil War's conclusion in 1865, while the primary conflict between cattle barons and settlers, along with indirect references to the Homestead Act of 1862, suggest a timeframe somewhere in the subsequent decades as well. In addition, despite its mythic dimensions and George Stevens's professed intention to create a story that would work allegorically rather than "just [on] the surface level,"[20] many have noted the similarity between the film's dispute and the conflict in the Johnson County Range War, which took place in Wyoming in 1892.[21] Thus, like *Red River* and *High Noon*, *Shane* presents itself as fictionalized history, creating the important combination of relevance and distance that characterizes works from the Western film and epic genres.

The film also exhibits useful parallels with epic values and ideologies, many of which emerge from the film's first scenes. For example, as we have seen, the Greeks held sacred *xenia*, a concept of hospitality that includes certain expectations and responsibilities between guest and host. As *Shane* demonstrates, a similar value-system is evident in stories of the Old West. When Shane first arrives at the Starrett homestead, he asks Joe if he minds him cutting through his land, a considerate attitude juxtaposed soon thereafter with that of the Ryker gang, who barge in aggressively, their horses trampling the Starretts' garden. This contrast helps delineate what constitutes proper and improper behavior. Joe, for his part, first offers water to his guest and then, once Shane's benign intentions become clear, invites him to dinner (where they bring out the "good plates" and an extra fork), shows him where to wash up, and later offers him lodging for the night, overtures that parallel the typical offers of banquet, bath, and bed we find in ancient epic, both Greek and Roman. A related parallel involves the Greek prejudice against questioning a man, even to ask his name, until he has had his fill of food and drink. Although Shane offers his name upfront and unprompted after Joe introduces himself, it is not until after dinner that in a similar aversion to intrusive questioning, Joe ventures to say, "I wouldn't ask you where you're bound," leaving Shane free to offer up the information or not. Furthermore, like with the Greek concept of *xenia*, as his guest – and soon, as his hired man – Shane enters into a relationship with Joe that entails certain responsibilities and expectations. Shane suggests this sort of relationship first when he picks up an ax unprompted and gets to work on the stump Joe has been wrestling with for two years; then later, when Ryker sees how well Shane can hold his own in a fight and offers him a job at double the wages Joe is paying, Shane refuses, exhibiting loyalty to his "patron" over his own safety and economic advancement. This parallel concern with hospitality in ancient epic and Western narratives is not coincidental, but reflects a necessity in societies at an early stage of development where social and political structures are not as firmly in place and life is more difficult and precarious.

The ancient epics also exhibit a profound concern with property rights that we saw reflected to some degree in *Red River*, but which in Westerns like *Shane* becomes central. In the *Iliad*, the quarrel between Agamemnon and Achilles is initiated when Agamemnon appropriates Briseis, whom Achilles has been awarded as a *geras*, or war-prize, while the primary conflict in the *Odyssey* centers on the suitors' abuse of Odysseus' household stores, along with the threat they pose to his wife's fidelity. In the *Aeneid*, the natives' right to their land, which goes hand in hand with the conflict over marital rights to Lavinia, spurs the great war that takes up the second half of the epic. In *Shane*, similarly, the dispute between Ryker and the homesteaders focuses on who has rights to the land, a conflict reinforced by repeated visual and verbal references to fences. Like the suitors in the *Odyssey*, the Rykers abuse the settlers' property – they not only allow their cattle to destroy crops and knock down fences, but even set fire to the Lewis family's home. In both cultures, because property is intimately tied up with identity, disputes over goods, women, or the land itself become vehicles for working out larger concerns about the self and its relation to society.[22] For Achilles, the loss of Briseis is not as important as the implication Agamemnon's appropriation of her has for his status and sense of importance; similarly, for Fred Lewis, the Rykers' arson is significant not so much because of its economic implications – the Lewises had already packed their belongings and abandoned the property intending to move – but because of its intimate connection to his identity: "That's our place," Lewis says, "[Ryker] had no right to do that . . . It was *ours*. I built it with my own hands." As with hospitality practices, this intense concern with property rights that epic and Westerns have in common results from their parallel positions as geographical and/or temporal "frontier" narratives that chronicle the tensions involved with early stages of societal development, illustrating again the parallel positions these two genres occupy in their respective societies.

A third correspondence is in the development of expectations for masculine and feminine behavior, which, as we have seen, is a crucial parallel between epic and Westerns. In *Shane*, both Shane and Joe help to develop notions of what constitutes ideal masculine behavior. Joe is the recognized leader of the homesteaders' contingent. He stands his ground against the Rykers bravely and refuses to consider giving up, repeatedly convincing other settlers who want to throw in the towel to stand firm. He also jumps into the fistfight at the bar with Shane despite the terrible odds, and in the end, is willing to risk his life to confront the Rykers. For his part, Shane exhibits reluctance to use a gun, but when he does pick one up, his superior skill is indisputable. He too shows courage, refusing to run away from a fight even when he stands alone against a small mob. Joe and Shane's shared claim to idealized manliness is clearly demonstrated in three episodes – first, when they work together to take out the monstrous stump, stubbornly using their "own sweat and muscle" rather than making an easier job of it by utilizing the horses; then in the bar-fight where they take on and defeat Ryker's men who outnumber them more than two-to-one; and finally, when they take on each other, Joe determined to fight his own battle with Ryker, and Shane determined to prevent Joe either being killed, or being changed by the taint of a killing. The two are clearly matched in some ways, as is emphasized by Joey's constant attempts to weigh the merits of the two against each other ("Can you shoot as good as Shane, Pa? . . . Could you whip him, Pa? Could you whip Shane?") and ultimately through the fact that Shane only wins the fistfight with Joe by breaking the code and knocking him out with his gun, though it is made clear that he does it for the "right" reasons. Both men, therefore, provide valid models for idealized male behavior, although as we will see, the model Joe provides is a human one in contrast to the heroic stature drawn for Shane.

Related to this is the connection between Greek and Western cultures seen in their attitudes toward male honor. The actions and attitudes of Homeric heroes are motivated primarily by a concern with *kleos*, or glory as measured by extrinsic considerations of what others say and think. Odysseus demonstrates a profound concern with his public standing when, at the Phaeacian Euryalus' suggestion that he is not participating in the athletic contests because he is not good enough, he indignantly rebukes him before jumping up to prove his mettle and repair his besmirched reputation (*Od.* 8.158–200). Indeed, Hector makes clear in Book 6 of the *Iliad* that a man's reputation was paramount when he refuses his wife Andromache's request to take up a safer but strategically sound defensive position rather than risk his life in the front lines by explaining that, no matter the dire consequences for them both, "I would be horribly ashamed before the Trojan men and the long-robed Trojan women if I shunned battle, holding back like a coward."[23] The film suggests a similar concern: like Odysseus among the Phaeacians, the reputation of Shane himself is initially called into question by his failure to take the bait the first time he enters the saloon and Chris Calloway throws a drink at him. When Shane next comes to town, therefore, he provokes a fight by throwing two drinks at Calloway, redeeming his reputation by one-upping Calloway's previous challenge. And like Hector, Shane demonstrates concern for his reputation over his safety: when little Joey tries to hold him back from the fight, saying, "Shane, there's too many!", Shane responds, "You wouldn't want me to run away would you?" The remarkable similarity in attitudes toward male public standing in the two cultures is demonstrated by parallel scenes where the wife tries to hold her husband back from battle. Like the *Iliad*'s Andromache, who asks Hector to "have pity . . . lest you make your son fatherless and your wife a widow" (6.431–2), Marian begs her husband to hold back from the dangerous showdown, asking "Don't I mean anything to you, Joe? Doesn't Joey?" Like Hector, Joe suggests that his *kleos*, in a sense, overrides all other considerations when he replies,

> Marian, honey, it's because you mean so much to me that I – I've got to go. Do you think I could go on living with you and you thinking that I'd showed yellow? And then what about Joey? How do you think I'd ever explain that to him?

Both epic and Westerns also highlight a tangible economic component to male honor. In the Homeric world, the word *timē* denotes the honor derived from public acknowledgment of one's value through the awarding of prizes. It is this aspect of Achilles' honor that is damaged when Agamemnon confiscates Briseis. Odysseus, likewise, is profoundly concerned with bringing home the booty that is an external measure of his worth. After he joins Shane in the fistfight in the saloon, Joe suggests that honor in the Old West has a similar economic aspect when he proudly asserts that "Ryker ain't paying for this damage, not with a nickel he ain't. I'm paying for what's broke. No, by Godfrey, *we're* paying for what's broke, me and Shane!"

In both cultures, too, the external basis of masculine honor is emphasized by a ritualistic exchange of taunts as prelude to battle. These insults, which frequently call a warrior's masculinity into question, are ubiquitous in the *Iliad*, as when Diomedes derides Paris, who has just shot him with an arrow in the foot, saying "Bowman, slanderer, curly-haired seducer . . . I don't care any more than if a woman had hit me, or a witless child" (11.385–9). A similar dynamic is seen in battle contexts in the *Aeneid*, as when the Rutulian Numanus taunts Ascanius and his comrades for their fancy attire, calling them "Phrygian women, not men" (9.614–18). Such provocations are present too in *Shane*, as when Calloway baits Shane by calling him "sody pop," and "sod-buster," implying his feminization when compared with "real men" who drink liquor and ride the range – an association made more explicit when he douses Shane in whiskey so that he'll "smell like a man." He later impugns Shane's masculinity, along with that of all the homesteading men, even more directly when he says, "They brought all their women with them to protect them," and asks, "Did you think you was goin' to come in here and drink with the men? . . . You'd better get back inside with the women and kids where it's safe." Jack Wilson's later baiting of "Stonewall" Torrey demonstrates another important facet of this phenomenon: aware of Torrey's southern roots, he derides Stonewall Jackson, Robert E. Lee, and "all the rest of them Rebs" as "trash" in order to provoke Torrey to draw his gun so that he will have an excuse to kill him, while Shane initiates his shootout with Wilson by calling him a "low-down Yankee liar." This sort of derision based on birthplace and background is reminiscent of the overriding concern in Greek and Roman epic with lineage and the prevalence of references to one's ancestors in pre-battle boasts and insults, as in Glaucus' long report of his noble ancestry in the *Iliad* (6.145–211). As such, *Shane*'s example suggests a concern in Western film with delineating what constitutes masculine virtue and honor that is strikingly similar to that found in ancient epic.

Just as these narratives work to shape notions of manhood and masculine honor, so too do they reflect ideas about what constitutes women's nature and delineate models for female virtue. Marian is unambiguously cast as a "good woman" and a model wife and mother. We first see her framed in the farmhouse window singing, suggesting not only her association with domestic space, but her contentment with her place as well. Throughout the film, Marian's primary duties are cooking, serving, nurturing (both her son Joey and the wounds Joe and Shane incur in the bar-fight), and assisting with mourning (when she is sent to help Torrey's wife after his murder). In many ways, Marian's role is not much different from the expectations for wives in antiquity, as is most fully explicated in Xenophon's *Oeconomicus*. Although this is a Classical period work, Ischomachus' recounting of how he trained his wife to manage the "inside" aspects of the household (including domestic duties, tending sick servants, and the like) is a close match to what we see in the ancient epics in expectations for virtuous wives, like Andromache in the *Iliad*, Penelope in the *Odyssey*, and Lavinia in the *Aeneid*. Feminine difference is also suggested in each genre by their opposition to male heroic achievement: in the *Iliad*, Andromache tries to pull Hector back from the front lines in battle, and Hecuba and Helen suggest a similar intention by offering him wine and respite (6.254–62 and 354–8). In the *Odyssey*, Circe and Calypso pose a threat when they detain Odysseus on their islands, removing him from the public arena of manly achievement. And in Book 4 of the *Aeneid*, Dido's attempt to hold Aeneas back from heroic duty is dramatically "punished" by her abandonment, loss of standing, and suicide.

In *Shane*, Marian fills a similar role. Though she is overwhelmingly cast as virtuous, her feminine weakness is suggested in her hysterical reaction to Joe's intention to confront the Rykers. Peter French notes that in this scene, "Marion is reduced to pathetic whining and pleading,"[24] a reaction that suggests the woman's inadequacy in the area of self-control, while also providing a counterpoint to the male impulse to act when action is needed. Related to this is Marian's idealized pacifistic notions: she tells Shane that "[w]e'd all be much better off if there wasn't a single gun left in this valley – including yours." Peter French suggests that Marion is averse to guns because she sees them as a "phallic symbol, a powerful and deadly icon of the masculine. Perhaps that is what she wants banned from the valley,"[25] a view that demonstrates the emasculating threat that women's values pose to men in these patriarchal cultures. While in the end Marian's wish is granted – after the climactic confrontation, Shane tells Joey, "run on home to your mother and tell her – tell her everything's alright, and there aren't any more guns in the valley" – this utopian state can only be achieved by masculine, heroic – and violent – action. In this way, as we have seen elsewhere, while feminine values are positioned as good in the abstract, masculine heroic action is shown to be both necessary and virtuous in the world of reality. Marian's primary function in *Shane*, then, as we have seen for Westerns in general and in ancient epic, is to help define masculine virtue through contrast, opposition, or support.

While Marian's feminine qualities help delineate the idealized manhood of both Joe and Shane, in the end the model of masculinity Joe provides is of a down-to-earth, workaday variety, a human brand in contrast to Shane's more heroic one, which is the kind that ultimately "saves" society. And despite its anchoring in violence, Shane's heroism is noble and selfless; he is a "savior" who sacrifices himself for the good of the community, leading many to identify him as a sort of Christ figure.[26] Indeed, he exhibits none of the traits that would be considered "flaws" in a Christian notion of a hero: he exhibits neither the rage of Achilles (which we saw in Tom Dunson), nor the tricky, deceptive nature of Odysseus, nor the weary reluctance of Aeneas (which we saw with Will Kane). He is simply "*so good*," as Joey puts it, from his adoring child's perspective.

Yet despite his overwhelming "goodness," in many ways Shane still conforms to the broad outlines of what constituted masculine heroism in ancient epic. Although he tries to shuck off his heroic mantle, he is still recognized as "different." Ryker suggests as much when he says "You don't belong on the end of a shovel," and though Joey sizes his father up against Shane, even he recognizes that Shane belongs to a different world when he says that, unlike with his father, Shane's gun "goes with" him. Moreover, as we have seen elsewhere, Shane's heroic identity is visually signaled through costuming: his fringed buckskin garb not only sets him apart, it suggests his association with the land and his position "outside" the community. Although he temporarily puts this, and his gun, aside, his heroic nature eventually emerges: in a parallel to an epic arming scene, Shane re-dons his heroic garb before the climactic battle,[27] in which he defeats three men, including the menacing Wilson and a hidden gunman, almost single-handedly in a realistic Western facsimile of the ancient *aristeia*. Like Achilles, who toys with the idea of quitting the battle permanently and going home, and like Aeneas, who temporarily puts his quest aside while he nests with Dido, Shane too tries to set aside his heroic identity. But in the end, like the heroes of old, he is compelled to re-assume it. And like the heroes of antiquity, Shane ultimately cannot join the society he has redeemed: the same violent acts that have saved the community exclude him from it, as he recognizes when he says, "I got to be goin' on . . . There's no living with – with a killing. There's no going back from one. Right or wrong, it's a brand. And a brand sticks. There's no going back." Although this violence puts a seal on his exclusion, Marian has recognized from the beginning that being part of a settled community runs counter to Shane's nature, as she indicates when she tells Joey, "Don't get to liking Shane too much . . . he'll be moving on one day." Like the epic heroes of antiquity, Shane exhibits an innate superiority to other men and a violent nature that necessitates his exclusion from the society whose development he enables through his heroic deeds.

Thus, not only does *Shane*, as a paradigmatic example of Western cinema, promote value-systems and ideologies and provide models for masculine and feminine virtue that parallel those found in ancient epics, it also contains strikingly similar notions of what constitutes the heroic nature. As Blundell and Ormand have contended, this overlap derives from the parallel functions these genres have as works that are anchored in formative periods in their respective societies' history and in their mutual concern with both reflecting and shaping national identity. We now again turn to more specific connections this film has with each of the three canonical epics of Greece and Rome in order to provide additional support for this view.

THE *ILIAD*

George Stevens was already an established director of successful films like *Swing Time* (1936) and *Gunga Din* (1939) when the Second World War broke out and he joined the Army Signal Corps, heading up a combat motion picture unit from 1944–46. The horrors he witnessed there – his unit covered both the liberation of Paris and of the Nazi concentration camp at Dachau – had a profound influence on him. He did not direct again until 1948 with *I Remember Mama*, followed by *A Place in the Sun* three years later. But "[a]s time went on," Stevens said, "I kept feeling I should do a picture about the war." In addition, he was becoming increasingly troubled about the violence in Westerns that were becoming so popular among children. As a response, he made *Shane*, which he described as "a Western, but really my war picture."[28]

Stevens's stated intentions with regard to the film's underlying meaning provide a broad basis for comparison with Homer's *Iliad*, the ur-war narrative of Western civilization. Many scholars like Simone Weil have noted that in the *Iliad*, "[t]he cold brutality of the deeds of war is left undisguised,"[29] with some concluding that the clinical accuracy of the descriptions of violent death and wounding are based on first-hand experience. Stevens, too, having seen war close-up, set out to present a realistic picture of gun violence in order to demystify it: "You know, the one thing I wanted to do with *Shane* was to show if you point a .45 at a man and pull the trigger, you destroy an upright figure."[30] As such, he purposefully increases the impact of the film's violence by withholding gunplay until almost halfway through the movie; then when a shot first rings out in the shooting demonstration Shane gives Joey, Stevens ramps up the effect by replacing the sound of the pistol with that of an eight-inch howitzer paired with a rifle shot.[31] The violent nature of fistfights, too, is intensified by the sounds of splintering furniture and shattering glass, or dogs barking, distressed horses whinnying, and panicked cattle breaking fences.[32] Stevens's strategy was to delay the violence, but when it came, to make it "startling in its ferocity"[33] rather than sanitizing the horrors of battle.

Despite this realism where violence is concerned, the film's hero is highly idealized, lacking even the rage that characterizes Achilles.[34] Stevens in fact seems to have softened the protagonist considerably from his original manifestation in Schaefer's novel, where Shane is repeatedly characterized as dangerous, with a seething anger that surfaces when he is provoked,[35] making him considerably more Achillean in print than he is on screen. His difference in the novel in fact is suggested in terms very similar to the metaphors that surround Achilles in his return to battle: as we have seen, Achilles is positioned as something not-quite-human when he is compared repeatedly to fire, light, and metal, while Schaefer describes Shane as having a "fire" inside him, and in his own return to battle he is compared to iron and steel, and his power called "elemental."[36] Stevens's Shane in contrast seems to act more out of noble selflessness than intensely felt emotion, so that in some ways his heroic superiority and difference seem more generalized. Yet Carl Rubino has noted that the two protagonists do share an important quality: they are men torn between two destinies. As Achilles tells Odysseus in *Iliad* 9, his goddess-mother has told him that if he stays and fights, his life will be short but his renown eternal, whereas if he goes home, he will live a long life but soon be forgotten (410–16). Here, Achilles toys with the idea of choosing this second path. As discussed above, Shane too attempts to renounce his heroic identity, symbolized when he exchanges his gunfighter garb for the drab workclothes of a farmhand. Both men, however, are eventually drawn back into battle, Achilles, by an intense need to avenge Patroclus' death, and Shane to safeguard the life of his friend following the death of their comrade. And while the hero's reaction is in each case somewhat different – for Achilles, it is rage and grief, while for Shane, it is a more implicit recognition that he alone can save the community – in both works his return to battle is cast as inexorable. In Book 15 Zeus himself characterizes the events of the *Iliad* as predetermined (59–71), while in his parting speech to Joey, Shane suggests a similar inevitability: "A man has to be what he is, Joey. You can't break the mold. I tried it and it didn't work for me." As Rubino puts it, both men "never really had a choice": their very nature makes suspension of heroic action unsustainable, so that they eventually must participate again in the violence which will result in their ultimate exclusion from the society they have helped to redeem.

Furthermore, as we have seen elsewhere, *Shane* exhibits a complex identification between hero, companion, and enemy similar to that which is found between Achilles, Patroclus, and Hector in the *Iliad*. In Stevens's film, Joe Starrett is cast as a foil for the titular hero, while first Ryker, then his menacing hired gun Wilson are cast as "shadow" figures, making the culminating battle as much an existential psychological struggle as it is a physical one, much as it was for Achilles. Like Achilles and Patroclus, Shane and Joe are bosom companions who are both closely matched but also categorically different. James Work has called the two men from Schaefer's novel "equal halves of a single force,"[37] a relationship Stevens suggests in the film with several carefully composed sequences: for instance, in the stump scene, the camera frames them as two balanced forces swinging their axes in productive harmony, while in the brawl at Grafton's saloon, similarly balanced shots present the two men as near mirror images throughout (Fig. 3.1a–b).

But like Achilles, whose divine heritage provides a superhuman

3.1a and b At left, Shane (Alan Ladd) and Joe Starrett (Van Heflin) take out a stump; at right, Joe and Shane take on Ryker's men in a fistfight. *Shane* (1953). Paramount Pictures.

superiority that sets him apart from Patroclus (and everybody else), Shane is set apart by his heroic nature, the mythic quality of which provides a near parallel to Achilles' semi-divinity. Shane's mythic stature is suggested by his appearance out of nowhere, his buckskin garb, his inscrutable past, his mysterious identity – "call me Shane," he says, offering no surname – and his abrupt departure into the night. In Schaefer's novel, the psychic function this is intended to suggest is made explicit in young Bob's description of Shane as he heads towards the final confrontation: "He was tall and terrible there in the road, looming up gigantic in the mystic half-light . . . He was the symbol of all the dim, formless imaginings of danger and terror in the untested realm of human potentialities beyond my understanding."[38] In the film, similarly, Shane's mythic qualities have divine associations, as has been noted by Harry Schein, who calls Shane's entry "as godlike as his exit" and concludes that "it is a higher being who comes, driven by fate-impregnated compulsion, to fulfill his mission"[39] – a description that could apply equally well to Homer's Achilles. And though Shane does not re-enter the battle for vengeance as Achilles does, his motivation – to prevent Joe being either killed or polluted by a killing – is not dissimilar in that it is anchored in the deep connection the two men share. Thus, just as Patroclus is the softer, more sympathetic counterpart to the hard, intractable Achilles, Joe's position as homesteader, family man, and community leader are the counterweight to Shane's nomadic, isolated, dangerous qualities, a dynamic which fulfills a similar function.

And as in the *Iliad*, just as Hector – despite his sympathetic, likeable qualities – serves as a reminder to Achilles of the mortality he is reluctant to accept in himself, in *Shane*, Ryker and Shane are paired through their imminent obsolescence, while the menacing gunfighter Wilson represents the violent traits that Shane wants to repress in himself. Shane is positioned as a first-wave Westerner much like Ryker when on his first entry he comments, "Didn't expect to find any fences around here," followed by "It's been a long time since I've seen a Jersey cow." That Joe soon thereafter takes him for a Ryker ally also suggests a certain likeness in their natures. In the end, the correspondence between the two men is made explicit when Shane tells Ryker, "You've lived too long. Your kinda days are over," and Ryker responds, "My days? What about yours, gunfighter?"

Wilson too, as an appendage of Ryker, is positioned as a negative facet of Shane's persona that he would like to repress. Like Wilson, Shane is a mysterious stranger with a shadowy past who rides in alone, and despite his attempt to put it aside, the fact that his gun is seen by Joey as part of the fabric of his being is an indication that he, like Wilson, is a gunfighter by nature. On Wilson's arrival, Shane's ability not only to identify Wilson from his description, but also to predict the tactics he will use lead to insinuations ("You seem to know an awful lot about this kinda business, Shane") that he, too, belongs to the same world of violence and conflict. And despite the idealized goodness Shane in some ways seems to embody – helped along by Alan Ladd's golden hair and handsome, unlined face – the hero's casting contributed to his "subtly menacing" air, as Ladd's work in *films noir* helped bring an "ambivalence to the title role, a dark side to his pin-up image."[40] And while Wilson's black hat and clothes provide a contrast to Shane's light-colored garb, as James Folsom has noted, the Wilson character's clothing in the film is "precisely that of Shane in the book,"[41] a transference that supports the sort of identification I am suggesting. In addition, while the foreboding martial music that accompanies Wilson's entry contrasts with the lilting pastoral music of Shane's first appearance, Shane's ride to town to face Wilson recalls Wilson's own entrance both visually and musically (Fig. 3.2a–b). And finally, in a striking innovation, Stevens implies the psychic function of the Wilson character as a counterpart to Shane with a rapid fade-out, fade-in sequence on his first entry into the saloon, suggesting his mythic dimension outside of real time and space (Fig. 3.3).

But despite these affinities, Shane also demonstrates difference when compared to both Ryker and Wilson: unlike Wilson, who uses his gunfighting skills maliciously and with apparent glee, Shane uses his reluctantly and in defense of the community. Unlike Ryker, who

3.2a and b At left, Shane (Alan Ladd); at right, Jack Wilson (Walter Jack Palance). *Shane* (1953). Paramount Pictures.

3.3 Jack Wilson (Walter Jack Palance) in *Shane* (1953). Paramount Pictures.

resists the changing nature of the West with bullying and violence, Shane recognizes and accepts societal development, even if that means the demise of his kind, as he demonstrates with his response to Ryker's query ("My days? What about yours, gunfighter?") with "The difference is, I know it." And just as Achilles must in the end confront Hector, coming face-to-face with his human side (made explicit through Hector's assumption of Achilles' mortal armor), so too must Shane confront both Ryker as an emblem of his own looming obsolescence and Wilson as a symbol of the darker aspects of his own character. Thus, as in the *Iliad*, the battle at the end of *Shane* is as much an existential psychological struggle as it is a physical one. In addition, the effect for Shane is the same as it was for Achilles: the extraordinary deeds of the protagonist redeem society, but the hero himself is ultimately excluded from the community he saves.[42]

THE *ODYSSEY*

Just as Shane's cool-headedness and mild temperament at a glance make him an odd comparison with Achilles, he likewise seems an unnatural fit with Odysseus at first due to his lack of guile and cunning, two traits that famously characterize the hero of Homer's *Odyssey*. Yet here again, there are several important points of comparison. Alan Ladd, who plays Shane, is a shorter man of slighter build – he stands a mere 5'6" – than is Van Heflin, who plays Joe Starrett, a point which the Schaefer novel on which the film is based suggests is purposeful, as Shane is there described as "not much above medium height, almost slight in build. He would have looked frail alongside father's square, solid bulk."[43] Likewise in the *Iliad*, the Trojans Priam and Antenor comment on Odysseus' slighter build when compared to his comrades Agamemnon and Menelaus (3.193 and 209–10). Both men, however, are presented as having traits – like charisma, ability, and experience – that elevate them above their peers. In the *Odyssey*, Odysseus is known for his heroic wariness – in addition to the lies and disguises he uses to safeguard his identity, for instance, he takes the precaution of asking Calypso to swear a great oath that she is not plotting some mischief against him when she informs him that she is letting him go (5.177–9). Shane too is constantly on his guard. As Schaefer puts it in his novel, "[his] brows were drawn in a frown of fixed and habitual alertness. Beneath them the eyes were endlessly searching from side to side and forward, checking off every item in view, missing nothing."[44] The film likewise makes clear that Shane possesses this characteristic: when he first arrives at the Starrett farm, he twice draws his gun at what are revealed to be harmless noises – young Joey cocking his toy gun and a calf that has gotten out of the fence – demonstrating his alertness and caution in new situations. And though he seems to lack guile quite utterly, like Odysseus he conceals his identity, giving only his first name and offering no information about his past. Also like Odysseus, whose gift of speech elevates him in the eyes of his peers,[45] Shane, despite the laconic nature so typical of Westerners, reveals a penchant for eloquent speech when inspiration is needed: when the homesteaders despair at Torrey's funeral and Joe falters when trying to convince them to stay, falling back on, "I – I don't know, but you've just got to, that's all," Shane steps in with a stirring plea for perseverance for the sake of family and community, re-instilling in Joe the heart he had momentarily lost.

Shane also has in common with the *Odyssey* a focus on the issue of restraint. Shane's heroic restraint is highlighted early on when he stoically endures the taunts of Chris Calloway, resisting engaging in a needless fistfight. Like Odysseus, who comes home to trouble in his house with the suitors' abuse of his property but restrains himself until the appropriate time for heroic action, Shane too comes "home" to trouble, with Ryker and his men destroying plowed ground, cutting fences, and killing sows, but he too holds back until the time is right. And like Odysseus, Shane's restraint is emphasized by the lack of it in others. Stonewall Torrey, most notably, is characterized as a hothead; even his own friends like to tease him good-naturedly because he is so easily riled. He is also cast as impulsive when he leaves town before the group when they had agreed to go together, and he demonstrates a weakness for drink. And like with Odysseus' companions, his lack of restraint ultimately contributes to his demise, as Wilson plays upon his impulsive nature to lure him into drawing his gun in order to kill him with impunity. As in the *Odyssey*, the juxtaposition between Torrey's lack of self-restraint and Shane's prudent use of it is important in shaping notions of what constitutes heroic masculinity.

Finally, rather like Achilles with his two destinies, Odysseus is a man divided by competing drives: his lust for action and adventure, and his longing for home and family. This split is reinforced by the *Odyssey*'s division into two roughly equivalent halves, the first dealing with Odysseus' journey home from Troy and the second centering on his attention to problems at home. And despite his constant focus on returning to Ithaca and ensuring the integrity of his family, Odysseus is the consummate wanderer: even at the epic's end, the resolution of his problems with the suitors and his successful reunion with his wife Penelope are diminished by the knowledge that he will soon have to set out again, venturing so far from home that he will encounter a people with no knowledge of the sea in order to appease the wrath of the god Poseidon.[46] Shane exhibits a similar tension between these two competing drives: not only do the opening and closing shots position him as a wanderer – a suggestion reinforced by the fact that the music that opens and closes the film is entitled "The Call of the Faraway Hills"[47] – he characterizes himself as such when he says he is headed "One place or another; someplace I've never been"; at the same time, in accepting the offer of work from Joe, Shane exhibits a longing for a more settled existence. But like Odysseus, Shane is unable to remain domesticated permanently: at the film's close, he sets off, telling Joey, "I got to be goin' on . . . A man has to be what he is, Joey." Thus, despite his lack of guile, Stevens's characterization of Shane shows an important kinship with Homer's portrait of Odysseus.

In addition to these affinities between heroes, another significant way in which *Shane* reflects the themes of Homer's *Odyssey* is in its concern with a young boy's coming-of-age. As noted in chapter 1, the first four books of the *Odyssey* focus on Odysseus' son Telemachus as he is prompted by Athena to make his initial forays into manhood by gaining experience in public speaking, seafaring, and diplomacy. At the end of the epic, this initiation into manhood culminates with his participation in the battle against the suitors, as he stands alongside his father and defends his home, his inheritance, and his own and his father's honor. Throughout the epic, Telemachus' movement toward maturity is illustrated by a corresponding movement away from his mother's influence: in Book 1, for instance, when he rebukes her for asking the minstrel to change his song and sends her back to her quarters, her clear surprise and dismay indicate that she is not used to having him assert himself in this way. Then when he embarks upon his journey to the mainland, he conceals his departure from his mother, knowing she would try to hold him back. And in the prelude to the climactic battle, he takes the reins of household authority from her completely when he asserts, "I am master in this house" and again sends her to her rooms.[48]

In *Shane*, Joey is substantially younger and, unlike Telemachus, has a secure father-figure in place. Nonetheless, this story is very much concerned with similar issues. In Schaefer's novel, the young Bob says that Shane came along about the time he was "beginning to feel [his] oats."[49] Shane's function as an instigator of the young boy's coming-of-age is then demonstrated through the discrepancy between Bob's father's view of him as a boy and Shane's treatment of him as a man: when his father responds to one of Bob's remarks with "Seems to you, eh? . . . Seems to me you're mighty young to be doing much seemsing," Shane follows this up with "You see, Bob . . .," prompting Bob to note that "Shane was speaking to me the way I liked, as if maybe I was a man and could understand all he said."[50] In the end, on Shane's final day with the family, Bob explains his newfound understanding of the increasingly serious situation with, "I guess I was growing up."[51] In Stevens's film too, Shane's arrival and departure bookend a coming-of-age experience for Joey. At the film's outset, Joey is securely identified as a little boy, signified by the fact that his father won't let him have real bullets in his gun. Shane's arrival, however, initiates the process of Joey's coming-of-age, just as Athena's did for Telemachus. This is signaled when Joey sheepishly admits that he had watched Shane's approach from afar, and Shane replies, "You know I – I like a man who watches things goin' around. Means he'll make his mark someday." Shane then serves as a mentor by initiating Joey into the masculine world of violence: Joey watches as Shane steps up to Chris Calloway's challenge in the saloon despite the odds, and later receives from Shane a lesson in gunmanship. As in the *Odyssey*, the mother functions as a repressive agent who threatens to stifle her son's masculine development: in *Shane*, Marian tries to protect Joey from the harsh realities of life ("Don't get to liking Shane too much . . . He'll be moving on one day, Joey; you'll be upset if you get to liking him too much"), and tries to direct his future away from the heroic lifestyle by telling Shane, "Guns aren't going to be my boy's life." Although still a boy, Joey exhibits resistance to his mother's influence much as his epic counterpart did, grumbling, "Why do you always have to spoil everything?" after she breaks up his first shooting lesson. Despite his youth, Joey even manages to play a role in the final showdown when he alerts Shane to the presence of a hidden gunman. In the end, Shane offers Joey some final words of advice that make clear that his role in Joey's life has been to spur him toward manhood: "You go home to your mother and your father and grow up to be strong, and straight. And Joey, take care of them. Both of them." As such, Shane works both as surrogate father to Joey and, like Athena, as a sort of divine instigator toward initiation into manhood. Fred Erisman suggests that the concern with the theme of growing up in Schaefer's writing relates to the development of the United States from "an idealistic experiment in popular government to a sophisticated, if unwilling, world power" in the same period in which his work is set.[52] This suggestion works equally well for the *Odyssey*, which was created in a period of rapid political, economic, and social change as the area that was to become Greece moved from the isolated kingdoms of the Bronze Age when the Trojan saga is set to the politically unified network of communities that developed into the *polis*, or city-state, in the Archaic period when the epics were written down.

Another important consideration when looking at works that share thematic concerns with the *Odyssey* is the treatment of women. As we have seen, throughout Homer's epic Odysseus is plagued by a constant anxiety regarding his wife's fidelity, fearing that if he delays his return too long, she will give herself to another man – a situation that proved fatal to Odysseus' comrade-in-arms Agamemnon. In *Shane*, concern with women's sexual integrity is apparent in both novel and film: in the novel, Wilson threatens Joe with "You wouldn't like someone else to be enjoying this place of yours – and that woman there in the window,"[53] whereas in the film, Ryker implies ("Pretty wife Starrett's got . . .") that Shane's loyalty is motivated by the allure of his wife Marian. The anxiety surrounding this issue is increased by Joey's attitude toward Shane, whom he clearly idolizes, and although

3.4 Shane (Alan Ladd) and Marian Starrett (Jean Arthur) in *Shane* (1953). Paramount Pictures.

his relationship to Joe is not problematized, Joey's confession to his mother that he loves Shane almost as much as he loves his father hints at the potential threat Shane poses to the family unit – both as a paternal figure and as a romantic alternative. Marian's recognition of this is implied by her understated admission to Joey that she "like[s Shane] too," followed by an emotional plea to Joe to "hold me, don't say anything, just hold me – tight." And visually, Stevens reinforces this notion by having Marian wear her wedding dress to the Independence Day celebration that also marks her anniversary to Joe: in symbolic terms, she is in a sense offering herself as a new bride, while Shane's role as potential groom is suggested by the dance they share (Fig. 3.4).

In addition, Shane and Marian are positioned as having complementary natures in a way that reflects the relationship between Odysseus and Penelope – but here, intensifying a non-marital connection and sharpening concerns about the threat Shane poses to the Starrett marriage. Scholars like Nancy Felson and Sarah Bolmarcich have demonstrated that Penelope is the model of an ideal wife not just because of her sexual virtue, but also because she acts as a complement to her husband's nature: for example, like Odysseus, she is cunning, as she makes clear with her famous shroud-trick; like Odysseus, she is wary, as she demonstrates when she holds back from embracing Odysseus until she confirms his identity by eliciting private information (23.173–206); and like Odysseus, she is more perceptive than others, as her epithet *periphron* ("thinking all around") suggests. Odysseus and Penelope's relationship thus exhibits the *homophrosyne* that Odysseus praised as ideal in Book 6 of the *Odyssey*, suggesting that they are "true companions" because of their exceptional like-mindedness.[54] A similar dynamic is evident in *Shane*. Like Penelope, Marian is quick, wary, and perceptive, watching comings and goings through the window and listening in on the male conversation at the settlers' meeting through the door. She understands before the others that Shane's nature means he will be "moving on one day"; indeed, in Schaefer's novel, Shane recognizes her astuteness explicitly when he comments, "You're a mighty discerning woman, Marian."[55] As in the *Odyssey*, these traits reflect similar ones in the hero-figure himself, so that the attraction between Shane and Marian, in the view of some scholars, should be seen primarily as an unspoken identification between the two in recognition of their spiritual kinship.[56]

Yet despite this clear attraction and its threatening potential, no serious crisis about infidelity results.[57] Indeed, Joe implies just the opposite when he says, "Honey, you're the most honest and the finest girl that ever lived, and I couldn't do what I gotta do if I hadn't always knowed that I could trust you." His statement, in fact, follows his nonjudgmental acknowledgment of the attraction between Shane and Marian when he says, "I – I've been thinking a lot, and I know I'm kind of slow sometimes, Marian, but I see things, and I know that if – if anything happened to me that you'd be took care of. . . ."[58] As Bob Baker suggests, the crisis here is conveniently averted by Shane's well-timed exit.[59] But while here it remains an undercurrent, *Shane*, much like the *Odyssey*, demonstrates a significant concern with the potential for adultery in a woman who ultimately provides a model for feminine virtue when her fidelity is affirmed – an affirmation only strengthened through its testing in the first place.

A final important connection between the *Odyssey* and *Shane* is that they both acknowledge in significant ways the validity of the antagonists' perspectives. In the *Odyssey*, we get a glimpse of the suitors' perspective in Book 2, where Telemachus calls an assembly to complain of their abuse of his household. In rebutting Telemachus' accusations, Antinous overviews Penelope's behavior from the suitors' perspective, characterizing her as a tease when he says,

> For now it is the third year, and soon it will be the fourth, since she has been cheating the hearts of the Achaeans in their breasts. She gives hope to everyone and makes promises to each man, sending them messages, but her mind desires other things. (2.89–92)

The fact that the citizens who are present fail to act on Telemachus' request for help suggests that Antinous' argument does indeed hold some sway. Near the end of the epic, in addition, Odysseus and his men are challenged by the suitors' families, who are outraged that their sons and brothers have been cut down in cold blood. However justified Odysseus' actions may have been, Homer makes clear here that the suitors' families, too, have a legitimate grievance, and it is only through the intervention of Athena as *dea ex machina* that an awkward peace is effected.

Likewise in *Shane*, we are asked to consider the perspective of the hero's principal adversary, a point that once again finds its roots in the novel when Shane himself acknowledges the validity of the perspective of the cattleman, there called Fletcher: when Joe complains that Fletcher sees the homesteaders as "nothing but nuisances," Shane responds, "From his point of view, you are."[60] This mere hint in the novel is taken further in the film: although Ryker and his men are throughout most of the narrative portrayed as the "bad guys" whose position is unjustified and who are unscrupulous in their methods, soon after the film's mid-point, Ryker gets the opportunity to speak in his own defense after Joe characterizes his own position as the "right" one: "Right?" Ryker responds,

> *You* in the right? Look Starrett, when I come to this country you weren't much older than your boy there. We had rough times, me and other men that are mostly dead now . . . We made this country. We found it and we made it, with blood and empty bellies . . . We made a safe range out of this. Some of us died doing it, but we made it. Then people move in who . . . [f]ence off my range, and fence me off from water. Some of 'em like you plow ditches and take out irrigation water, and so the creek runs dry sometimes. I've got to move my stock because of it. And you say we have no right to the range. The men that did the work and ran the risks have no right? I take you for a fair man Starrett.

Ryker's eloquent defense is soon answered, but his position is not definitively undercut by any means, so like the audience of the *Odyssey*, the viewer is left understanding that there are no absolutes and no monopoly on a sense of entitlement.

THE *AENEID*

As we saw with Homer's works, Stevens's hero at a glance does not strikingly resemble Virgil's. But Aeneas and Shane do share one enormously important quality: they are heroic men whose special skills are needed to further the project of nation-building, and both sacrifice their personal needs and desires for the sake of this heroic project. Shane's desire to set aside his heroic identity and settle down parallels both the two destinies of Achilles and the competing drives of Odysseus, and here again, it can be seen as an important correspondence with the conflict between Aeneas' personal desires – emblematized by his dalliance with the lovely queen Dido – and the divinely compelled quest to found Rome. While the burden Shane feels as a result of his heroic nature is merely hinted at in the film, Schaefer's novel makes his weary reluctance clear by noting that in quiet moments of reflection, he exudes an air of sadness; at other times, like Aeneas, he sighs, and his very movements convey a sense of "unutterable weariness."[61] Stevens's film mostly elides reference to the weight the hero bears as a result of his heroic duty, but the scale of the sacrifice he makes for the good of the progress of civilization remains paramount. By facing Ryker in defense of the homesteaders, Shane is facilitating Western expansion and the promise of Manifest Destiny, but at the same time guaranteeing his own obsolescence. When just before the climactic battle Marian asks Shane if he is taking up his gun again and facing Ryker for her, he makes clear that his motivation is not his romantic interest, but a defense of family, and by extension, community, when he responds, "For you Marian; for Joe, and little Joe." Despite his desire to settle down (and his desire for Marian), Shane puts aside his yearnings in order to ensure the progress of civilization, a sacrifice that parallels that of Aeneas. And like Aeneas, who, as Carl Rubino puts it, "never truly reached the promised land," Shane too is excluded from the community by virtue of the very heroic qualities that have preserved it: as Rubino notes, "Once the crisis has been averted and the violence has passed, there is no longer any real place for [these men] in the communities they have rescued and restored."[62]

The self-sacrificing nature of the hero, moreover, contributes to a similar strategy in both works where the superficial promotion of current regimes and ideologies is called into question by more subtle undercurrents that emphasize the sacrifice and loss on which these empires were built. In the second half of Virgil's epic, the hero and his people reach their destination, but butt heads with the natives, headed by Turnus. In our allegiance to the Trojans and Aeneas himself, we as the audience are predisposed to see Aeneas' cause as "right," not only because he is the central protagonist, but also because Virgil has framed his quest repeatedly as a divinely sanctioned mission to found a new home. This tendency would only have been strengthened for the original Roman audience, as Aeneas was already known to them from other sources as a semi-divine ancestor and legendary founder of their homeland.[63] So too does the film's perspective predispose us to see Joe Starrett and his fellow homesteaders as the "good guys": as James Cortese notes, Stevens's depiction of the homesteaders, with their emphasis on family, hard work, and respect for law, order, and community, reflects the self-image of the post-war American middle class, positioning them as "the vanguard of our ancestors who made our country what it is," thereby predisposing the 1950s audience to see their side as the "right" one.[64] In both cases, this predisposition is strengthened by the audience's foreknowledge, which helps to frame the protagonists' goals as "destined": we know, after all, that Aeneas' cause eventually won the day and led to the glories of Rome and the *Pax Romana*, just as in the American West the settlers eventually won out over the cattlemen and the land became "civilized" in a seeming validation of the notion of Manifest Destiny. Cortese has also examined this aspect of Stevens's film, noting that Shane's cause, and his heroic stature, is bolstered by the sense that "destiny is on his side, that the next stage in the 'winning of the West' is the triumph of domestication and law." The effect, he argues, is that "*Shane* not only fictionalizes history, but mythologizes it into the history we think we deserve." And although we know this narrative to be fiction, nevertheless we take it to have an important element of truth, one "meant to affirm a society's sense of historic inevitability, cultural supremacy and worthiness to rule"[65] – a tactic highly reminiscent of Virgil's narrative strategy.

Yet neither work sets forth these views unreflectively. Although this promotion of national identity and justification of the means by which empire was built is the most prominent narrative thrust, both works include elements that trouble this line of thinking. For instance, both epic and film actively acknowledge the sound bases of the antagonists' perspectives – Virgil, by suggesting that from the Rutulians' point of view, the Trojans are invaders trying to appropriate their homeland (and their women); and Stevens, as we have seen, by including a speech in which the primary antagonist reminds us of the primacy of the cattleman and very compellingly characterizes his own position as morally right. In addition, the fact that Virgil promotes Augustus' regime and the *Pax Romana* he has ushered in with an epic focused on the ancient war that enabled it reminds the audience that the Augustan peace is rooted in violence. Indeed, by featuring scenes from the recent civil war on Aeneas' shield in Book 8 (675–713), Virgil pointedly acknowledges Augustus' own participation in the bloody conflict on which his peace was predicated. A similar irony is present in *Shane*: when Shane tells Joey in the end to "run on home to your mother and tell her – tell her everything's alright: there aren't any more guns in the valley," the fact that this utopian state has only been achieved by violent masculine heroic action is driven home by its following close on the heels of the gunfight that killed three men. And finally, while both works finish with the death of the adversary who impeded the nation-building project, thus opening the way for the glorious future of the nation to come, they both end on a less than optimistic note: Virgil, of course, closes with Aeneas' succumbing to the same *furor* that the epic has positioned as opposed to Roman values and ideals, revealing a fissure in the picture he has drawn of idealized Roman-ness; and Stevens closes his film – unlike the novel – with the mournful cry of Joey, desperately calling for Shane to come back, emphasizing the loss that is the cost of empire. Both works, then, on one level work as a promotion of the status quo, but offer a more nuanced view for those who want to look deeper.

CONCLUSION

We will look in vain for clear evidence of direct classical influence in Stevens's film – aside from an isolated "by Jupiter" on Ryker's part, there is none to be found. In addition, the smoothed-over edges of its comely, unfailingly noble hero are in some ways a sore match for those of epic heroes, who are remembered as much for their rage, wiliness, and lassitude as they are for their strength, power, and near-invincibility. Yet like the heroes of antiquity, Shane provides the yardstick against which masculinity is measured, and the model he provides is strikingly similar to the one Homer first delineated over 3,000 years ago. And with its fictionalized historical anchoring, *Shane* provides a good example of how Westerns, much like ancient epics, are an ideal generic vehicle for promoting and reinforcing ideologies, for articulating national identity, and for justifying national ascendancy by positioning it as both fated and "right." While *Shane* thus is not a close model for any of the three ancient epics, its many and significant points of contact help to illustrate Blundell and Ormand's notion that, standing as it does on the frontier of civilization, and concerning itself with similar problems and anxieties, Western film is indeed the epic genre for modern America.[66] Recognition of this relationship can not only help us understand the more remote works of antiquity better, but ourselves as well.

NOTES

1 Graves and Engle (2006: 268).
2 McCarthy (1997: 445). The third was *The Ox-Bow Incident* (1943), which also did not take the Best Picture Oscar.
3 Warshow (1954: 200–1); Sarris (1968: 111); Bazin (1971: 151–2).
4 Cortese (1976: 125); Baker (1996: 217).
5 In Schaefer's novel the narrative is recounted by the Joey character, there called Bob, as a grown man reflecting back on the past. Shaefer's story first appeared in 1946 as a three-part serial entitled "Rider from Nowhere" in *Argosy* (Marsden 1984a: 339; see also Nuwer 1984: 279) before it was published (with additions and revisions) in novel form in 1949. For more on the evolution of this story and for a discussion of the differences between novel and film, see Marsden (1984a) and Folsom (1984: 374–82).
6 Perkins (1962: 33).
7 Hughes (2008: 50); Baker (1996: 216). Baker's article, "*Shane* through Five Decades," looks at how the film took on different meanings at various times in response to "a revised set of contexts" (1996: 216).
8 www.imdb.com/list/ls002124326/; www.afi.com/10top10/category.aspx?cat=3 (both accessed May 13, 2015).
9 Hughes (2008: 51).
10 See Hughes (2008: 51); Cloutier (2012: 122).
11 *Shane* was filmed just before widescreen became the rage, and since the film was significantly over-budget, Paramount decided to release it in widescreen format to maximize profits, though this meant chopping off the tops and bottoms of the picture. It is notable that Loyal Griggs won his Oscar for Best Color Cinematography despite this lamentable mutilation. See Fenin and Everson (1973: 336); Hughes (2008: 50).
12 Haslam (1984: 17); see also Nuwer (1984: 277); Marsden (1984a: 344); Rubino (2014).
13 Haslam (1984: 20).
14 Marsden (1984a: 344).
15 French (1997: 77, 79).
16 Holtsmark (2001: 32–3).
17 Schaefer (1984: 71, 77).
18 Baker (1996: 215).

19 Qtd. in Hyams (2004: 11).
20 Qtd. in Fisher (2004: 28).
21 See e.g. Rankin (1984: 11–13); Countryman (1988: 297).
22 For more on this in *Shane*, see Erisman (1984: 290–1).
23 6.441–3. See Katz (1981: 32–3).
24 French (1997: 32).
25 French (1997: 16).
26 See Marsden (1984b) for a discussion of Shane's Christ-like nature.
27 Rubino (2014); see also Holtsmark (2001: 33).
28 Harris (2014: 443). See McGilligan and McBride (2004: 116) for similar comments.
29 Weil (1965: 26).
30 Qtd. in Hughes (2004: 73).
31 Hughes (2004: 73). See also McGilligan and McBride (2004: 116); Hughes (2008: 50).
32 See Hughes (2008: 48).
33 Hughes (2008: 47).
34 This mixture of an idealized, virtuous hero and the undisguised consequences of violence is reminiscent of Homer's work, where too, "[w]hatever is not war, whatever war destroys or threatens, the *Iliad* wraps in poetry; the realities of war, never" (Weil 1965: 26).
35 See Schaefer (1984: 88–9, 122, 125).
36 Schaefer (1984: 169, 242, 245).
37 Work (1984: 316).
38 Schaefer (1984: 249).
39 Schein (1955: 319).
40 Hughes (2008: 44–5, 47).
41 Folsom (1984: 381). See Schaefer (1984: 62).
42 See Rubino (2014).
43 Schaefer (1984: 63).
44 Schaefer (1984: 63). See also pp. 121–4 and 135.
45 i.e. *Il.* 3.221–3.
46 11.119–34 and 23.266–81.
47 Composed by Victor Young and Mack David. Performed by the City of Prague Philharmonic Orchestra.
48 1.345–61; 2.372–6; 21.353.
49 Schaefer (1984: 122).
50 Schaefer (1984: 206).
51 Schaefer (1984: 235). For more on Jack Schaefer's concern with the theme of growing up, see Erisman (1984).
52 Erisman (1984: 289–90).
53 Schaefer (1984: 232).
54 See Felson (1997: 43–65); Bolmarcich (2001).
55 Schaefer (1984: 176). Even young Bob recognizes his mother's astuteness, as he comments that "[s]he always knew when to talk and when

not to talk" (Schaefer 1984: 199). In the novel, however, it is Joe, not Marian, who warns Bob of Shane's transient nature.

56 In Schaefer's novel, that Marian constitutes a "true companion" to the Joe/Shane dyad is made explicit when Shane draws a parallel between the tenacity they show in working to tear out an old stump and Marian's persistence in baking a perfect apple pie after the first one was burnt (1984: 105–12), achievements which symbolize masculine and feminine virtue respectively.

57 Marian's attraction to Shane is a more serious threat in the novel (Folsom 1984: 377).

58 The post-fight scene in Schaefer's novel is even more explicit in demonstrating the triangular nature of the relationship between the three (1984: 201–3).

59 Baker (1996: 217–18).

60 Schaefer (1984: 73). For more on the tensions between cattlemen and farmers, see Rankin (1984).

61 Schaefer (1984: 170, 218; 196, 260).

62 Rubino (2014).

63 i.e. Cato the Elder's second-century BC *Origines* and Livy's first-century BC *Ab urbe condita* (with the first five books, in which Aeneas' role in the founding of Rome appears, published ca. 27–25 BC).

64 Cortese (1976: 123).

65 Cortese (1976: 123–4, 129).

66 Blundell and Ormand (1997: 536).

4 *John Ford's* The Searchers[1]

FILM SUMMARY

The Searchers opens in Texas in 1868 with Ethan Edwards (John Wayne) riding up to the homestead his brother Aaron (Walter Coy) shares with wife Martha (Dorothy Jordan) and their three children. Although he is welcomed, some uneasiness is evident, stemming in part from questions about Ethan's activities since the Civil War's conclusion three years earlier, and in part from the clear attraction between Ethan and Martha. When the Edwards' adoptive son Martin Pauley[2] (Jeffrey Hunter) joins them for dinner, Ethan is openly hostile to the young man, seemingly due to his part-Cherokee heritage.

The next morning, Ethan and Martin join the Reverend Captain Samuel J. Clayton (Ward Bond) and a handful of other men in pursuit of cattle rustlers, realizing too late that this is a Comanche diversion for a murder raid. Ethan and Martin return to the Edwards' homestead to find it in flames, with Aaron and his son Ben (Robert Lyden) dead, Martha both raped and killed, and the two girls Lucy (Pippa Scott) and Debbie (Lana Wood) kidnapped. After a hasty funeral, the men set out again in the hopes of rescuing the girls. When one of their group is wounded in a skirmish with the band of natives who have kidnapped the girls, Clayton and the others turn back, leaving Ethan, Martin, and Lucy's beau Brad Jorgensen (Harry Carey, Jr.) to search on alone.

Ethan later finds Lucy raped and murdered in a canyon and buries her, but keeps it from the younger men until Brad, having scouted ahead, reports with excitement that he has spotted Lucy in the Comanche camp. When Ethan confesses the truth, the distraught Brad charges off in a frenzy and is killed. Ethan and Martin search on, returning a year later to the Jorgensen homestead, where we learn that the pretty young Laurie (Vera Miles) has been impatiently awaiting Martin's return. The next morning, though Laurie tries to prevent him, Martin sets off after Ethan, who has ridden ahead.

The search continues for several years, during which time Ethan kills the dishonest trader Jerem Futterman (Peter Mamakos), who identified Debbie's captor as the Nawyecka Comanche chief Scar, but then tried to ambush them for the withheld reward money; Martin inadvertently obtains a Comanche wife Look (Beulah Archuletta), who is soon after killed in a US cavalry raid; and the two investigate a US military camp, where they encounter a handful of maddened white women recovered from the Comanche, but no sign of Debbie. Finally, their old friend Mose Harper (Hank Worden) puts them in touch with a Comanchero (Antonio Moreno) who facilitates a meeting with Scar. There, they find the grown-up Debbie (now played by Natalie Wood) identified as one of Scar's wives. They leave abruptly, aiming to continue negotiations the next day, but Debbie soon appears at their camp, asking them to go and leave her with her people. Ethan draws a gun, intending to kill her. Though Martin shields her, Ethan is only stopped by a Comanche arrow to the shoulder. They make their escape without Debbie.

When they later return to the Jorgensens' homestead, they interrupt the wedding of Laurie and Charlie MacCorry (Ken Curtis), which is soon cancelled due to Laurie's clear feelings for Martin. Clayton initiates Ethan's arrest for Futterman's murder, but in the nick of time the cavalry arrive with a report that Scar's Nawyecka Comanche are camped nearby. Ethan and Martin join Clayton and his Texas Rangers and they ride out to confront the threat.

Clayton and Ethan plan to charge the camp, but Martin insists on sneaking in ahead of them in the hopes of saving Debbie. He enters Scar's tent and wakes Debbie, who agrees to leave with him; when Scar returns unexpectedly, Martin shoots him. Ethan, arriving too late to kill his enemy, takes what vengeance he can by scalping him. As he exits the tent, he sees Debbie, and nearly trampling Martin who tries to stop him, charges at her wildly as she runs for her life. When he catches up with her, rather than killing her, he lifts her up as he'd done when she was a child, takes her in his arms and says, "Let's go home, Debbie."

Ethan and Martin then return Debbie to the Jorgensen homestead, where Lars (John Qualen) and his wife (Olive Carey) welcome her inside, followed by a euphoric Laurie on Martin's arm. Ethan stands alone outside the door looking in, before turning to walk silently into the desert as the door swings shut behind him.

INTRODUCTION

John Ford's *The Searchers* made a respectable showing at the box office in 1956, but coming in eleventh with returns at $4.45 million[3] it trailed far behind leader *The Ten Commandments*' $68.2 million domestic haul.[4] It not only failed to win any major awards, but its sole nomination was for an Outstanding Directorial Achievement in Motion Pictures award for Ford from the Directors Guild of America. Contemporary reviews, too, were mixed: Jack Moffitt gushed that it was "undoubtedly one of the greatest Westerns ever made," praising the film for "sheer scope, guts, and beauty," but although their assessments were generally favorable, *Time* complained of "lapses in logic" and a "general air of incoherence"; the *New York Times*'s Bosley Crowther criticized its length and the "obviously synthetic surroundings of the studio stage" in some of the outdoor scenes; while admiring Wayne's acting and Ford's handling of the material, *Newsweek* saw the plot as "nothing unusual per se"; Ronald Holloway in *Variety* admired the "eyefilling and impressive" cinematography, but assessed the film as "somewhat disappointing" in that it was "[o]verlong and repetitious"; and *The New Yorker*'s John McCarten afforded the film but one terse paragraph, seeing it, like most contemporary audiences, as unexceptional.[5] Even *Sight and Sound*'s Lindsay Anderson, previously a champion of Ford's work, bemoaned the "unmistakeabl[y] neurotic" nature of the hero and Ford's own "unease with his subject."[6] What's more, if I mention the film today when asked about my work, at least half of my inquirers have never even heard of it: as Glenn Frankel puts it, "*The Searchers* is perhaps the greatest Hollywood film that few people have seen."[7]

Nevertheless, *The Searchers* is now regularly recognized by critics not only as one of the best Westerns – if not the best[8] – of all time, but as one of the greatest Hollywood movies ever produced.[9] In 1989 it was one of two Westerns (the other being *High Noon*) among the first twenty-five films selected for preservation by the Library of Congress's National Film Preservation Board. Western directors including Howard Hawks, Sam Peckinpah, Clint Eastwood, and Sergio Leone have been influenced by the film, and filmmakers in other genres, including Steven Spielberg, Martin Scorsese, and George Lucas, have acknowledged its impact on their work as well.[10] Films from *Once Upon a Time in the West* to *Lawrence of Arabia* and *Star Wars* contain homages, as does the final episode of Vince Gilligan's *Breaking Bad*;[11] Stuart Byron noted structural parallels in *Taxi Driver*, *Close Encounters of the Third Kind*, *The*

Deer Hunter, and many other films, while A. O. Scott sees influence in *Punch Drunk Love*, *Kill Bill*, and *Brokeback Mountain.*[12] Indeed, Stuart Byron went so far as to argue in 1979 that much as Ernest Hemingway saw all modern American literature as coming from Mark Twain's *Huckleberry Finn*, "in the same broad sense it can be said that all recent American cinema derives from John Ford's *The Searchers*."[13] Influence is seen in other media as well: Buddy Holly's classic "That'll Be the Day," recorded by the Crickets in 1957, was inspired by John Wayne's catchphrase in the film, and a 1960s rock band took its name from the title.[14] And in September 2001, visual artist Douglas Gordon created a video installation piece called "The 5 Year Drive-By" in which projection of the film was slowed to such a speed that it would require five years – which many see as the timeframe of the film's search – to view the whole movie.[15]

In addition, much ink has been spilled analyzing the film, including at least two full-length books, and unlike the other works in this study, this film has received sustained attention from classicists: James Clauss has examined its relation to both Greek and Roman epic in his analysis of the film's *katabasis* theme, Martin Winkler has examined it as an *Iliad*, and I myself have written on its relationship to the *Odyssey*.[16] Clauss and Winkler both nodded at connections with the *Aeneid* in these earlier publications, and more recently, Winkler has positioned Ford himself as "America's Virgil" in two conference presentations.[17] What more can there be to say? In a film as full and complex as Ford's masterpiece, I would argue, the answer is "plenty," and because of the pride of place both Ford and the film itself have in the canon of Western directors[18] and works, this film deserves consideration in a foundational study such as this one.

THE EPIC TRADITION

I noted in the introduction Ford's tendency to sprinkle Homeric allusions throughout his films, and numerous scholars even outside the field of classics have recognized him as an epic poet in the Homeric vein. Andrew Sarris calls Ford a "storyteller and poet of images"; Robin Wood sees him as "the American cinema's great poet of civilization"; Giannetti and Eyman call him "the nostalgic poet who most effectively captured a sense of time lost and time remembered, of the breadth of the American experience"; and Jim Kitses credits him as "[o]ne of the creators of the Western genre, America's national epic," describing his attempt to dramatize America's development drawing on history and myth as a "Homeric struggle."[19] The contemporary *Time* magazine review referenced above also made the comparison with Western civilization's first bard explicit with a reference to Ford's "Homeric appetite for violence of spirit and action," and subsequently, Scott Eyman has called Ford "America's Homer," J. A. Place has written, "Ford uses [Monument Valley] as Homer used the sea," and filmmaker John Milius has said, "He's a storyteller like Homer. When Homer got through with a story, you had something you could read forever."[20] In regards to this film in particular, like with other works in this study, some have seen it in light of Greek tragedy,[21] but far more common are comparisons with Homeric epic. Kitses has called Ethan's reception at the film's beginning "momentous, as if Ulysses or the prodigal son were returning," while critic and filmmaker Jean-Luc Godard compared its ending to "Ulysses being reunited with Telemachus"; and both contemporary reviews and commentators like McBride and Wilmington and Michael Böhnke have framed Ethan and Martin's quest as an Odyssean journey.[22] It is not surprising, then, that this film has been the subject of the attention of classical scholars as well.

Like the other films in this study, *The Searchers* presents itself from the outset as a hybrid of history and myth: Ford offers a specific 1868 date and Texas setting, but immediately undercuts the historical implication by opening on the recognizable landscape of Monument Valley, Utah, "a subtle announcement that what follows is a fable."[23] So too does the narrative itself offer a mix of fact and fiction: the plot is based on Alan LeMay's 1954 novel of the same name, which itself has roots in the historical tale of Cynthia Ann Parker, a white settler kidnapped by the Comanche at age nine when most of her family were massacred in Texas in 1836. As in *The Searchers*, Cynthia Ann's uncle James Parker obsessively tracked her and her fellow captives for years, and like Debbie, she married into the tribe but was eventually recovered and reunited with her white family. However, LeMay researched sixty-four Indian abductions and ultimately drew on features from several of these in writing his fictionalized account.[24] Unlike in book and film, James Parker eventually gave up his quest, leaving Cynthia Ann to be recovered later by Texas Rangers; and unlike Debbie, having lived with the Comanche for twenty-four years and with three children by her Comanche husband, Cynthia Ann was never able to assimilate to the white community, and according to some accounts eventually either committed suicide after trying to escape or died of a broken heart longing to return to her adopted people.[25]

Ford himself showed both interest in and disregard for historical accuracy: he told Peter Bogdanovich that in his films, he "tried to do it the real way it had been in the West," relying on lessons from old lawmen like Pardner Jones; Ford additionally noted that he knew Wyatt Earp personally, and some of Earp's Tombstone associates (Jones among them) were in the John Ford Stock Company.[26] Yet he disregarded historical authenticity in important ways – most notably, in his use of Navajos and their accouterments in his portrayal of the Comanche.[27] Likewise, although he cast Harry Carey Jr. as Olive Carey's son, a reflection of their actual relationship, he chose the blue-eyed German-born Henry Brandon as the Comanche chief Scar, a clear transgression of the appearance of reality and an indication that the historical and factual markers are only a veneer placed over a largely fictional account. Like classical epic, then, this film too is a mishmash of myth and history.

In addition, *The Searchers* recalls the ancient epics in its heroic focus: at the most fundamental level, John Wayne's Ethan Edwards is a hero of epic proportions on a standard heroic journey. He is not only a skilled warrior, but he stands out from others in knowledge and perception – he is the first to recognize the cattle theft as a ruse and understand its purpose; he also identifies the Comanche death song, knows the Comanche habit of sleeping with a pony tied to one's side, and both perceives and adeptly thwarts Futterman's ambush. He is stubborn and persistent, determined to see his mission through no matter how long it takes ("Seems like [an Injun] never learns there's such a thing as a critter'll just keep comin' on. So we'll find them in the end, I promise you. We'll find them. Just as sure as the turnin' of the earth"). And his near-invincibility is suggested when he withstands a poisoned arrow that would have killed most men without complaint, and again when he responds to Martin's angry "I hope you die!" with an unperturbed, "That'll be the day."

Like the epic hero, he is deeply concerned with honor, as he demonstrates with his willingness to kill his own niece to protect what he sees as the integrity of his family. And like the epic hero, he exhibits an ideal relationship to language, which, as we have seen, for Westerners involves extreme linguistic economy: he uses terse, clipped phrases ("Name's Ethan"); he is impatient with a long-winded sermon at his own brother's funeral ("Put an amen to it!"); and he is irritated by unnecessary wordiness in others ("I'd be obliged if you'd come to the point, ma'am"). His skills are indisputable and his confidence complete, as is suggested when Martin, having been used as an unwitting decoy, asks him accusingly, "What if you'd missed?" and his dismiss-

4.1 Ethan Edwards (John Wayne) in *The Searchers* (1956). Warner Bros., C. V. Whitney Pictures.

ive response is, "Never occurred to me." And like the standard epic hero, although Ethan's particular skills are necessary for redeeming society, he himself is unable to be part of the community he eventually saves, as is poignantly symbolized by the film's famous final shot of Ethan walking out alone into the desert as the door to the Jorgensens' home, which encloses the restored community, swings shut behind him (Fig. 4.1). As we shall see, however, Ethan's heroic qualities are not simply generic, but he demonstrates a close connection to each of the heroes of antiquity's canonical epics as well.

THE *ILIAD*

Edward Buscombe notes in *The BFI Companion to the Western* that the first Western stories center on kidnap by Indians, commonly termed captivity narratives. These tales were "at first based upon actual experiences but [were] increasingly fictionalized, dramatiz[ing] the deep-seated racial and sexual fears of the whites confronted with the unknown occupants of a strange land."[28] But when Alan LeMay interviewed Ben Parker, a descendant of Cynthia Ann's family, in preparation for writing his book, Parker was surprised to find that LeMay was more interested in Cynthia Ann's "angry, vindictive, self-justifying uncle James," who had searched for her for eight years than he was in the recovered captive herself.[29] Clearly, it was not the suffering of the victim that LeMay found most compelling, but the complex motivations that underlay her uncle's obsession, and it was this figure rather than the captive maiden who became the central focus of LeMay's novel and the film it inspired. To me, all this recalls Homer's *Iliad*, an epic that centers on a conflict triggered by Helen's abduction by a foreign people, but the heart of which is Achilles' heroic rage, which stems as much from his internal struggles as he seeks to come to terms with life, death, and his own limitations as it does from external events. In both cases, then, as so often in epic and Westerns, a woman motivates the plot, but the real focus is male heroic action, while the woman herself is shunted to the periphery.

In addition to his more generalized heroic traits, Ethan Edwards, Ford's version of the intriguing protagonist initially inspired by James Parker, shows a particular kinship with Homer's Achilles through his burning rage.[30] Of course, Achilles' famous rage is in fact the epic's formal topic, just as with *The Searchers*, as Kitses puts it, when it comes to Ethan, "[r]age is all."[31] In Book 1, Achilles is first angered when the great king and his nominal superior Agamemnon unjustly takes away his war-prize Briseis. Outraged by this affront to his honor, Achilles removes himself from battle, in effect isolating himself from the main body of the Greek forces. So too in *The Searchers* does Ethan early on become nominally subordinate to Captain Clayton, and like Achilles and Agamemnon, the two former Confederate soldiers clash over issues of honor: when Clayton prods Ethan with "I didn't see you at the surrender," Ethan's response is heavy with implications: "Don't believe in surrenders. Naw – I still got my saber, Reverend; didn't turn it into no plowshare neither." As their initial quest to catch the cattle rustlers turns into pursuit of the native band who attacked the Edwards' ranch, Clayton remains in charge despite Ethan's clearly superior strength, knowledge, and suitability for leadership. But after the stand-off at the river, Clayton pushes Ethan too far, and Ethan explodes: "Well Reverend that tears it! From now you stay out of this! All of you! I don't want you with me! I don't need you for what I gotta do." Like Achilles, this break with sanctioned authority propels Ethan into separation from larger society. Although both men retain a few loyal supporters – for Achilles, Patroclus and the rest of his Myrmidons, and for Ethan, Martin and Brad – the implication is the same: this rift signifies that the men's epic heroism is too big to be contained by society's usual constraints, and suggests the isolation this necessarily entails.

In both works, however, while this break with authority causes anger and isolation, a more visceral, existential rage is at the heart of the narrative, and in each case, this more deeply seated fury is motivated by the murder a dear companion – for Achilles, that of Patroclus, and for Ethan, that of Martha.[32] For both men, moreover, this rage is anchored in similar feelings of loss, failure, guilt, and powerlessness. As we have seen, Patroclus functions as Achilles' softer, more feminine counterpart, so that when Patroclus dies, Achilles loses not just a close companion, but part of himself. For Ethan, Martha too represents his feminine side – like Ethan, tough and relentless (as Aaron says, "that Martha – she just wouldn't let a man quit!"), but able to tap into the domestic impulse and social connections that Ethan cannot access; when she dies, Ethan then too loses part of himself. Achilles' feelings of loss are compounded, as Jonathan Shay has observed, by feelings of failure and guilt. He bemoans the fact that he failed to protect his friend in his hour of need ("Let me die now, since I was not fated to help my comrade in his final hour; at a far remove from his fatherland he perished, lacking me as his protector to ward off his doom": 18.98–100), while his notion that the wrong man has died ("before this, the heart in my breast had hoped that I alone should die here in Troy, far from cattle-rich Argos, and that you should return to Phthia. . .": 19.328–30) indicates feelings of guilt.[33] Although Ford leaves Ethan's feelings unspoken, it is clear that he too is tormented by a sense of failure: in his emotion-laden expression as he unsaddles his horse after comprehending the danger (see cover image), scholars like Sam B. Girgus see not only the horror of his imagining what may be happening to Martha, but also self-censure at the fact that he was not there to protect her.[34] And like Achilles, Ethan's grief is compounded by guilt, but his of a more unspeakable nature – Ethan is plagued by the unconscious recognition that Scar has done what he himself wanted to do: kill his brother Aaron and have sex with his wife.[35] Both men also share a profound anxiety at the lack of control these events highlight for them: Achilles must come to terms with his own death, which he is powerless to prevent, and Ethan must reconcile himself to the lack of control he has over his niece's purity and what he sees as his own family's honor.

These catastrophes propel our heroes into grief-fueled quests for revenge, notable in Achilles' case for its superhuman intensity, and in Ethan's for its impressive duration; and in both cases, the hero is pushed out of the bounds of normal human experience, becoming at once super- and subhuman. Achilles' superhuman nature is expressed by the divine aid given him – his immortal armor, the ambrosia Athena drips into his veins (19.350–4), and the assistance Athena renders him in battle (22.214–47). His subhuman nature, on the other hand, is illustrated through comparisons with beasts, particularly predatory creatures, metaphors that are made near-reality when Achilles tells Hector before he kills him, "I wish my soul and spirit would permit me, having carved it up, to eat your flesh raw" (22.346–7) – a gruesome image that positions Achilles as radically isolated not only from society, but from his own humanity as well. Likewise, although explicit divine interference would run contrary to generic conventions, as his quest grows longer, Ethan "nearly obtains superhuman proportions," as Girgus puts it.[36] For instance, he achieves near-invulnerability, as suggested when he is barely slowed by the poisoned Comanche arrow, and Martin Winkler compares the role of Mose, as a helper figure and "holy fool," to the function of Athena and Thetis in the *Iliad*, suggesting that like Achilles, Ethan receives a sort of divine aid.[37] At the same time, however, as he becomes increasingly determined to kill his own niece, he also becomes more and more separated from his own humanity. Indeed, as Garry Wills puts it, Ethan becomes both "divine and bestial in the scale and ferocity of his willpower."[38]

In both cases too, the terrible fury that has hold of these men does not abate with the death of the enemies on whom they sought revenge: after he kills Hector, Achilles is still driven to drag his body behind his chariot, mutilating it horribly in front of Hector's own parents' eyes in a dramatic transgression of societal norms; likewise for Ethan – in this case, denied the satisfaction of killing Scar himself, as Martin has beaten him to it – the violent death of his nemesis does not offer him comfort or satisfaction; instead, he pulls out his knife and scalps the fallen leader, becoming in effect the subhuman animalistic savage he has all along made the Comanche out to be.[39]

The Searchers, like the other films in this study, also has in common with the *Iliad* an important identification between hero and enemy that attaches symbolic significance to the culminating conflict. We have seen that for Achilles, Hector signifies his human weakness and the mortality to which he will ultimately succumb. For Ethan, Scar represents the repressed desires he is reluctant to acknowledge in himself. This relationship has been well recognized: McBride and Wilmington describe Scar as the "crazy mirror of Ethan's desires"; Arthur Eckstein and Martin Winkler have both called him Ethan's "alter ego"; Jim Clauss has discussed Scar as Ethan's "counterpart in the underworld"; Peter French calls Scar "Ethan's scarred psyche"; Jim Kitses refers to the two men as "doubles"; Robert Pippin says "[t]hey are in fact mirror or twinned characters"; and Glenn Frankel has called them "two sides of the same mirror."[40] Just as the relationship between Achilles and Hector is suggested through Hector's assumption of Achilles' armor, so too is the connection between Ethan and Scar made clear through the exchange of a battle token: Scar draws Ethan's attention to the fact that he now wears around his own neck the medal Ethan had given Debbie. In numerous other ways, too, Ford makes clear that Scar is to be seen as a projection of what Ethan denies in himself: for instance, just as Scar kills cattle to carry out his murder raid, Ethan shoots buffalo to deprive the Comanche of their food source;[41] just as Scar mutilates the bodies of Ethan's family, so does Ethan shoot out the eyes of a dead Indian

4.2 Emilio Gabriel Fernandez y Figueroa (Antonio Moreno), Martin Pauley (Jeffrey Hunter), Ethan Edwards (John Wayne), and Scar (Henry Brandon) in *The Searchers* (1956). Warner Bros., C. V. Whitney Pictures.

and scalp Scar himself; just as Ethan pursues Scar to avenge Martha's murder, so too is Scar motivated by revenge ("Two sons killed by white men. For each son, I take many [scalps]"). Their equivalence is made clear when in response to Ethan's loaded question "You speak pretty good American – for a Comanche; someone teach you?" Scar soon after echoes the implication, saying, "You speak good Comanche; someone teach you?" (Fig. 4.2).[42]

And just as Patroclus serves as the softer, more feminine balance to Achilles' hardness and aggression, Martin serves a similar role for Ethan.[43] Like Patroclus, who passionately argues for a more sympathetic course of action that will spare the suffering Greeks, Martin too advocates compassion and seeks to preserve life where Ethan's masculine aggression wants to obliterate it, so that Martin in effect acts as "the willing agent of the feminine counternarrative" in the film.[44] Ford makes explicit the importance of Martin's role in tempering Ethan's excesses when Martin tells Laurie, "He's a man that can go crazy wild, and I intend to be there to stop him in case he does." Martin's "eighth Cherokee and the rest Welsh and English" heritage likewise positions him as a balance between Ethan and Scar[45] – a three-way connection emphasized by the blue eyes all three actors share – creating a triad much as we have seen with Achilles, Hector, and Patroclus.

In the end, the resolution of the existential crisis the hero's loss has ignited is achieved in each case not by the punishment of his foe, but by a catharsis that enables him to finally relent his murderous rage and regain his lost humanity.[46] For Achilles, this takes the form of Priam's touching supplication, which reminds him of his own father's grief, and allows Achilles to grieve appropriately not only for Patroclus, but for his own mortal nature. For Ethan, this is his interaction with the terrified Debbie, whom he lifts up when he catches her as if on instinct, replicating his playful greeting in her youth, and thus awakening in him long-suppressed familial connections. While some critics have scorned Ethan's sudden change of intent,[47] others have defended the action here as "entirely credible."[48] I too see this seemingly abrupt switch as perfectly plausible in much the same way that Achilles' is: with Scar, not only as Martha's killer but also as the husband who represents Debbie's unacceptable sexual activities, dead; with a barbaric act of vengeance having been performed in scalping Scar; and with Debbie herself having renounced the Comanche and agreed to go with Martin,[49] circumstances have altered considerably. Even if he cannot accept her miscegenation (and thus cannot rejoin the family himself), Ethan can accept a now less threatening Debbie, whose ties to the Comanche have been severed and whose allegiance to the white community has been restored.

Despite this catharsis-enabled re-engagement with their humanity, both heroes suffer the common fate of Western and epic heroes who, as we have seen, are unable to rejoin the society they helped to redeem.[50] Achilles will die before the war is finished, destined not to return to his homeland. Ethan likewise returns Debbie to the Jorgensens, but is excluded from the restored community. In Ford's justly famous ending, first Debbie and the Jorgensens, then Laurie and Martin walk past him and into the house as if he is invisible. He stands at the door looking in for a moment before turning to walk alone into the desert as the door swings shut behind him. No hand initiates the action, rather the door closes firmly and silently on its own as if fate itself is at work.[51] Just as firmly is Achilles excluded from the conclusion of the epic that has featured him: in an ending just as poignant, despite his death it is Hector who rejoins the community at the *Iliad*'s end, as Priam brings his body back to the bosom of his family and into his homeland, where he is grieved, praised, mourned, and given due burial, while Achilles is as shunted out of sight as if a door had closed on him as well.

In addition to the conspicuously Achillean nature of the hero, Ford's film demonstrates a gendered framework similar to that of the *Iliad*, in which the female characters function to demonstrate positive and negative roles for women. Mrs. Jorgensen, for instance, as a motherly figure who offers an emotional plea for the safety of her son ("Don't let the boys waste their lives in vengeance!"), demonstrates maternal roles and virtues in much the same way as does Hecuba for Hector in the *Iliad*. Her daughter Laurie, despite her impatience and near-betrayal of Martin, fills a role similar to Andromache in that she ultimately proves herself a faithful and supportive "wife", despite her attempts to pull Martin back from his heroic duty, as Andromache did with Hector.

But most strikingly, as we have seen, the larger conflict in both epic and film is predicated on the abduction of a woman, Helen and Debbie, respectively. In both cases, these women are positioned as threatening through their shifting allegiances. The ancient tradition in general is ambiguous about whether Helen was abducted willingly or by force, and within the *Iliad* in particular she both berates herself for following Paris to Troy (3.173–5), and positions herself as a victim of the gods (3.399–404); in addition, she expresses loathing for Paris and a wish that Menelaus had killed him, but is easily seduced by him thereafter (3.428–47). Likewise in *The Searchers*, although Debbie was initially taken against her will, she eventually becomes one of Scar's wives and expresses allegiance to the Comanche when she tells Martin, "These are my people." It is perhaps this spiritual "contamination" that Ethan finds even more threatening than her physical miscegenation, as it is only after she expresses this sentiment that he draws his gun. In classical period Athens, seduction was considered a greater crime than rape, because, as Lysias puts it, "those achieving their ends by force are hated by the ones they have forced; but those using persuasion have corrupted [their victims'] souls" (*On the Murder of Eratosthenes* 32–3). In a similar way, Ethan is deeply disturbed by the idea of Debbie's miscegenation; but it is her expression of loyalty to her Comanche lover and his people that prompts him to actualize his intention to kill her. Thus, like Helen, Debbie is threatening both through her sexuality and through her shifting loyalties.

And as is the case with Debbie, in the larger myths of the Trojan cycle Helen's primary male connection in her natal culture – her husband Menelaus – finds the sexual violation she commits so threatening that he considers killing her; but like Ethan, Menelaus in the end changes his mind, restoring her to her Spartan home and her previous position. Moreover, this reversal takes place only after Troy has been sacked, Helen's Trojan husband Paris killed and his successor Deiphobus killed and mutilated, in the latter case by Menelaus himself, and after Menelaus has had an intimate interchange with Helen – in vase paintings, he is frequently portrayed as overcome by her beauty, sometimes when she bares her breast to him – that serves to remind him of their past connection as lovers and her status as the mother of their child. Likewise, while Ethan's change of heart about killing Debbie is enabled by Debbie's own restored loyalty,[52] the destruction of the Comanche camp, Scar's death at Martin's hands, and the mutilation Ethan himself executes, it is prompted most directly by the intimate interchange that reminds him of their previous relationship.[53]

While the destruction of Troy and the events that follow take place outside the action of the *Iliad*,[54] they are well-known parts of the epic tradition of which it is a part, and thus help to demonstrate the similar premium placed on women's fidelity in highly patriarchal societies like pre-historic Greece and the nascent United States. Overall, women's roles in Ford's film, much as in Homer's *Iliad* and the surrounding traditions, provide a gendered framework that works to delineate patriarchal notions of what constitutes women's virtue both by demonstrating as its highest manifestation support of the male heroic agenda through sexual fidelity, and also by signaling the danger posed by women who threaten through their sexuality.

THE *ODYSSEY*

Ethan Edwards is often recognized as one of Ford's most complex characters, and indeed, in many ways he resembles not just Homer's Achilles, but also his *polytropon* (*Od.* 1.1) hero Odysseus, the man of many twists-and-turns. Each is a brave, heroic soldier and leader who relies on his superior wits and shows restraint where other men are undone by the lack of it; but each is also cast as an anti-hero who achieves his goals through questionable means and exhibits both hypocrisy and serious failures in leadership and judgment.

Odysseus, as we have seen, is known for his cunning: as Helen tells us in Book 4, he manages to sneak into Troy in disguise on an intelligence-gathering mission (4.240–64); he figures a way out of the Cyclops' cave when he and his men are trapped and seemingly doomed (9.318ff.); he saves his own ship and the men on it by taking the precaution of mooring it outside the bottle-necked harbor where the rest of his fleet are trapped and killed by the Laestrygonians (10.87–132); and he slyly procures a cloak from the swineherd Eumaeus through a pointedly suggestive tale (24.462–506). Ethan demonstrates a similar mental acuity: he is well-versed in both Comanche and Spanish, he knows Native American customs and tricks, and he fully perceives the danger of Futterman's ambush while Martin remains oblivious.

Both men, too, demonstrate heroic self-restraint where other men are undone by the lack of it. For example, Odysseus' men, falling victim to hunger, feast on Helios' cattle and are destroyed, while he alone resists this temptation and survives (12.339–425). In *The Searchers*, whereas Martin rushes off in a frenzy once the posse have understood the Comanche intent, Ethan resists, despite his anxiety for his family; instead, he takes the time to feed and refresh his horses, and thus soon overtakes Martin, who is now on foot, having ridden his horse to death.[55] Ethan's restraint is further emphasized by the contrast with Brad Jorgensen, who upon learning that the Comanche have raped and killed the woman he loves, races forth in a suicidal charge,[56] a stark contrast to Ethan's far more methodical pursuit of the Comanche in response to a similar loss. Moreover in both works, concern with the concealment of information is an important component of the restraint both men show. Odysseus comes home in disguise, hiding his identity even from his wife in order to assess where the household members' loyalties lie, and thus he regains control of his house and his queen – a success emphasized by the counter-example of Agamemnon, who returned home rashly in triumph and was killed by his adulterous wife and her lover. Ethan, too, uses disguise, posing as a trader to infiltrate a Comanche camp to gather intelligence. And like Odysseus, Ethan keeps his cards close to his chest, illustrated again through a contrast with Martin, who asks too unguardedly if Ethan has learned anything about Scar, so that Ethan cuts him off angrily: "When are you going to learn to keep your big mouth shut?"

Although both men are cast as traditional epic heroes on standard heroic journeys, both Odysseus and Ethan exhibit behavior that calls their heroism into question, making them equal parts hero and anti-hero. Odysseus, for instance, is known for his cunning – and his lies. In the course of the epic, he offers at least three extended, elaborate fictional biographies to support his disguise as a beggar.[57] And although some of his lies and disguises are motivated by self-preservation and were likely seen as morally neutral in ancient Greek culture,[58] in Book 24 he pulls the same trick on his elderly, grieving father without any motivation, it seems, but knavery (24.303–14). His moral ambiguity was such that, as we have seen, the more straightforward hero Achilles implicitly condemned Odysseus for false-dealing, and in later literature, the portrayal of his character became increasingly dark and unscrupulous. At the beginning of the Cyclops episode, he demonstrates greed and poor judgment that results in six men losing their lives, and at the end his need to boast once again brings his ship and the men on it into mortal danger. Moreover, Odysseus is willing to achieve his goals in ways that run counter to prevailing notions of heroic conduct: he defeats the suitors by taking them by surprise at a banquet, having disarmed them and cut off their escape routes.

Ethan, too, is cast as an anti-hero whose villainous traits are clear: this is a man who, as Pippin puts it, "spews racist invective at every opportunity, who mutilates the bodies of the dead . . . who slaughters buffalo in an insane rage just to deprive Indians of food, and who is out to murder a child."[59] At the beginning of the film, his brother Aaron implies that the "fresh-minted" cache of coins Ethan offers to pay for his board has been obtained unscrupulously, and just before the film's climax, Captain Clayton confiscates Ethan's gun and initiates his arrest for Futterman's murder. And like Odysseus, Ethan is not above using methods that run counter to societal notions of fair play: he shoots at both Comanches and Futterman as they turn their backs in retreat, the latter after using Martin as an unwitting decoy and just before depriving Futterman's corpse of the gold piece he had paid out to him earlier.

Odysseus' anti-heroic qualities are also evident in his hypocrisy: he censures his men for a lack of restraint – for instance, when they open the bag of the winds and when they eat the Cattle of the Sun

– but he too can demonstrate a ruinous lack of restraint, both in his imprudent boast to Polyphemus (which in fact draws down the curse that proves devastating to them all) and again when he dallies in Circe's bed, delaying their return for an entire year. He also exhibits the same behaviors he condemns in his enemy: he slaughters the suitors in retribution for entering his home uninvited, appropriating his food, and wooing his wife, but this is not unlike his own behavior with Polyphemus, whose cave he enters uninvited after appropriating his sheep and cheese, and whom he later symbolically emasculates by putting out his eye in an act of phallic dominance.[60]

The Searchers contains a similar dynamic in the alter ego relationship established between Ethan and Scar outlined above, which also contains elements of a profound hypocrisy: as Arthur Eckstein has shown, the conflict is initiated when Scar does what Ethan himself "wants to do but cannot do and cannot even admit to wanting: he annihilates Ethan's brother's family and seizes the women for himself."[61] Ethan, then, spends the rest of the film trying to do the same thing – wipe out Scar and his people and recapture Debbie. Just as Scar had infiltrated the Edwards homestead using the ruse of cattle-rustling, so too does Ethan infiltrate Scar's camp under the pretense of trade, when his intentions are far more threatening. Both the film and the epic undercut notions of cultural superiority and problematize the issue of "us vs. them" by blurring the lines between hero and villain and by demonstrating the protagonist's participation in the same behaviors he scorns in others.[62]

In the end, both men exhibit important failings in achieving their goals: Odysseus loses all his men in the course of his journey, a failure noted even in the epic's proem ("He did not save his companions, for all his longing [to do so]": 1.6). Ethan likewise loses Brad Jorgensen – a failure he attributes to himself ("I got your boy killed") even though Brad's father does not hold him responsible – and as several commentators have noted, it is not he but Mose Harper who twice finds Debbie, and it is Martin who kills Scar.[63]

In a related parallel, both Homer and Ford interrupt their narratives with a long tale-within-a-tale that emphasizes the unreliability of perspective and brings the questionable qualities of the protagonist into sharp relief. In Books 9–12 of the *Odyssey*, Odysseus recounts his adventures to the Phaeacians. The episodes he discusses include far-fetched elements more appropriate to folk-tales than to real-world experiences: he encounters giants and six-headed monsters; his men are turned into pigs and back into men; and he travels to Hades and meets famous warriors and mythological superstars. Even if these fanciful tales are taken at face-value, Homer inserts several strong hints that Odysseus may be stretching the truth: careful scrutiny of his account of his departure from the Cyclops' island reveals his assertion that Polyphemus hears him shout, though he has just characterized the distance as twice as far as a man's voice could carry (9.473ff.); he reports a private conversation between the gods Zeus and Helios, then covers his tracks by saying he had heard it through the divine grapevine (12.374–90); and he reports seeing the shade of Heracles in Hades, but, remembering his apotheosis, quickly explains that it was just his specter, as the real Heracles is found on Olympus (11.601–4). The reasons for such embellishments are revealed when he abruptly interrupts his narrative at a climactic point and suggests that it is bedtime, prompting his audience to offer him lavish gifts in order to entice him to continue, just as he had surely anticipated they would. His willingness to lie in order to advance his interests reminds us of this hero's wiliness, while emphasizing his unreliability and the bias of individual perspectives.

Likewise, Ford includes in the narrative heart of his film an extended sequence in which Laurie reads a letter from Martin aloud to her parents and suitor Charlie MacCorry.[64] The events she relates contain a notable shift in tone and perspective from that of the main narrative: whereas throughout most of the film, Ethan is presented as a complex character who, for all his faults, feels deeply, in this sequence he is cold and callous. Whereas Martin is generally good-natured and compassionate, here he is cruel and abusive to his inadvertently acquired Comanche wife. As in the *Odyssey*, the reasons for this are emphasized by a break in the narrative at a strategically important point: when Laurie learns of Marty's "marriage," she is hurt, but upon hearing that his new wife is a squaw, she is so outraged and appalled that she jumps up and throws the letter into the fire – a contrast in reactions that points to the virulent racism she will later vocalize so shockingly. This interruption then reminds us that the events the letter relates are filtered through the perspective of Laurie's jealousy and bias, depicting Ethan as she (and others) see him,[65] and Marty as she wants to believe he behaves toward her Indian rival.[66]

In addition to their similar hero/anti-hero natures, Odysseus and Ethan are alike in their attitudes toward home: both men exhibit an intense longing for home, but they are estranged from the domestic space by their wandering natures and by sexual considerations. Throughout the first half of the *Odyssey*, Odysseus strives to return home, but even after he reaches Ithaca he is distanced by the disguise he dons in order to assess his wife's loyalty and that of the other members of the household. As *The Searchers* opens, Ethan returns to his brother's house having been away for years, and like Odysseus, he approaches cautiously as if unsure of how he will be received, a tentativeness emphasized by the contrast with Martin's carefree and energetic approach soon thereafter.[67] Even after he has been accepted into the home, his disconnectedness is suggested by fraternal tension, his own hostility toward Martin, and his desire for a woman whom he cannot have.[68]

In the main narrative thread of each work, moreover, each man is engaged in a long and difficult quest to preserve the integrity of a woman, a mission in both cases made urgent by the sexual threat these women pose. Odysseus strives to return to his home and reunite with his wife Penelope before she gives herself to another, while Ethan pursues the Comanche in a race to recover Debbie before she is of an age to have sex with her captors. The theme of women's sexual integrity in *The Searchers* is replicated in a less menacing way by the relationship between Martin and Laurie Jorgensen, whose courtship also reflects the *Odyssey*'s themes: much like Penelope, Laurie loves Martin and waits for his return as he roams far and wide for years on end. But also like Penelope, her need for a male protector necessitates limits to Laurie's loyalty ("I ain't cut out to be no old maid!" she tells him) so that we are given to wonder whether she will remain true to him or give herself to another before Marty can assume his proper place as her husband. Like Penelope, Laurie does agree to another marriage; and like with Penelope, her proper husband returns just in time to participate in a contest for the bride's hand (in this case, a comic fistfight), saving her from entering into a disloyal and improper union.[69] Both works, then, are deeply concerned with women's sexuality and the threat inappropriate use of it poses to a man's honor and very identity.

While this theme gets a somewhat comic treatment in this secondary storyline, so serious is the threat in the primary heroic thread that both protagonists exhibit a capacity for violence in reaction to infidelity. In the *Odyssey*, the example of Clytemnestra is constantly held up as a cautionary tale to Odysseus that illustrates the dangerous potential in his own wife; the fact that Clytemnestra is killed by her own son in vengeance implies the seriousness of the consequences that may be in store for Penelope should she also prove unfaithful. Any doubt about this dissipates when Odysseus, having been recognized by his faithful elderly nurse Eurycleia, grabs her by the throat and threatens to kill her if she does not keep his identity to herself (19.479–90), dramatically demonstrating the potential for violence

4.3 Ethan Edwards (John Wayne), Martin Pauley (Jeffrey Hunter), and Debbie Edwards (Natalie Wood) in *The Searchers* (1956). Warner Bros., C. V. Whitney Pictures.

that surrounds this issue. Ford's film is even more explicit: as Debbie matures, Ethan shifts from a mission to rescue her to a mission to kill her. That his intentions are serious is made perfectly clear when he points a gun at her and orders Martin to step aside (Fig. 4.3).

Both women, moreover, demonstrate that the protagonists' fears regarding their loyalty are not unfounded: even after her fidelity has been safely established, Penelope defends Helen, the most famous of adulteresses, by attributing her transgression to divine interference: "Surely a god set her about this shameful deed, and never before did she set such a baneful folly in her heart" (23.222–4) – to Nancy Felson, an acknowledgment that she too might have ended up in Helen's position.[70] Similarly, after Ethan and Martin have confirmed that she has in fact become one of Scar's wives, Debbie indicates complicity in this betrayal by expressing allegiance to the Comanche people. In the end, however, both heroes restrain themselves from this sort of violence. Having exacted revenge on the suitors and the betraying serving-women; having seen Penelope's caution and restraint even with him; and having received reasonable reassurance through her bed-trick that she has not betrayed him sexually, Odysseus relents and embraces Penelope in a symbolic restoration of the home and community. Likewise, with Debbie having shifted her allegiance back to her natal family and with the Comanche destroyed, Ethan is able to see her once again as her mother's daughter, and thus sets aside his murderous intentions and restores her to the white community.[71]

Both works thus foreground the extreme cultural importance placed on women's chastity along with the profound threat that women's infidelity poses to male honor and identity. As scholars have shown, in the highly patriarchal culture of ancient Greece, identity was intimately tied up with paternity and progeny; because of the vital role women played in the transfer of status, a premium was placed on their fidelity which was ensured at all costs, while failure to defend it was a cause for shame and dishonor.[72] In the American West, the tenuous position of the white settlers who were attempting to establish a claim by encroaching on Native American territory led to a similarly strong impulse to control women's sexuality in the interest of racial purity: as McBride and Wilmington observe about this period, "If a white man impregnates a dark woman, he is planting his seed in an alien culture; but if a dark man impregnates a white woman he is, in the eyes of the primitive white, violating her,"[73] and threatening, in effect, the integrity of the white culture. The extreme importance of women's chastity in both cultures is dramatically illustrated in Homer's work and in Ford's through the implication that a woman who poses this sort of threat needs to be eradicated.

A final significant correspondence in epic and film is the coming-of-age story of the hero's son (or son-figure). As we have seen, at the outset of the *Odyssey* Odysseus has been separated from his son for nearly twenty years, their estrangement heightened by Telemachus' uncertainty regarding his paternity (1.215–16). In *The Searchers*' opening scenes, a similar estrangement is established between Ethan and Martin, also due to their long separation – Ethan at first doesn't even seem to recognize Martin, so that Martha is prompted to prod him: "Martin? Martin Pauley!" – and to issues of ancestry: Ethan comments accusingly, "Fella could mistake you for a half-breed," suggesting his racist discomfort with what Martin soon clarifies as his "eighth Cherokee, the rest Welsh and English" heritage.

Despite this tension, the similarity between the young men and their father-figures is emphasized in both works. First Athena as Mentes and later Helen and Menelaus all comment on Telemachus' likeness to his father (1.206–12; 4.141–50). He later shows himself to be Odysseus' equal in more than just looks: when he tries to string Odysseus' great bow, we are told that he would have succeeded, but holds off at a sign from his father (21.125–9). He is thus positioned as like his father in ability – since all of the suitors, in contrast, fail utterly in their attempts – and in nature – like his father, Telemachus exercises heroic restraint by concealing information that would tip off the suitors to their game. Ford likewise suggests that Martin and Ethan have similar natures: not only are they are paired as the "searchers" of the title, but Martin's wandering nature is reinforced when Charlie MacCorry, wooing Martin's girl Laurie, serenades her with "Gone again, skip to my Lou," immediately after she learns that Marty will not be home for Christmas again.[74]

In each work too, the youth serves a period of apprenticeship to the older man that provides him the experience he needs to become a full-fledged hero in his own right. Telemachus' journey toward heroism is first prompted, as we have seen, by Athena, his father's divine helper, so that in the *Telemachia* he gains experience in public speaking, seafaring, and diplomacy, while forging ties in his own right with important leaders on the mainland. After he is reunited with his father in Book 16, he learns from him important lessons about information management, restraint, and strategy, before taking his proper place beside him in battle in Book 22. His heroic development is suggested as well by his shift from a deferential attitude toward a more assertive stance, suggested immediately after Athena as Mentes first prompts him toward manhood when first his mother, then the suitors, marvel that he now speaks so boldly (1.360 and 381–2). By the end of the epic, he asserts his authority over them both unambiguously when he proclaims that "I hold authority in this house" (21.353). The fact that he has come into his own fully is demonstrated when he deviates from his father's instructions (though importantly, not against his interests) by hanging the disloyal serving-women rather than putting them to the sword, denying them a more dignified death (22.435–45 and 461–73) while demonstrating that he is a man in his own right rather than merely his father's minion.

In *The Searchers*, similarly, Martin is initially young and inexperienced: in his first battle with the Comanche, he is overcome after his first kill and covers his face in distress. His apprentice status is suggested in his complete deference to Ethan, even in the face of abuse. Ethan in turn repeatedly stresses his authority ("*I'm* givin' the orders") and superior strength ("I can whup you to a frazzle"), along with Martin's inferior knowledge and "tainted" ethnic heritage ("What does a quarter-breed Cherokee know. . .?"), while preventing him from full participation in the quest, as when he rebuffs Martin's attempt to join in negotiations with a Comanchero over whiskey with "Wait'll you grow up." As the film progresses, however, Martin begins to assert himself ("Well you told me that already, so shut yer mouth!") and to insist on full participation in the quest: when Ethan tells him to wait outside Scar's tent while they confer, for example, Martin pushes past him with a defiant "Not likely!" And in the end, like Telemachus, Martin develops independence and resolve: he insists on implementing his own plan of action by entering the Comanche camp alone in the hopes of saving Debbie, arguing against the strategy endorsed not just by Ethan, but by Captain Clayton as leader of the Texas Rangers. And just as Telemachus emerges at the end of the *Odyssey* as a full-blown warrior to equal his father, at the end of *The Searchers*, Martin establishes himself as a hero in his own right not just by initiating Debbie's rescue, but by killing Scar.[75]

Despite this similarity, however, after they achieve their goals, the period of wandering and searching for both Telemachus and Martin is over, the period of quest and adventure merely an episode that marks a transition from boyhood to manhood.[76] At the *Odyssey*'s end, Telemachus is firmly entrenched in his home on Ithaca, but now with his inferior status as a subordinate member of the household firmly cast off. Martin's domestication is more conspicuously demonstrated in the closing scene of *The Searchers*, when Laurie takes his arm and they enter the Jorgensens' house together, presumably soon to marry and start a new family over which he will rule as *paterfamilias*. Not so for Odysseus and Ethan. For these men, the quest is not a temporary state but part of the fabric of their being, as is suggested by the fact that both are fated to wander on after the action of the works themselves: Odysseus must set out again to lands so far distant, the people have no knowledge of the sea,[77] while at *The Searchers*' conclusion, Ethan sets off alone into the desert. The very titles of the works in which these heroes appear point to the pervasiveness of their wandering natures: the *Odyssey* – the title of the epic as it has come down to us – is derived from the hero's name, but has in recent centuries come to describe any long, adventurous journey or quest, while the film's title labels Ethan a "searcher," as it does Martin; but unlike for Martin, Ethan's search will not end, as the theme song suggests as Ethan walks away: "A man will search his heart and soul/ Go searchin' way out there;/ His peace of mind he knows he'll find,/ But where, oh lord, lord where?" Despite a deep longing for home and family, Ethan, like Odysseus, is the paradigmatic wanderer. He may stop in, but eventually his very nature will compel him to "Ride away . . . ride away . . . ride away."

THE *AENEID*

While Ethan demonstrates Achilles' rage and the *polytropon* nature of Odysseus, he also shows a close affinity to Aeneas. At the beginning of both Virgil's epic and Ford's film, the focal heroes have been somewhat diminished by a defeat in war – for Aeneas, the conflict with the Greeks at Troy, and for Ethan, the US Civil War, in which he fought for the confederacy. Neither man, moreover, is fully able to move past this defeat: Ethan still wears his "Johnny Reb" coat, and proudly proclaims that he cannot be sworn in by the Rangers because "[I] figure a man's only good for one oath at a time. I took mine to the Confederate States of America." For his part, Aeneas repeatedly expresses longing for his lost city, even (somewhat undiplomatically) telling his lover Dido as he abandons her, "If the fates had left me to live my life by my own devices and to order my cares by my own will, my first concern would be the city of Troy . . ." (4.340–3). Both men, nonetheless, are engaged in efforts to forge a new and glorious nation, and in the process come into conflict with natives who disrupt their efforts, a conflict which in both cases is triggered by a dispute over a woman – Aeneas and Turnus clash over the hand of the Latin princess Lavinia, and Ethan pursues the Comanche who have abducted his niece Debbie.

In addition, both writer and director highlight the costs involved in these nation-building efforts, in both cases signified by the sacrifice of women. Both men must abandon women they love, as these unions are incompatible with the male heroic agenda: Aeneas, compelled by the gods themselves, must leave behind Dido and the city she has built in order to found Rome, while Ethan, in pursuit of the manly action which is vital to his nature, leaves behind Martha, who then weds his less charismatic brother Aaron. Both men are pained at this necessary abandonment – Aeneas leaves "groaning deeply, his soul having been shaken by so great a love" (4.395), and Ethan appears forlorn as he sits outside watching while Aaron takes his lost love to bed in what Garry Wills calls a "silent but very telling *paraklausithyron*" (a convention of ancient elegy in which a lover sits lamenting outside his mistress's door).[78] Both men, in addition, must face the sudden loss of women they love in a violent and unexpected invasion: Aeneas has lost his wife Creusa as they fled Troy, and Ethan loses Martha in a Comanche death-raid.

In both works, the sacrifice of women is not only highlighted, but even fetishized: as Alison Keith has shown, the *Aeneid* has a tendency to linger over and lovingly describe the dying and dead bodies of women like Dido and Camilla, sexualizing them in a way that is not done with men's deaths.[79] Likewise in *The Searchers*, we are invited to imagine the raped and mutilated corpses of Martha and Lucy; we are even given a glimpse of the murdered Look. In contrast, the deaths of Aaron, Ben, and Brad are shunted off-screen, and they do not offer the same invitation to linger over the image of the dead bodies as the deaths of the women do. Furthermore, the women's deaths in both works are framed as necessary to the heroic agenda: Creusa and Dido must die because these connections hamper Aeneas' efforts to found Rome, as he is destined to wed Lavinia in order to forge ties of kinship with the natives and because it is this union that will produce the line of Alban kings;[80] Camilla, too, must go, as she is not only a strong, active woman in contrast to the Roman ideal (much like Dido), but she also fights against the side of destiny. Martha's and Lucy's deaths, on the other hand, act as motivations to the heroic action Ethan, later accompanied by the Texas Rangers and US Cavalry, will take in exterminating the Comanche who threaten the progress of the developing nation. Look's death, in addition, is necessary so that Martin can marry Laurie, a union that will help restore the fragmented white community by bonding his adopted sister Debbie to the Jorgensen family, and eventually contribute to its development by producing offspring that are more white than Indian. Both works do, however, provide a model for women who will take some part in the new world: in the *Aeneid*, it is the modest, silent, and passive Lavinia who plays a role in the founding of Rome, and thus offers us a guide to the virtues valued in a Roman matron, while in *The Searchers*, Debbie can be spared and reintegrated into white society only after she tacitly capitulates to the dominant (white) male viewpoint and renounces the Comanche, situating subordination to the male agenda as a prime female virtue.

Finally, the heroes of these works are also alike in that both are ultimately excluded from the society whose development they enable: Virgil's acknowledgment that Aeneas himself will not live to see Rome's founding parallels Ethan's exclusion from the restored white community in *The Searchers*' famous ending. Moreover, Aeneas' chronological remove from the establishment of the city of Rome proper – not to mention from the Golden Age of the *Pax Romana* – finds an additional analogy in Mrs. Jorgensen's matter-of-fact recognition that her generation of settlers and homesteaders will not live to see the glories of the country yet to come. And importantly, in both cases the glorious zeniths of national development that lie in the narratives' future are implied to be located in the audience's present.

This relationship between the foundational past and the "glorious" present points to even more compelling connections between these two works in authorial intention and strategy. Like the *Aeneid*, *The Searchers* is a self-questioning, multi-layered reflection on heroic achievement, an epic that utilizes the epic form to extol traditional subject matter while at the same time subtly subverting it.[81] As we have seen in previous chapters, recent scholars have shown that Virgil's epic functions both to promote the glories of Rome and to point out the problems with and sacrifices inherent in the process of its establishment. The critique these scholars discern, however, is subtle enough that generations of commentators missed it, misled by generic expectations and by the propagandistic elements Virgil makes more overt. Even Augustus, whose glorious national vision is scrutinized and dissected in the *Aeneid*, seems to have been blind to the epic's more cynical aspects, as he ordered the work saved despite Virgil's own deathbed request that it be destroyed. In much the same way, Ford uses the genre most closely associated with chronicling, promoting, and elevating the foundation of America's national identity to expose some of the darker facets of its character. And as with Virgil's epic, contemporary audiences and critics – and many casual viewers since – seemed oblivious to the film's darker, more disturbing implications and the largely counter-heroic nature of its protagonist.[82]

Virgil's epic outwardly promotes the glories of Rome and the imperial regime through a genre most closely associated with the promotion of national identity; through a semi-divine warrior-hero who demonstrates key cultural virtues while emphasizing Augustus' noble lineage; by positioning the Roman Empire as the fated culmination of all that has come before; and by inserting explicit and exalting references to the events leading up to Augustus' reign. He punctuates these themes with patriotic imagery, such as the long line of Aeneas' descendants his father overviews for him in the Underworld (6.756–886) – a scene that would have recalled the sculptural program of the Temple of Mars Ultor in Rome, which similarly places Augustus in a historical continuum to justify his rule[83] – as well as offering an ekphrasis of sorts when Venus presents her son with his immortal arms, the heart of which features Octavian's victory at the Battle of Actium (8.675–713).

So too does Ford draw on the Western tradition, its standard iconography, and a prototypical Western hero to promote the taming of the West and the doctrine of Manifest Destiny. The basic plot of the film seems amenable to such a project: a man is out to recover the niece kidnapped when the rest of his family was massacred, suggesting an "us vs. them" theme, with the assumption that the honor will attach to "us" and the blame to "them." Repeated references to the savagery of Native Americans, along with their characterization as murderers, rapists, and kidnappers, contribute to the outwardly comforting notion that Westward expansion was a triumph of civilization over savagery as a way to rationalize imperialism and near-genocide. This perspective is linguistically reinforced by Mrs. Jorgensen's moving speech:

> It just so happens we be Texicans. A Texican is nothing but a human man way out on a limb, this year, and next, maybe for a hundred more. But I don't think it'll be forever. Someday, this country's gonna be a fine good place to be. Maybe it needs our bones in the ground before that time can come.

Like Virgil, Ford includes patriotic imagery, like the smartly dressed Seventh Cavalry advancing triumphantly to Custer's jaunty marching tune "Garryowen," enhanced with blaring bugles and military flags on proud display. Ford thus offers a film with a basic framework that reinforces and validates America's self-image as a tough, hard-working, self-sacrificing nation whose conquering of the West was a benevolent civilizing project and the incidental violence morally justified. And all this was reinforced by the casting of John Wayne, a man who had by this time become the virtual embodiment of the Western hero in a role that might have drawn on Robert Warshow's influential 1954 essay on the paradigmatic Westerner as a "blueprint."[84]

Yet as we have seen, Virgil undercuts the patriotic thrust, for instance by having Aeneas exit the Underworld through the gate of "false dreams" rather than that of "true shades" (6.893–8), and by juxtaposing images of Octavian's triumph with scenes of unchecked imperialism, such as long lines of the conquered peoples, the Euphrates moving with "humbled waves," and the Araxes offended by his bridge (8.714–28). Likewise in his film, Ford juxtaposes depictions of brutality on the part of the white community with his patriotic scenes in order to undercut the nostalgic idealism. Sandwiched between inspirational scenes of the Seventh Cavalry, for instance, are images of strewn corpses and the pitiless herding of whipped captives following the massacre of a Comanche village. Many scholars see these scenes as reminiscent of the massacre of the Cheyenne at the Washita River in 1869 or of the Lakota Sioux at Wounded Knee in 1890,[85] making them visual reminders of the more shameful chapters in the historical "taming" of the West. In addition, among the dead Ethan and Martin find Look, a character who had previously been a target of mockery and derision from the searchers themselves. While Look's comic treatment in the preceding sequence may offend our current sensibilities in terms of both race and gender, she is also presented as harmless and innocent, as Marty drives home with his distressed query, "Look? What did them soldiers have to go and kill her for, Ethan? She never done nobody any harm!" The inclusion of such a character in the wholesale slaughter of a village shifts the implication of the military's *modus operandi* from defending civilization to wholesale genocide.

In a similar way, the spunky, likeable Laurie Jorgensen is throughout the film cast as the forerunner of the All-American girl – warm, pretty, spirited, smart, and hard-working. But in what many critics characterize as the most shocking scene in the film, Laurie, upset that Martin is setting out to find Debbie again, asks,

> Fetch *what* home? The leavings of Comanche bucks sold time and again to the highest bidder with savage brats of her own? . . . Do you know what Ethan'll do if he has a chance? He'll put a bullet in her brain. I tell you, Martha would want him to.

That this vicious, hateful, racist speech spews from the mouth of a woman we have come to identify with – and who in her dogged pursuit of the mixed-race Marty had seemed to disregard racial differences in an important way – once again disrupts our view of the moral basis of Western expansion.[86]

Ford undermines racist assumptions about the "savage" character of Native Americans in other ways. For instance, he first suggests that the white women captives the Seventh Cavalry have recovered have been maddened into sub-humanness by their experiences with the Comanche;[87] but when we meet Debbie, she is lovely, eloquent, and perfectly sane, undercutting the racist fears of Ethan (as well as Laurie, and thus the white community as a whole). And it is the mixed-race Martin who in the end succeeds not only in killing Scar, but also in reintegrating into the white community.[88] In effect, Ford demythologizes the national project by calling into question the view of the subjugation of native peoples as a heroic, civilizing act.

Ford also puts the American dream under a microscope by suggesting the profound similarity between Ethan and Scar: not only are both men tough, determined soldiers and leaders, they both murder and mutilate in pursuit of vengeance, holding an entire race responsible for the actions of a few. Most strikingly, just as Virgil ends his epic with Aeneas succumbing to the same *furor* that his nemesis Turnus has demonstrated and that has been implicitly condemned as anti-Roman throughout the epic, so too at the end of Ford's film does Ethan give in to the same savage impulses he despises in the Comanche when he scalps his fallen enemy. In this way, both Virgil and Ford dramatically problematize their protagonists' heroic natures, and in doing so, again call into question the integrity of the national project they embody.

CONCLUSION

As has been noted, many of the film's initial viewers "hardly noticed Ethan's pathological racism";[89] some commentators, in addition, have mistaken Ethan's racism for Ford's.[90] I have elsewhere defended Ford from the latter charge, noting that Ford was a friend to the Navajo, who dubbed him "Natani Nez" (Tall Soldier) and inducted him into their tribe in gratitude for the income he brought to the reservation by shooting some seven films at Monument Valley over the course of his career and employing many Navajo as extras at fair wages.[91] In addition, many of the seemingly problematic elements of *The Searchers* can be explained away as part of a larger anti-racist agenda (the treatment of Look, for instance, is filtered through Laurie's perspective as a jealous lover and soon-to-be-revealed racist herself; the casting of the white Henry Brandon as the focal Native American is symbolic of his function as Ethan's alter ego; the conflation of Comanche attributes with Nez Perce, Navajo, and others are due to cinematic considerations and practicalities).[92]

But Ford was no saint: he is regularly described as a cruel and tyrannical bully on set,[93] and he was certainly not immune to the less enlightened views on race that were prevalent in his lifetime. Ford played a bit part as a Klansman in D. W. Griffith's groundbreaking but profoundly racist *Birth of a Nation* in 1915, and in his own 1924 *The Iron Horse*, he unrepentantly depicts Native Americans as the vicious, savage "bad guys." Even in the generally much more nuanced 1939 *Stagecoach*, they appear chiefly as nightmarish, murderous apparitions.[94] Glenn Frankel, moreover, notes that in Ford's 1961 *Two Rode Together* – which followed *The Searchers*, and dealt with a similar plot much less successfully – "the racist sentiments . . . are endorsed rather than undermined" as they were in the earlier film.[95]

For these sins, Ford is often condemned wholesale, as by Quentin Tarantino who noted his role in Griffith's film with outrage before proclaiming, "To say the least, I hate him."[96] Ford's supposed racism is often illustrated by noting his famous proclamation, "I've killed more Indians than Custer,"[97] but as often happens, this does not tell the whole story, as Peter Cowie suggests by letting Ford finish his thought: "Let's face it, we've treated them very badly – it's a blot on our shield; we've cheated and robbed, killed, murdered, massacred and everything else, but they kill one white man and God, out come the troops."[98] To be sure, Ford's uses of race in his narratives, including this one, are not above criticism; yet by the standards of his time, Ford's decision to take on racial and sexual issues of these sorts was bold, and his depiction of Native Americans in this film groundbreaking, as is suggested by the assessment in *Films in Review* of Courtland Phipps, who was upset by the "sentimental attitude toward the Indian which is the equivalent of an indictment of the white man."[99] What Phipps was threatened by was the seeming legitimization of Scar's atrocities – "Two sons killed by white men; for each son, I take many [scalps]" – with a motive not unlike the one that drives the white hero, along with the fact that, as McBride and Wilmington put it, "As the search progresses, it becomes increasingly difficult to appreciate the difference between Ethan's heroism and the villainy of Scar. . ."[100]

Yet by the 1960s the film's critical assessment began to rise as Ford came to the attention of the French *auteurists*, while in 1971 McBride and Wilmington eloquently pleaded a case to an American audience for its artistry and complexity.[101] As with most great works of art, Ford's film is many things to many people, as perhaps is evident from the narrative's close connection to all three of the canonical ancient epics. Today, despite the vigorous objections of a few dissenters,[102] the film has firmly entered cinema's artistic canon, recognized as groundbreaking not only generically, but also as a serious, if flawed, examination of racism and as courageous criticism of the hypocrisy inherent in America's national narratives.

NOTES

1 Some material in this chapter was first published in *Arethusa* 41.1: 11–49, Copyright © 2008 The Johns Hopkins University Press. Reprinted with permission.

2 Often spelled "Pawley" in scholarly analyses (as well as on IMDb). I am following the spellings of names as they appear in LeMay's novel (if applicable) and the film's shooting script (found at sfy.ru/?script=-searchers, accessed July 28, 2015).

3 Byron (1979: 48); Davis (1995: 279); McBride (2011: 569); Eckstein (2004a: 44 n. 105). Buscombe (2000: 67) notes that "[b]ox-office figures are notoriously unreliable," but his figure is in the same ballpark.

4 According to IMDb (www.imdb.com/title/tt0049833/business?ref_=tt_dt_bus, accessed July 20, 2015).

5 Moffitt (1956: 3); *Time* (1956); Crowther (1956: 121); McCarten (1956: 54); Holloway (1956); *Newsweek* (1956).

6 Anderson (1956: 94–5).

7 Frankel (2013: 326).

8 As on AFI's list of the top ten Westerns (www.afi.com/10top10/category.aspx?cat=3; accessed July 17, 2015)

9 The film was listed twelfth on AFI's "100 Years 100 Movies" 10th anniversary edition in 2007 (www.afi.com/100years/movies10.aspx, accessed July 21, 2015) and seventh on the 2012 *Sight and Sound* critics' poll, the latest available as of this writing (www.bfi.org.uk/news/50-greatest-films-all-time, accessed July 21, 2015).

10 See Cowie (2004: 207); Kitses (2007: 102); McBride (2011: 570–1); Frankel (2013: 7, 320–1); et al.

11 Snierson (2013).

12 Byron (1979); Scott (2006); see also Frankel (2013: 322). Byron notes that both Spielberg and Cimino have denied direct influence in their films, but argues for it anyway (1979: 46).

13 Byron (1979: 45).

14 See Byron (1979: 48); Hughes (2008: 85); McBride (2011: 570); Frankel (2013: 315); et al.

15 See Lehman (2004: xi). This event took place in 29 Palms, California, and one *Arethusa* reader noted that it also was offered in Berlin and Fornebu, Norway. There is some debate over whether the search in the film lasts five or seven years (see Eckstein 2004a: 37 n. 7).

16 Clauss (1999); Winkler (2004); Day (2008).

17 Clauss (1999: 7); Winkler (2004: 164). Winkler presented a paper on Ford as "America's Virgil" at the 2008 annual CAMWS meeting in Tucson, and spoke again on this topic at the fall 2015 Film & History meeting in Madison WI.

18 Ford's importance as a director is suggested by his four Academy Awards and six nominations, more than any other American film director, along with five New York Film Critics' Awards, and in 1973, an AFI Lifetime Achievement Award (see Bogdanovich 1968: 28; Byron 1979: 46; Davis 1995: 3; Eyman 2004: 7). Not just this film, but his work in general influenced other directors such as Ingmar Bergman, who called Ford "the best director in the world," and Orson Welles, who listed the old masters of American film direction as "John Ford, John Ford, and John Ford" (qtd. in Davis 1995: 3; see also Tynan 1967: 58).

19 Sarris (1968: 49); Wood (2001: 31); Giannetti and Eyman (2001: 164); Kitses (2007: 44, 41).

20 *Time* (1956); Eyman (2004: 7); Place qtd. in Cowie (2004: 166); Milius qtd. in Frankel (2013: 321).

21 E. Christian Kopff, drawing on Jean-Pierre Vernant's comment that Greek tragedy stopped using the hero as a model and started treating him as a problem, uses this film and Ford's *The Man Who Shot Liberty Valance* as an illustration of this same movement in 1950s–60s Westerns (1999: 240); Clauss looks at the *katabasis* theme in *The Searchers* in relation to Euripides' *Heracles* (1999: 13); and Kitses (2007: 96–7) compares Ethan to "a hero in a Greek tragedy," calling his love for Martha in particular "an intolerable, Oedipal sin." Most

comprehensively, Martin Winkler (2001b) devoted an essay to examining this film's relation to Greek tragedy.

22 Kitses (2007: 99); Godard qtd. in Byron (1979: 48); *Look* (1956: 90); McBride and Wilmington (1971: 210–11); Böhnke (2001: 58).

23 Frankel (2013: 306).

24 Frankel (2013: 199).

25 See Eckstein (2004a: 43 n. 89) for the former; the latter is according to Elsie Hamill qtd. in Frankel (2013: 179). McBride (2011: 552) says she starved herself to death. For a comprehensive account of the Parker's Fort massacre, the search for Cynthia Ann and her fellow captives, her eventual fate, and her descendants, see Frankel (2013: 11–182). Other historical touches include the character of Mose Harper, purportedly based on the half-crazy Indian fighter "Mad Mose" who also had a predilection for rocking chairs, as well as scenes of a Seventh Cavalry attack on a Comanche village that recall historical massacres of Native Americans in the same era (noted below).

26 Bogdanovich (1968: 40, 84). The John Ford Stock Company commonly refers to the large group of actors on whom Ford drew repeatedly.

27 Henry Brandon told Joseph McBride (2011: 566) that Scar's hair is done in Nez Perce fashion, and that Ford instructed costume designers to incorporate Navajo styles, which were better suited to the film's desert setting than was the dress of the Comanche as Southern Plains Indians. See also Frankel (2013: 250) et al.

28 Buscombe (1988: 18).

29 Noted in Frankel (2013: 182).

30 This connection has been discussed by Wills (1997: 257–8, 261) and Winkler (2004).

31 Kitses (2007: 97).

32 As Winkler (2004: 154–5) has noted.

33 See Shay (1994: 69–70).

34 Girgus (1998: 34). See also French (2001: 52).

35 See Eckstein (1998: 3; 2004a: 200; 2004b: 15ff.)

36 Girgus (1998: 44).

37 Winkler (2004: 156).

38 Wills (1997: 261).

39 See Winkler (2004: 155, 159).

40 McBride and Wilmington (1971: 212); Eckstein (1998: 13); Winkler (2004: 153); Clauss (1999: 9); French (2001: 55); Kitses (2007: 101); Pippin (2009: 236); Frankel (2013: 307). McBride more recently has called Scar Ethan's "alter ego" and "doppelgänger" (2011: 557, 563, 565).

41 French (2001: 55).

42 See Day (2008: 29–34) for further development of this equivalence.

43 Kitses (2007: 100) calls Martin "[o]ne of Ford's feminised males"; Winkler (2004: 166 n. 11) also touches on this relationship: "Martin

may be seen as Ethan's good side or as the embodiment of the good qualities in himself which Ethan denies or represses."

44 Frankel (2013: 314).

45 Strengthening this reading is McBride's analysis that Ford identified closely with Ethan, while he could "assign nobler aspects of himself" to characters like Martin (2011: 559).

46 See Winkler (2004: 159–60).

47 In LeMay's novel, the protagonist (there called Amos) does not shift his intention, but is in fact killed by a young Indian maiden whom he at first mistakes for Debbie (2013: 299–300).

48 McBride (2011: 564). Winkler argues for the rightness of Ethan's abrupt change of mind based on ancient comparanda (2001b: 137–41).

49 The film does not show that Ethan knows about Debbie's change of heart, but he may have gleaned it from how she comports herself as she flees Scar's tent with Martin.

50 Winkler (2004: 160–1); see also Blundell and Ormand (1997: 550).

51 See Winkler (2004: 160–2) for further discussion.

52 McBride (2011: 564), along with other critics (Pye 1996: 235; see also Gallagher 1986: 335–6n.), sees Debbie's change of mind as the film's "most glaring flaw." This flabbergasts me, as I see it is a profound piece of psychological realism. When they first come upon Debbie, she tells Martin, "At first I prayed to you, come and get me, take me home. You didn't come," suggesting that she gave up, and accepted her lot as part of the Comanche people. She now learns that her kinfolk *have* been looking for her, which awakens in her a longing for her past life and the family she loved, and which has now been revived as a real possibility. By the time Martin comes to rescue her the second time, these yearnings have had time to grow and develop. (Martin Winkler sees this change as abrupt, but argues for its merits too based on a literary tradition of abrupt changes of mind going back to Greek tragedy: 2004: 137–41.)

53 See Winkler (2001: 160).

54 Menelaus' dilemma is dramatized in Euripides' *The Trojan Women*; the murder and mutilation of Deiphobus is recounted in Virgil's *Aeneid* 6.509–30; for discussion of vase paintings depicting this scene, see Blondell (2013: 40); Powell (2012: 585) notes the breast-baring variant.

55 Wills (1997: 256).

56 See Clauss (1999: 6).

57 The so-called Cretan Lies: 13.256–86; 14.199–359; and 19.165–202, 221–48.

58 As suggested by anthropological studies of the honor and shame-based traditional societies in the Mediterranean culture basin: see again Du Boulay (1994: 172–3, 188–200) and Winkler (1990: 133–7).

59 Pippin (2009: 230).

60 I developed this point more fully in Day (2008: 29–34), showing that Odysseus has an alter ego relationship with his enemies much like the one I argue for throughout this book between Achilles and Hector, and demonstrating the parallel with the relationship between Ethan and Scar. While I still discern this as an important dynamic in the *Odyssey*, in this monograph I have focused more exclusively on its manifestation in the *Iliad*, as I believe there is it both more pronounced and more fully developed.
61 Eckstein (1998: 3). See also Eckstein (2004a: 15ff.; 2004b: 200).
62 Again, I explore the implications of this more fully in Day (2008: 37–45), where I argue that Ford here exposes racism and other forms of prejudice as part of a pattern of excluding the Other as a scapegoat for weaknesses in the self, revealing more about the subject's lack than about real deficiencies in the object of discrimination.
63 O'Brien (1998: 22), et al.
64 In LeMay's novel, the corresponding events are not related through the device of a letter.
65 See Gallagher (1986: 326).
66 Stowell (1986: 139–40) and Wills (1997: 257) also see this sequence as colored by Laurie's anger and jealousy. Many commentators, however, take this sequence more at face value, and thus are far more critical of what they see as Ford's racist presentation of Look and the abusive behavior directed toward her (see, for instance, Pye 1996). See Day (2008: 36–7) for an argument that Homer and Ford each make their audience complicit in the negative behaviors of their protagonists.
67 See Gallagher (1986: 334).
68 Ford communicates this primarily through meaningful looks and gestures, along with Ethan's sole concern for Martha when he returns to the burning homestead, but he reinforces it musically, using Rev. H. D. L. Webster's Civil War ballad *Lorena*, which has as its theme an unconsummated, socially taboo love, as "Martha's Theme" (Eckstein 2004a: 6; 2004b: 200–1; Kalinak 2004: 121ff.).
69 Scholars like Nancy Felson (1997) argue that Penelope does, or may, know of Odysseus' identity and that she sets up the marriage contest so that he himself can win her hand and to facilitate his revenge. While I subscribe to this view, Penelope's plan does involve the real risk that the beggar is not in fact Odysseus, and that even if he is, one of the suitors will best him and win her hand.
70 Felson (1997: 39–40).
71 In Nugent's original screenplay, on the verge of killing Debbie Ethan shifts his intention with the explanation, "You sure favor your mother" (qtd. in Eckstein 1998: 14).
72 See Carson (1990); Rose (1993: 220); French (2001: 148–9).
73 McBride and Wilmington (1975: 162). In LeMay's novel, the sexual

threat is much less pronounced, as Scar himself is presented as a father-figure rather than as a potential husband.

74 Clauss (1999: 8).

75 Martin's initial "apprentice" status is less prominent in LeMay's novel, while the specific movements toward manhood discussed here are absent from the novel entirely.

76 See McBride and Wilmington (1975: 158).

77 As prophesied by Teiresias at 11.119–37.

78 Wills (1997: 256).

79 Keith (2000: esp. 114–17).

80 As prophesied by his father in the underworld (6.760–6).

81 Although I have not had access to his paper, Winkler's 2008 CAMWS abstract (camws.org/meeting/2008/program/abstracts/08d4.Winkler, accessed July 28, 2015) indicates that he examines something along these lines in Ford's later work.

82 See Pippin (2009: 230, 243); McBride (2011: 557); Frankel (2013: 315).

83 Zanker (1988: 210–15).

84 Frankel (2013: 309–10). See also Kitses (2007: 34). The audience's identification with John Wayne's character worked almost too well: the movie was both promoted and received as nothing less than a "standard-issue" John Wayne action film (Frankel 2013: 15; see also Pippin 2009: 243; Frankel 2013: 304–5).

85 e.g. McBride (2011: 564).

86 See McBride and Wilmington (1971: 213–14); Pye (1996: 229–30); Day (2008: 40–1). In LeMay's novel, Martin Pauley is all white.

87 Winkler (2001b: 131) suggests that the women's screams at the sight of the sergeant and doctor entering implies that it is the women's treatment at the hands of the Seventh Cavalry that has maddened them, but the film is not conclusive. Frankel (2013: 299) says that in a pre-production note, Ford firmly attributes their madness to their time with the Comanche.

88 Eckstein (2004a: 15); McBride and Wilmington (1975: 162). Pye (1996: 234) notes that with his Cherokee ancestry, the "well-balanced Martin," like the "well-integrated" Debbie, suggests at least the possibility of harmonious racial intermixing.

89 McBride (2011: 557).

90 e.g. Pye (1996); see Frankel (2013: 312–13).

91 Day (2008: 42–3). For Ford's treatment of the Navajo and their appreciation of him, see Bogdanovich (1968: 8, 14–15); Gallagher (1986: 341); McBride (2011: 555); Frankel (2013: 274–5, 277, 293); et al.

92 See Stowell (1986: 139–40); Wills (1997: 257); Day (2008: 34–6); McBride (2011: 565–6).

93 Examples abound. See e.g. Davis (1995: 274); Frankel (2013: 221–2,

233–4); et al. Henry Brandon explained, "When you're working with a genius, you put up with a lot" (qtd. in McBride 2011: 569).

94 See Frankel (2013: 216–17, 235–6).

95 Frankel (2013: 316–17). See also Whitehall (1966–67: 21).

96 Qtd. in Yamato (2012).

97 Ford qtd. in Hughes (2008: 86), et al.

98 Qtd. in Cowie (2004: 151).

99 Qtd. in McBride (2011: 563); see also McBride (2011: 558–9); Pippin (2009: 231); et al.

100 McBride and Wilmington (1971: 212).

101 See Frankel (2013: 319–21).

102 For instance, Stephen Metcalf in a 2006 online article in *Slate* rakes the movie over the coals, mocking its adherents as Ivory Tower "nerd-cultists" in an astounding display of anti-intellectualism that may also contain a kernel of truth. Still, even Metcalf admits to being moved by the film's climax.

5 *John Ford's* The Man Who Shot Liberty Valance

FILM SUMMARY

The Man Who Shot Liberty Valance opens in 1910 with the return of Senator Ransom "Ranse" Stoddard (James Stewart) and his wife Hallie (Vera Miles) to the small western town of Shinbone, where they immediately arouse the interest of the local press. They are met by the aged ex-marshal Link Appleyard (Andy Devine), who soon escorts them to the undertaker's office, wherein lies a plain pine coffin containing the body of Tom Doniphon. The newspaper editor Maxwell Scott (Carleton Young), who has followed them, has never heard of Doniphon and demands to know more about the man whose death has brought the Senator all the way from Washington. Ranse agrees to tell his story at last, initiating the long flashback that constitutes the bulk of the film.

Many years before, Ranse was a green Easterner headed to Shinbone where he intended to practice law, but on the outskirts of town his stagecoach was robbed and he himself whipped by the brutal outlaw Liberty Valance (Lee Marvin). He is later found by Tom Doniphon (John Wayne), a local rancher, who takes him to the town café where he is nursed back to health by the pretty young Hallie, whom Doniphon plans to marry. Once he has recovered, Ranse helps out at the café to pay his room and board, but hangs his shingle in front of the newspaper office operated by Dutton Peabody (Edmond O'Brien), ignoring warnings that it will provoke Valance. He also opens a one-room schoolhouse to educate the illiterate of Shinbone – Hallie included – and becomes an advocate for law, order, and statehood.

At a town meeting called to elect delegates to the Territorial Convention, Doniphon declines a nomination, after which Ranse and Peabody are elected over Liberty Valance, who is employed as a hired gun by the cattlemen who want to preserve the open range, and are thus against statehood. Valance retaliates by wrecking the newspaper office and beating Peabody near to death, after which Ranse resolves to confront Valance despite his moral objection to violence and his inexperience with guns. At the ensuing shootout, Ranse is wounded, but it is Valance who drops to the ground dead. Afterwards, Doniphon interrupts a relieved Hallie tending to Ranse and understands that she has developed feelings for him. Doniphon gets drunk and burns down his house, onto which he was building a room in preparation for his marriage to her.

Later, at the Territorial Convention, Ranse is nominated to run for Congress against the cattlemen's candidate on the strength of his reputation as the man who killed Liberty Valance. Upset at the thought of a career built on violence, he tries to leave, but is stopped by Doniphon, who tells him the truth: it was he, not Ranse, who shot Valance from an unseen position in the shadows of a nearby building, and he did it for Hallie. This knowledge inspires Ranse to return and accept the nomination. He not only wins the election and serves multiple terms in the senate, but he also goes on to become a three-term governor, ambassador to the court of St. James, and a vice-presidential contender, while Tom Doniphon falls into obscurity.

As Ranse finishes his story, the newspaper editor destroys his notes, explaining, "This is the West, sir. When the legend becomes fact, print the legend." Later, on the train ride back to Washington, Ranse thanks the conductor, who shows him extra attention. The film ends with the man's response: "You think nothing of it. Nothing's too good for the man who shot Liberty Valance."

INTRODUCTION

Like *The Searchers* some six years earlier, John Ford's *The Man Who Shot Liberty Valance* was not immediately embraced by critics. Nominated for only one Oscar (Best Costume Design, Black-and-White, for Edith Head), its only wins were a relatively minor Laurel Award for John Wayne as Top Action Performer and a slew of genre-specific Western Heritage Awards.[1] Partly influenced by its old-fashioned stylization, almost in the manner of silent Westerns, as well as the lack of Ford's characteristic "buoyant energy" and scenic vistas,[2] most American reviewers were critical: *Variety* thought that Ford and his writers had "taken a disarmingly simple and affecting premise, developed it with craft and skill to a natural point of conclusion, and then . . . proceeded to run it into the ground"; the *New York Times*'s Bosley Crowther called it a "baffling oddity"; the *New Yorker*'s Brendan Gill called it "a parody of Mr. Ford's best work"; and in his review in *Film Quarterly*, Ernest Callenbach compared it to "one of those TV programs you watch with a hand on the switch, but never quite turn off."[3] And although it was financially successful, taking in a little over $3 million domestically, this was below the norm at this time for a Wayne vehicle.[4] A few contemporary critics, however, showed greater vision – Andrew Sarris, for instance, said that it "achieves greatness as a unified work of art with the emotional and intellectual resonance of a personal testament," while Peter Bogdanovich described it as "perhaps [Ford's] most deeply felt personal statement."[5] Over time, these views prevailed, as gradually the film came to be seen not only within the broader context of Ford's work, but also within the long-term trajectory of the Western genre. *The Man Who Shot Liberty Valance* was at last entered into the National Film Registry in 2007 and has come to be viewed not as a lesser work of a fading, once-great artist, but as the "artistic summation" of one of America's most influential directors and "the most important American film of the 1960s."[6]

While the film itself is not quite as high on the cultural radar as *High Noon* or *Shane*, the exhortation to "Print the legend" is familiar enough, though often mistakenly taken as a justification for myth-making (Ford's own, and more generally).[7] On the contrary, it is in fact Ford's fairly pessimistic unmasking of the ways in which we shape history to suit the narrative most in line with our national self-image and which best suits our goals.[8] And although it does have important connections to Greek epic as well, the film's concern with the role mythologizing plays in the advancement of civilization and in politics most strongly evokes the subtle questioning of imperial propaganda that many scholars discern in the *Aeneid*: that is, each work glorifies the heroic past that forms the foundation of its respective civilization, while at the same time questioning how society draws on and uses that past, thereby calling attention to what has been lost in the process.

In addition, because of the self-questioning, retrospective nature of this film, I would like to expand my reach in this final chapter to consider *The Man Who Shot Liberty Valance*'s affinities with Greek tragic drama, and in particular to what is perhaps the most famous and well-known of the Greek tragedies today, Sophocles' *Oedipus the King*, in which similar issues of knowledge and identity are intertwined with themes of murder, marriage, power, and reputation.

While this is a departure from my practice in previous chapters, along with the important generic relationship between Westerns and epic, scholars, as I have noted, have also acknowledged important connections between Westerns and the Greek tragedies that have been equally influential in Western literary history. Moreover, fifth-century Greek tragedy and Virgil's first-century epic are similar in that they both draw so heavily on Homeric plots, themes, and values that they can be seen as receptions of Homer's work in themselves; because it stands near the end of a long line of Ford Westerns, *The Man Who Shot Liberty Valance* functions as a response to these earlier, foundational works in much the same way. In addition, the context of production and authorial motivation for these later ancient works means that each has at its heart a shift from individual to more communal concerns as well as a more explicit focus on the relationship between past and present than do Homer's earlier oral epics, an emphasis clearly evident in Ford's film as well. While some might object that arguing for connections with both epic and tragedy undercuts the notion of a significant relationship between Western film and epic, or even works from antiquity more generally, I hope to show that on the contrary, it strengthens it by demonstrating how later Westerns served as a cultural response to the earlier foundational narratives in much the same way as fifth-century Greek tragedy and Virgil's literary epic built upon and responded to earlier material preserved in Homer's works.

THE EPIC TRADITION

Ford's film is based on a short story of the same name by Dorothy M. Johnson, a rare – and very successful – female writer of Western fiction. Johnson's story first appeared in *Cosmopolitan* magazine in 1949 and was later reprinted in a collection of short stories in 1953. The Ranse character in Johnson's story reads Plato in the original Greek, and taking this as her cue, Nancy Warfield has analyzed the film, alongside other of Ford's movies, as a reflection of ideas set forth in Plato's works,[9] suggesting the film's deep-seated roots in classical antiquity.

As has already been noted, Ford had a tendency to sprinkle Homeric allusions into his films, and *Liberty Valance* is no exception. When Peabody is surprised in the middle of a grandiose, drunken monologue taken from Shakespeare's *Henry V* by a menacing Liberty Valance and his gang, he adapts the speech to the occasion, barely missing a beat: "when the blast . . . of war blows in our ears, then we summon up – Liberty Valance . . . and his Myrmidons." While this parallel is not developed, Peabody's allusion points to the important connection that Blundell and Ormand later argued for: namely, that epic and Western film fill equivalent cultural roles, inaugurating the heroic tradition that established the foundational ideologies on which later society was built.[10]

Although clearly positioned as the villain, Valance exhibits many of the characteristics of the epic hero. He is a formidable warrior who carries a special weapon – a silver-knobbed whip – the fetishization of which is suggested by the orgiastic nature of his beatings: indeed, as Tag Gallagher notes, his henchman Floyd (Strother Martin) "experiences something resembling a sadistic orgasm" while watching one of Valance's assaults.[11] Valance is also stubborn and confident, and like ancient warriors, taunts his foes as a prelude to battle, gleefully disparaging Ranse for participating in unmanly activities: he mocks him as "hash-slinger" and "waitress," while also calling attention to his Eastern dress and manners by repeatedly referring to him as "dude"[12] – much like the taunts and jibes that in both epic and Westerns tap into and reinforce established notions of idealized masculinity.

Tom Doniphon, of course – also stubborn, confident, and fiercely independent – is set against him as an equally formidable warrior, and his "epic" stature is reinforced by casting: at this time, Wayne was the quintessential Western hero, his star power demonstrated by the fact that out of a total budget of $3.2 million, he earned $750,000 to Ford's $150,000, and he had appeared on the Quigley Poll's list of Top Ten Money Making Stars every year but one since 1949.[13] As producer Howard W. Koch put it, "the Big Cowboy was really the whole thing."[14] His imposing size – Wayne was a burly 6'4" – paired with the contrasting star qualities of the two lead performers – as James Stewart put it, "People identify with me, but dream of being John Wayne"[15] – meant that both physically and metaphorically he was, like Homeric heroes, mightier than men "such as men are now" (*Il.* 5.304, 12.383, et al.).

Both Doniphon and Valance, moreover, exhibit an "epic" concern with honor, as is evident in the scene where Valance trips Ranse, who is carrying Doniphon's dinner, sending his plate flying.[16] When Doniphon insists that Valance himself pick it up rather than one of his minions, Ranse only averts a violent end to the tense stand-off by picking it up himself, angrily scorning the deadly potential in an argument over "one measly steak." Ranse's incredulity highlights what is in fact at stake – notions of honor and manhood that he cannot understand, but which penetrate to the core of epic heroes like Doniphon and Valance.

And like the heroes of epic, these two come into conflict over property rights –Valance standing with the older generation of cattle barons who want to preserve an open range, and Doniphon defending the new wave of homesteaders, much as we saw with Ryker and Shane in Stevens's film.[17] In both cases, as is typical, these representatives of the old guard, both good and bad, are ultimately excluded from society – Valance, like Ryker, through death, and Doniphon, like Shane, through exclusion from the very society his heroism makes possible. As Scott Eyman has said, "In . . . *Liberty Valance*, the kind of men needed to master the wilderness are the kind of men that can only function in wilderness; they are men who [*sic*] civilization must expel."[18] Lastly, the film demonstrates a concern with burial in common with ancient epic: Ranse insists that Tom Doniphon be buried with his boots, gunbelt, and spurs, the trappings of his heroic warrior identity. Despite the challenge, as we will see, that the film poses to the sort of legends that underlie the Western genre, this film anchors itself – and America's historical narrative – firmly in a "heroic" tradition much like that which we have seen in classical antiquity.

THE *ILIAD*

As noted above, Ford himself prompts us to consider the film's villain Liberty Valance as an Achilles figure, a resemblance most pronounced in his excess of passion, which typically manifests itself as rage. Also like Achilles and the other heroes of his time, Valance's concerns are for the interests of the individual over those of the community – an interest suggested in the name "Liberty," though taken to a negative extreme[19] – a concern related to his antagonistic relationship with authority (represented in the *Iliad* by Agamemnon and in *Liberty Valance* by "the law"). And like Achilles, who famously was taken down by a shot from Paris' bow, this great warrior is felled – or seems to be – at the hands of Ranse, a far inferior warrior whose masculinity, like Paris', has often been called into question. Despite the fact that it is not Ranse's bullet that kills him, a heroic figure suffering an ignominious defeat at the hands of an inferior warrior is a familiar trope of both epics and Westerns.[20]

Unsurprisingly, as we have seen repeatedly elsewhere, Ford here develops an identification between hero and villain similar to the one Homer develops in his *Iliad* between Achilles and Hector. This identification is suggested early on in a scene where Ranse tells Doniphon that he does not want to kill Valance for assaulting him, but to put him in jail, to which Doniphon, placing his hand on his gun, responds skeptically, "Out here, a man settles his own problems." Ranse's incredulous reaction – "Do you know what you're saying to me? . . . You're saying just exactly what Liberty Valance said!" – sets the two up as counterparts. Doniphon reinforces this equivalence when he warns Ranse as he takes his leave that Liberty Valance is the "toughest man south of the Picketwire – next to me." This relationship has not been unnoticed by Western scholars: Jim Kitses, for instance, calls the two men "mirror images of overbearing authority and aggressive manhood" with Valance as "the extreme, psychotic version of Doniphon," while Scott Eyman suggests the two men's function as alter egos when he says that "[Doniphon] knows that, on some level, when he kills Valance, he is killing himself" by rendering himself unnecessary.[21] An argument can be made, then, that Doniphon is the Achilles figure and Valance the alter ego who represents the negative aspects of his self.

Moreover, in Ranse Stoddard Ford offers us the softer, more sympathetic third party set in opposition to these alter egos, completing the triangle we have seen in the *Iliad* and elsewhere. Although, unlike Patroclus, he would be hard to classify as a formidable fighter, Ranse does achieve heroic status of a different sort with his knowledge of the law and his political prowess, as well as exhibiting extraordinary bravery by facing almost certain death in the showdown with Valance. And like Patroclus, he is clearly cast as a feminine balance to the overbearing masculinity of Doniphon and Valance (Fig. 5.1): he waits tables, washes dishes, and even wears an apron to the climactic showdown, all of which Valance uses to disparage him. And just as Homer signaled that Achilles, Hector, and Patroclus worked as facets of the same *ego* through the exchange of armor, Ford suggests a similar relationship through imagery: as Robert Pippin has noted, first Ranse (wounded), then Valance (dead), and then Doniphon (drunk) are shown laid out on a buckboard in similarly positioned shots,[22] suggesting this sort of essential identification (although Ranse is being ushered into town, symbolizing his ascendancy, while both Valance and Doniphon are driven out, suggesting the death of the heroic age in which they have thrived). And like Patroclus, Ranse attempts to face the enemy who more properly should be set against Doniphon as the better warrior. And though Ranse does not die, Doniphon does kill his alter ego in defense of the lesser man, much as Achilles had done for Patroclus.

5.1 Liberty Valance (Lee Marvin), Ransom Stoddard (James Stewart), and Tom Doniphon (John Wayne) in *The Man Who Shot Liberty Valance* (1962). Paramount Pictures, John Ford Productions.

Despite this similarity, the outcome in Ford's film is quite different than in Homer's *Iliad*: unlike Achilles, Tom Doniphon lives a long life and dies in obscurity – indeed, we might say that he chose the second fate that might have been Achilles', but wasn't – while Ranse ends up with the glory that should rightly have been Doniphon's. And though Ford resembles Homer in drawing on this triangle of relationships to explore issues of existential import, his endgame is considerably more pessimistic. In the *Iliad*, Achilles works toward coming to terms with his humanity and his mortality, deriving comfort in the epic remembrance that will be his for millennia to come. In *The Man Who Shot Liberty Valance*, Doniphon comes to terms with the death of his way of life, but in doing so, he knows that he will not become part of the heroic tradition.

This more pessimistic strain in Ford's film is illuminated by Dutton Peabody, who in his role as "founder, owner, publisher, and editor of *The Shinbone Star*" serves in some ways as a bard with the power over epic remembrance, a function he himself suggests when he butters up the incompetent town marshal with, "My dear friend Link Appleyard, the fearless fighting marshal of the West? Oh ho ho, your name will go down in history with Buffalo Bill. . .!" Although Peabody throughout the film is depicted as a champion of truth in journalism, reporting events even at peril of his life, his statement here begins to suggest how legends are made and history subject to distortion, foreshadowing the film's famous ending. When Mr. Scott,

Peabody's successor and editor of the *Star* in the frame story, tears up his notes, he not only denies Tom Doniphon the posthumous glory he deserves, he also pulls back the curtain on the process of myth-making. As Bogdanovich has put it, unlike Scott, "Ford prints the fact." In doing so, he "ruthlessly exposes the mythmaking apparatus that underlies much of history and much of the director's own work in the Western genre."[23]

THE *ODYSSEY*

When *The Shinbone Star*'s editor demands to know the story behind Senator Stoddard's reasons for coming to town, Ranse is at first reluctant, putting him off with "He was a friend, Mr. Scott, and we'd like to be left alone." Once pressed, however, he concedes, but makes clear through his mournful reluctance that relating this tale from the past will cause him pain. Nonetheless, he launches into an extended narrative, and the bulk of the film is told in flashback. In this, Ford makes an important change from Johnson's original story, where the earlier events are also recounted retrospectively after we learn of the death of the Doniphon character, there called Bert Barricune, but significantly are not narrated by Ranse (there named Ransome Foster) or anyone else.[24] With this change, Ford's film develops an important relationship to Homer's *Odyssey*, which contains the first extended – and perhaps most famous – "tale within a tale" in Western literature. Like Ranse, Homer's narrator Odysseus makes the pain reliving his sorrows will cause him clear, initiating his tale with "My lord Alcinous . . . your heart is inclined to ask of my baneful woes, so that I might mourn and sigh still more" (9.2, 12–13). Like Odysseus, who is known for his ability with words, Ranse, too, is a man of words, as is indicated by his roles as lawyer, teacher, and politician. And although most readers and viewers tend to take the recollections of these men at face value, both Homer and Ford insert subtle suggestions of narrative bias to suggest something important about the character of the tale-teller.

In the *Odyssey*, as we have seen, Odysseus betrays a tendency toward exaggeration in the Cyclops episode when he has Polyphemus hear him after he has placed his ship twice as far away from the giant as a man's voice could carry; and he suggests embellishment again when he reports a conversation between Zeus and Helios, so that he has to cover his tracks afterward. The Underworld episode in Book 11 also rings false in numerous ways: in addition to its basic premise, Odysseus includes a "greatest hits" roster not only of his companions from the Trojan War, but also of mythological superstars, suggesting a desire to give his audience what they want to hear. In addition to the *kleos* this sort of heroic adventure might bring him, Odysseus implies an additional motivation for this exaggeration when he breaks off his narrative at a climactic point and oddly suggests that they all go to bed – which, of course, prompts the Phaeacians whom he is regaling with his adventures to prod him to continue by offering him rich gifts (9.328–61). As he wraps up this portion of his story, he crowns his experiences in Hades by reporting that he saw the Elvis of his time, Heracles himself – but quickly, again, must cover his slip, clarifying that it was just Heracles' "phantom," for as we all know, Heracles himself was taken up to Olympus as an immortal (9.601–4). When Heracles – or his phantom – then compares Odysseus' trials and sorrows to his own (9.617–19), the narrative strongly hints at Odysseus' underlying agenda of bolstering his reputation by assimilating himself to the paradigmatic hero of antiquity.

For the careful observer, Ford likewise positions Ranse as a questionable narrator. Gallagher has pointed out that in Ranse's narrative, Valance is totally evil, a black-and-white characterization unusual for Ford. Tom Doniphon, moreover, is inscrutable, Hallie is soft and radiant, the loveable drunk Peabody comes off as Ranse's "lesser and foolish rival in the game of words," and Pompey exhibits a "slave mentality,"[25] whereas everyone seems to look up to Ranse. And both Gallagher and Pippin have pointed out discrepancies in the characterizations of Link Appleyard, who in the frame narrative is fairly dignified, but in the flashback sequences is a cowardly, gluttonous, bumbling clown.[26] In addition, much of the flashback is presented from Ranse's perspective – for instance, with the camera looking down at Hallie, or focusing on Valance's face as he whips Ranse.[27] In addition, Ranse relates a few scenes where he was not present at all – such as Valance's beating of Peabody in the newspaper office, and Doniphon's burning of his house; these episodes, of course, Ranse will have had to recreate from hearsay or imagination. While these seem somewhat "natural" by-products of storytelling, there are other indications that we are supposed to take this narrative with a grain of salt. It is well recognized that James Stewart, who was over fifty when this film was shot, was far too old to be playing a "youngster, fresh out of law school," while John Wayne too, also in his fifties, is older than his character would suggest. This of course can be explained in part by casting considerations, as the star power of Stewart and Wayne would practically guarantee a box-office hit. Yet it also might suggest a distortion of memory, a possibility that takes on new significance when a wider net is cast. For instance, while the minor character of Amos Carruthers was played by Denver Pyle, his hooky-playing, lollipop-licking young son was played by O. Z. Whitehead, who at fifty-two was almost a decade older than Pyle. While this odd casting decision is enough of a sidebar that it doesn't detract from the film's impact, it does impinge subtly upon the absolute veracity of the narrative's content, positioning Ranse, much like Odysseus, as a somewhat unreliable narrator.

Unlike Odysseus, of course, Ranse does not seem to be motivated by material gain or hopes for boosting his reputation. Instead, his speech functions as more of a confession in order to cleanse his own guilt for taking credit for someone else's act, and as an attempt to posthumously offer Doniphon the recognition he deserves but did not get in life. Yet in some ways too, it is an *apologia* wherein the embellishments function to present him in the best light while relieving him of the burden of the deception he has lived with all these years. As such, both Odysseus' narrative and Ranse's are manipulations of the past as a means of influencing the present. Because Odysseus is positioned as a bard in the *Odyssey* – his tale, for instance, follows the performance of a "real" bard, whom he praises to the skies before launching into his own "song" (9.2–11) – if his tale is revealed as subject to embellishments and distortions, this has direct implications for the work as a whole, which is also a product of the heroic oral tradition. Thus, Homer subtly asks us to question the epic remembrance he himself offers by giving us an example of myth-making in process. In much the same way, of course, does Ranse's embellished tale replicate the overall lesson that Ford wants to impart – that the "facts" of history are not above scrutiny.

THE *AENEID*

Although Ford has nudged us toward Homer through Peabody's reference to Liberty Valance as an Achilles figure, unlike Achilles, whose rage is ennobling and who is generally a sympathetic character, Valance is a rare Fordian character who is all bad, with his rage presented as an unambiguous character flaw. In this sense, Ford, like Virgil, inverts his Achilles figure, offering us instead a character more akin to Turnus, whom Virgil describes as "a second Achilles" (6.89), but whose rage works against the fated progress of civilization rather than for it. This dynamic signals that despite the Iliadic reference, Ford's work has a deeper connection to the *Aeneid*. Indeed, this is supported when Valance's more negative Achilles function is paired with the alter ego quality we have seen he shares with Tom Doniphon: like Aeneas and Turnus, who, according to Viktor Pöschl, embody the *imperium* and *furor* that are the "moral poles" of the epic,[28] so too do Doniphon and Valance suggest these principles, and as such work as "flip sides" of the same coin.

The close relationship of Ford's film to the *Aeneid* is perhaps most readily illustrated through Tom Doniphon's connections to Aeneas. We have already seen that Doniphon manifests the more general qualities of an epic hero, but as one who must sacrifice his personal desires for the project of nation-building and who cannot himself actively take part in the benefits of the society he helps to create, Doniphon recalls Virgil's somewhat reluctant, duty-bound hero Aeneas in particular. Doniphon's personal desires are clearly demonstrated when he declines the nomination for the state convention by explaining, "I got other plans. Personal plans," a reference to his intention to marry Hallie and create a life with her on his ranch. Unlike Valance and Achilles, whose personal objectives are for individual glory or economic advancement, Doniphon's inclinations are more like those of Aeneas, who also exhibits a yearning to settle down when he stumbles into a marriage of sorts with Dido, queen of Carthage, and seems more than content to stay put, even adopting royal Carthaginian dress and throwing himself into Dido's project of building her own city (4.259–67).

Yet the personal fulfillment our heroes long for is not destined to be. Both the *Aeneid* and *The Man Who Shot Liberty Valance* are set in times of societal transition – in the *Aeneid*, of course, Aeneas is charged with founding a new home for the Trojans, one which was destined to become the great Roman Empire, while Ford's film is set in the crucial period when the West was transitioning from wide-open ranges into fenced-off homesteads, from territories into organized communities moving toward statehood. Just as Virgil's epic situates Aeneas as a vital conduit in this transition to a new world he does not fully understand and cannot fully participate in, Ford's film suggests something similar: as the pioneers who paved the way for civilization, cattlemen and ranchers like Tom Doniphon are a dying breed whose usefulness has passed, and they must now step aside so that the merchants, homesteaders, and townsfolk can prosper and civilization advance. This dynamic is clearly signaled in Peabody's impassioned nomination speech, when he traces the development of the territory from wilderness, when there was "no law . . . except the law of survival, the law of the tomahawk and the bow and arrow," to the first influx of pioneers, adventurers, and cattlemen, whose law was "the law of the hired gun," and finally to the present day, with the coming of homesteaders, shopkeepers, and "builder[s] of cities," as he advocates for statehood to promote development, infrastructure, and law and order without violence. Although Aeneas needed the gods to nudge him and Doniphon (unlike Valance) is able to recognize and accept this inevitable progression on his own, these two heroes are analogous in their noble sacrifice of personal desires in the interests of the larger goal of nation-building.

Of course an important part of Doniphon's sacrifice is Hallie: in ceding credit to Ranse, he loses his intended wife to him in the bargain. And while unlike with Aeneas this is not his own choice, both heroes' sacrifices are once again driven home by the sacrifice of women in particular. In addition, in each case a union based on passion must give way to a marriage of political expedience. In the *Aeneid*, Aeneas must forego Dido because he is destined to marry Lavinia, a girl who is a passive, silent specter, and certainly no match for the vibrant, intense Dido in the personality department. So too in *The Man Who Shot Liberty Valance* does the union of Hallie with Tom – by whom she is "sexually awed," as Gallagher puts it[29] – give way to the tender but less passionate union of Hallie and Ranse. As Peter French has argued, Ranse's effect on Hallie is one of taming – he educates and civilizes her, but she is diminished by it.[30] The dynamic here thus is somewhat inverted – Doniphon does not abandon Hallie for a marriage with a more suitable, though bland and spiritless, woman, but instead she becomes one by marrying Ranse rather than him. But in both works, the glory of the present is called into question by associating it with the repression of the full potential of the feminine.

Finally, the sacrifice both Aeneas and Doniphon make entails putting on a false front: as Georgia Nugent points out, Aeneas' character is marked by the necessity to mask his suffering and his anxieties for the sake of others.[31] So too does Doniphon's character falsify the credit for the act of shooting Valance for the sake of the greater good and the benefit of society. In both cases, the discrepancy this false front indicates between action and interior yearnings works to emphasize the personal cost of each man's dedication to duty, sharpening his heroism. By setting aside his own hopes and facilitating Ranse's rise to power instead, Doniphon, like Aeneas, does not fight the fates but accepts them, sacrificing his own desires to pave the way for an empire he cannot truly be a part of. Yet Ford does not focus on the nobility of Doniphon's action, but on the tragedy: he emphasizes the loss this sacrifice entails, not just for Doniphon, but also in the watered-down tameness of "modern" Shinbone in contrast to the boisterous energy of old Shinbone[32] and by juxtaposing the self-important arrogance of the emergent hero – and the ultimate hollowness of his achievements – with the tragic, lonely death of a man who deserved better. Ultimately, by focusing on the tragedy of Doniphon's sacrifice, Ford, like Virgil, emphasizes the cost of nation-building, complicating traditional foundational narratives that emphasize glory while eliding loss.

Doniphon's ceding credit to Ranse points to an additional correspondence in these works: that the period of peace and prosperity to which the violent warrior society must ultimately give way is ushered in by a leader who styles himself as a patriotic, peace-loving "man of the people." In Virgil's epic, this is the emperor Augustus, who in fact commissioned the work: although he appears explicitly in only a handful of allusions, Augustus looms large symbolically as the leader whose regime represents the culmination of all that Aeneas is struggling for. Likewise in *The Man Who Shot Liberty Valance*, Ransom Stoddard is the civilized Easterner who acts as an advocate for law, order, and statehood and who symbolically represents the new, more civilized era for which Tom Doniphon's work lays the foundation. On the surface, both works seem to glorify this new age of peace and prosperity. In the *Aeneid*, this is most conspicuous in the parade of heroes in the Underworld in Book 6 that not only connects Augustus to Aeneas (and thus to the gods), but in which Aeneas' father Anchises also explicitly lauds the glory of Augustus and the *Pax Romana* he will usher in: "This is the man," he says, "this is he whom so often you hear promised to you, Augustus Caesar, son of a god, who will establish a golden age once again in Latium. . . ." (6.791–3). In Ford's film, the modern audience knows that Ranse, as an advocate for statehood, also has "destiny" on his side, and the "good people" of the film support the younger Ranse as an agent of progress and revere the older Ranse as an eminent statesman. In both cases, this superficial glorification is in line with nationalistic rhetoric and patriotic propaganda – in other words, with the vision that Augustus and "Uncle Sam" would have us accept without question.

However, Virgil and Ford do not elevate these leaders unthinkingly, but interrogate the public identity each man would promote in a similar way. In the *Aeneid*, Virgil explicitly conjures up the propaganda-driven images of Mark Antony that Augustus had disseminated in order to justify his conflict with a noble Roman. In Book 4, Aeneas' marriage to an exotic African queen positions him as a "potential" Mark Antony, whose affair with Cleopatra the then-

Octavian had positioned as feminizing and a dangerous personal distraction from his duty to Rome. Aeneas' ultimate abandonment of Dido in favor of fulfilling his duty, then, realigns him more suitably with his proper Roman virtue, so that in effect he resists becoming a Mark Antony in favor of manifesting a more proper Octavian-nature. In Ford's film, identity issues are similarly made central when at their first meeting, Liberty Valance challenges Ranse with the question "Now, what kind of man are you, dude?" At the time, Ranse takes this literally -"I'm an attorney at law! And I'm duly licensed for the territory!" he responds – but in the broader scope of the film, Valance's question touches on a much larger issue, when soon, as in the *Aeneid*, the moral framework of this seemingly upstanding leader is called into question.

Despite the conscious association of both men's public image with peace and order, the success of each as a leader is, in fact, built on a foundation of violence: in Augustus' case, not only the bloody civil wars that followed the assassination of Julius Caesar, but also the proscriptions that helped secure his power. In Ranse's case, his initial election to public office is indebted to his reputation as the man who killed Liberty Valance.[33] In recognition of this conundrum, both works take pains to problematize the new order rather than accepting it wholesale. As noted throughout this book, many modern scholars discern indirect challenges to the unambiguous promotion of the Augustan regime that punctuate Virgil's work: for instance, by highlighting Aeneas' reluctance as a hero and emphasizing what he gives up to achieve his divine goal, Virgil encourages his readers to acknowledge the sacrifices on which the glories of Rome are built. In addition, in an epic in which the hero is virtually equated with the Roman Empire itself, subtle challenges to imperial propaganda are sprinkled throughout the *Aeneid*: for instance, the divine sanction of Aeneas' initial entry into the Underworld is subtly undermined when the Golden Bough that signifies his chosen status hesitates before Aeneas can remove it (6.210–11); then, Aeneas' exit from the Underworld through the gate of "false dreams" (6.896) suggests a questioning of the glorious vision of Roman history that has just been presented; and in the end, Aeneas succumbs to the sort of emotion-driven Achillean rage that has been condemned throughout and kills the defeated, suppliant Turnus, complicating the unambiguous association of Augustus with governance guided by *gravitas* and *pietas* rather than *furor.* Thus, the epic's conclusion complicates the simplistic black-and-white categorizations Augustus has promoted and effectively calls Augustus' presentation of his own character into question.

A similar questioning of identity is present in *The Man Who Shot Liberty Valance*: although Ranse promotes law and order over rule by violence, he ultimately meets Valance on his own terms. And though we learn that Doniphon is in fact the one whose bullet brought Valance down, Ranse, as Pippin puts it, "for all his high-mindedness, is willing, without much visible struggling with his conscience, to build his life on a lie"[34] – at the expense, I would add, of Doniphon's happiness. The revelation that Ranse's career is built on a falsehood and enabled by another's loss makes his success ring hollow and calls into question not only the upstanding image he wants to promote but also the greatness of the more "civilized" society he represents. Ford calls direct attention to the problematic relationship of propaganda and history with the editor's famous oxymoronic aphorism: "This is the West, sir. When the legend becomes fact, print the legend." While Virgil was unable to be so explicit, his epic clearly demonstrates a parallel strategy: indeed, the words Pippin uses to describe Ford's film might just as well be applied to Virgil's work: "*The Man Who Shot Liberty Valance*," he says,

> is not itself a mythological treatment of a founding. It is rather about mythological accounts of foundings (indeed about the distorting and self-serving effects of even normal narration), and it is quite a qualified, even skeptical cautionary account of such mythologizings. . .[35]

This is not to say that the intention in either work was to undercut national identity entirely. When questioned in an interview about the value of such legends, Ford answered that "the positive ones were 'good for the country'"; Kitses, moreover, finds in the film "a postmodern complexity, at once nostalgic and critical, a celebration of myth and its deconstruction."[36] Virgil too, perhaps, might have argued that promotional strategies had their uses. But as Pippin puts it in reference to Ford's film, both authors ask us to recognize that

> This glorifying legend is also quite likely a fantasy, and there will come a time when the less than glorious truth must out, or when it at least powerfully threatens to be revealed . . . It is dishonorable and unworthy of a great civilization to continue to indulge such fantasies.[37]

Thus both Virgil, by inserting subtle challenges to the *Pax Romana* Augustus would have him unambiguously promote, and Ford, by challenging us to question rather than take for granted patriotic notions of Manifest Destiny and the glory of the nation's "progress," encourage us to scrutinize our national narratives and achieve self-knowledge, however difficult, rather than idle in a comfortably deluded self-image.

OEDIPUS THE KING

While most Westerns are known for the wide-open spaces that contribute to the "epic" feel I have been discussing throughout this book, in the case of *The Man Who Shot Liberty Valance*, scholars and critics have more frequently compared the film to a play rather than characterizing it as an epic. Noting that *Liberty Valance* is set primarily in the enclosed space of the town of Shinbone with interiors prevailing and most outdoor scenes taking place at night, Nancy Warfield says that the film has a "cramped, theatrical" appearance; Tag Gallagher and Joseph McBride, too, have noted its "theatrical" quality, with McBride saying it has "more in common visually with the chamber dramas of Carl Theodor Dreyer than with *The Searchers* and other Ford Westerns in which the physical milieu is as important a presence as the characters."[38] The frame narrative, in addition, has a bit of the feel of a play's prologue, while the opening sequence of the flashback which constitutes the main part of the narrative, as Peter Stowell has pointed out, seems to have the intentional look of a soundstage.[39]

In addition, I have noted that scholars of many stripes have connected Western films with Greek tragedy, both in a broader sense and in individual films, including each of the films in the previous four chapters. Here, too, in addition to Warfield's identification of Platonic ideas in *The Man Who Shot Liberty Valance*, critics have touched on strong connections with Greek tragic drama: Peter French has pointed to this film as an example of a "transition Western" (one which depicts the death of the West with the ascendance of the modern industrial era) and finds a parallel with Aeschylus' *Oresteia* in its depiction of the move from blood vengeance to a system of law; E. Christian Kopff has applied the French Hellenist Jean-Pierre Vernant's observation that in Greek tragedy the hero ceased to be a model and instead was treated as a problem to the shift in Western film in the 1950s and '60s exemplified by this film (along with Ford's earlier *The Searchers*); and Jim Kitses has noted that the two minor characters Kentuck' and High Pockets "weave through the action like a two-cowboy comic chorus, stand-ins for the community at large."[40] In contrast to Kitses, I would argue that a much closer parallel to the Greek chorus is provided by Dutton Peabody, who as a newspaperman functions partly as bard bestowing remembrance, but also as a commentator and intermediary between the major players and the community. Like the Greek chorus, he expounds the play's themes in elevated, dramatic orations that punctuate the storyline, while in objecting to his nomination for the Territorial Convention ("Good people of Shinbone ... I'm your conscience! I'm the still small voice that thunders in the night...!"), he suggests a view of himself that is reminiscent of the chorus of Greek drama: he is outside the action, but profoundly concerned with it. I will also add that the theatrical feel of this film noted by scholars diminishes the audience's perception of the hero of the Old West, who now seems unnaturally confined and bounded, while suggesting a land that is becoming settled and populated rather than being a blank slate. As Robert Warshow has argued, in Westerns, "the land and horses have ... a moral significance: the physical freedom they represent belongs to the moral 'openness' of the West."[41] The "closed-ness" of this film's setting, in contrast, implies the narrowing of moral codes that the laws and customs of developing society bring, a suggestion which better corresponds with the context of fifth-century Greek tragedy.

Gallagher, moreover, has identified "something above man" in this film: "call it fate ... the pilgrim has become a spectator of his own life, an actor in a play whose ending he cannot anticipate."[42] Gallagher's observation not only supports a theatrical quality to this film, but also points to a particular play which, to my mind, shows the most intimate tragic connections with it: Sophocles' *Oedipus the King*. This famous work is a detective play of sorts anchored in dramatic irony, as Oedipus works to solve a murder that he himself committed. *The Man Who Shot Liberty Valance* also is grounded in elements of mystery and irony, traits underscored by the enigmatic title. The film's trailers, too, emphasized this "who done it?" quality: one example, for instance, included both a verbal tease ("strangely enough, only one of these people could be sure he knew the identity of the man who shot Liberty Valance") and a visual one that included the scene where Liberty Valance is shot, but blacked out the left side, concealing his opponent (Fig. 5.2).[43] Although unlike in *Oedipus*, it is the audience who is oblivious to the killer's identity throughout the film, not the protagonist, both works utilize the interplay between knowledge and ignorance to explore issues of identity and self.

Moreover, although Tom Doniphon works well as an Aeneas figure, the Ransom Stoddard character is a decidedly un-epic sort of hero. Instead, as an Easterner and an educated professional determined to bring law and order to the territory, he is, as we have seen, a new kind of leader, and one who resembles Oedipus in that he functions as "an appropriate symbol of civilized man, who was beginning to believe, in the fifth century B.C., that he could seize control of his environment and make his own destiny ..."[44] Like Oedipus, Ransom

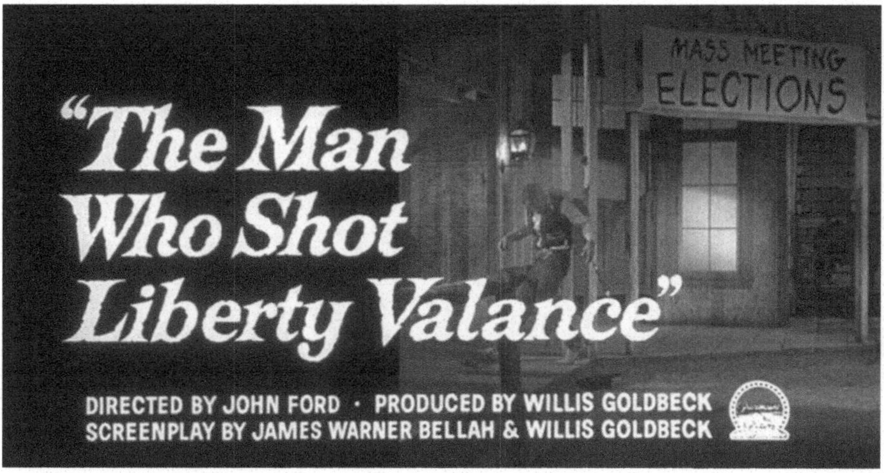

5.2 Liberty Valance (Lee Marvin) in a trailer for *The Man Who Shot Liberty Valance* (1962). Paramount Pictures, John Ford Productions.

Stoddard is at the narrative's outset a successful leader revered by the people; the position and reputation of each, however, is grounded in a murder that has been attributed to the wrong man. In Oedipus' case, he has killed his father without recognizing the victim's identity, and because of this, the throne of Thebes is left vacant for him to obtain. In Ranse's case, the credit he has received for a murder he did not commit provides the notoriety he needs to launch a political career. Each man, moreover, wins his position based on a reputation for having rid the land of a violent menace – the sphinx and Liberty Valance. And although each man demonstrates some merit on his own – Oedipus did in fact save Thebes by solving the riddle of the sphinx, while Ranse knows the law and presumably advances in his career on his own merit (both cognitively based achievements) – each man's glory is built on an ignoble foundation. The contrast between appearance and reality in each case is demonstrated through an emphasis at the outset of the narrative on the hero's self-important, even arrogant, attitude, seen in Oedipus through dialogue – he introduces himself to the audience at the play's outset as "I, Oedipus, celebrated by all" (line 8) – and in Ford's film primarily through Ranse's condescending tone and puffed-up demeanor (Fig. 5.3).

In addition, the critical role of the deaths of Laius and Liberty Valance in these works positions generational tensions as a central theme: in *Oedipus*, the oracles that originally set the plot in motion by indicating that Oedipus will kill his father and marry his mother

5.3 Maxwell Scott (Carleton Young), Charlie Hasbrouck (Joseph Hoover), and Ransom Stoddard (James Stewart) in *The Man Who Shot Liberty Valance* (1962). Paramount Pictures, John Ford Productions.

situate succession anxiety as fundamental. Generational issues are also highlighted in the riddle of the sphinx, with its suggestion of the natural progression of generations, while Laius' exposure of his infant son and Oedipus' murder of an older man who refuses to cede the road to him each enact an extreme version of this succession anxiety.[45] Ford's film includes similar tensions. Despite their generational equivalence (Wayne was born in 1907 and Stewart in 1908), Tom Doniphon works as a sort of father-figure to Ranse, a dynamic signaled in myriad small ways: not only does Doniphon save the "tenderfoot" Ranse after he has been beaten, he also offers him advice on how to get along in the West, gives him a shooting lesson, and even praises him for "throw[ing] a good punch," suggesting a certain pride in Ranse's assimilation to Doniphon's way of life. At the same time, Valance, who as we have seen works as Doniphon's darker counterpart, acts as a negative aspect of Ranse's father-figure,[46] a function signaled with his own taunting offer to teach Ranse law – "Western law!" – before he bullwhips him. Their generational difference is further signaled by the "might makes right" approach to life embraced by both Doniphon and Valance, which is contrasted with Ranse's attempted rejection of these in favor of law, order, and a civilized community.[47]

Of course, in the end Ranse's ideological position is "destined" to win out, for as we know the Wild West eventually gave way to the more ordered, law-based society we live in today. The ultimate

5.4 Tom Doniphon (John Wayne) tends to the wounded Ransom Stoddard (James Stewart) in *The Man Who Shot Liberty Valance* (1962). Paramount Pictures, John Ford Productions.

triumph of the way of life Ranse represents – and the necessity of the older generation eventually giving way to the next – has its roots in Johnson's original short story in which the Tom Doniphon figure is described as "an unwanted relic of the frontier that was gone, a legacy to more civilized times that had no place for him."[48] In Ford's film, Doniphon's rapidly approaching obsolescence is visually suggested early on when, as he tends to the wounded Ranse, the shadow of his hat appears to fit perfectly onto Ranse's head, foreshadowing that he is heir to Doniphon's position as the most powerful and prominent man in the community (Fig. 5.4). Doniphon and Valance are thus depicted as "the benevolent and malevolent surrogates of the vanished landscape,"[49] men who must inevitably give way to the "progress" that Ranse's arrival heralds.

This yielding to the newer generation, however, entails a loss of power and position that is often traumatic. In Sophocles' play, this transition is achieved through violence: even if he does so in ignorance, Oedipus must kill his father in order to take his throne. In Ford's film too, the incompatibility of rule by the gun and rule by law means that for Ranse to take over as a new kind of community leader, the older generation must be eliminated. While Valance is killed outright, Doniphon survives; but although Ranse does not literally kill him, by accepting his sacrifice he condemns him to a metaphorical death, taking away both his position in the community – the newspapermen in modern Shinbone have never even heard of him

– and his dreams for personal fulfillment.[50] Much as Oedipus did by assuming Laius' throne and marrying his queen, Ranse therefore kills one father-figure (Valance) and takes over the identity of the other: he becomes the husband to Hallie Tom Doniphon had intended to be, he becomes the most prominent man in Shinbone (and beyond), and he, not Doniphon, becomes known as "the man who shot Liberty Valance."

Of course, an important element of Oedipus' notoriety is that the woman he takes from his father is his own mother, by whom he then unknowingly sires his own siblings. While there is no literal incestuous element in Ford's film, a parallel exists nonetheless. Because Doniphon serves as a father-figure to Ranse, when Ranse and Hallie stumble into a relationship, pushing Doniphon aside, all three are aware that a transgression has taken place. In addition, throughout the flashback sequence, Hallie either acts as a nurturing caretaker to Ranse – as Gallagher says, she is "always mothering Ranse, tending his wounds"[51] – or he treats her as an uneducated, uncultured inferior – more or less as a child[52] (indeed, Vera Miles was born in 1929, and was therefore more than twenty years younger than both James Stewart and John Wayne). Thus, their relationship, while not technically incestuous, does exhibit a disturbing imbalance in age and in its power dynamics, a characteristic that heightens the generational tensions exhibited in Ranse's relationship with Doniphon and Valance.

In addition, the film's ending highlights the gulf between Ranse and Hallie in two ways. First, Hallie's placement of the cactus rose on Tom Doniphon's coffin suggests both to the viewer and to Ranse that she is still in love with him, an implication Ford himself indicated was intentional.[53] Then in the interchange between Ranse and Hallie at the film's conclusion, when Ranse asks if she would be "too sorry" if they left Washington and moved back West, Hallie replies, "If you knew how often I'd dreamed of it." This response suggests that though he has lived with her all these years, he has not really known her[54] – a situation reminiscent of Oedipus and Jocasta. Indeed, in a statement that could equally as well describe Oedipus, Pippin says that his failure to truly know his wife "goes to the root of Ranse's lack of self-knowledge, a certain blindness about the costs to be incurred by the kind of order he proposes for the town. . .."[55]

At the beginning of Sophocles' play, Oedipus is ignorant of both his identity and the implications of his actions, and thus confident that his position is deserved. The audience[56] – and sooner or later, all the players *except* the titular hero – come to know what Oedipus does not, and this balance of knowledge and ignorance adds poignancy to the tragic situation. As the "mystery" unravels, his *anagnorisis*, or tragic recognition, is sudden, as the horrifying truth hits Oedipus like a hammer blow, shattering his confidence and his sense of self. His *peripeteia*, or tragic reversal, is complete when following this horrific realization, he loses his wife/mother to suicide, his eyesight through self-mutilation, and his position and power through deposition and exile. Ford reverses this ironic element, with both the audience and the bulk of the film's characters kept in the dark through most of the film, rather than the protagonist, who does not remain oblivious to the truth for long:[57] soon after Valance's death, Doniphon enlightens him to the fact that he, not Ranse, fired the fatal shot from an unseen location. And unlike Oedipus, who pursues the truth relentlessly, Ranse hides the truth, allowing everyone else to live with an erroneous perception of his achievements.[58] For Ranse, his recognition does not come in a rush: instead, his punishment is the silent knowledge that he has built his success on another, perhaps better, man's achievements rather than deserving them wholly. This punishment is made more acute by the editor's decision to "print the legend" rather than allowing Ranse to finally come clean, so that unlike Oedipus, whose wounds are obvious, Ranse is wrecked internally. Moreover, Ranse is compelled to acknowledge tacitly that the dynamic of his success in politics is replicated in his marriage: Hallie's placement of the cactus rose on Doniphon's coffin as a reminder of their history together and her statement that "I guess my heart is here [in the desert]" suggest that Ranse's marriage, like his career, has been based on a false assumption.[59] Although Hallie remains very much alive, Ranse, like Oedipus, is forced to face the loss of the wife he thought he had. And also like Oedipus, he is in the end a man without a home: moving back to Shinbone may return Hallie to her roots, but her statement only serves to emphasize that Ranse started out as an outsider. Thus while it is Mr. Scott and the local press – and we the audience – who undergo an *anagnorisis* of sorts as we come to recognize the true nature of the outwardly venerable Senator Ransom Stoddard, it is Ranse who undergoes a *peripateia* much like Oedipus', in that each endures the loss of identity, of a place to call home, and of the wife they thought they had. In the end, the initially idealistic Ranse, who developed into a self-important, even arrogant statesman, has to confront the reality that he is not, in fact, the man he pretends and aspires to be, a realization very similar to the one Oedipus comes to.

CONCLUSION

The Man Who Shot Liberty Valance was not Ford's last Western,[60] but as the grand summation of the genre's acknowledged master, in some ways it brings the Golden Age of Westerns to a close. As Joseph McBride puts it, "*Liberty Valance* represents the true closing of the frontier, both [Ford's] own mythic frontier and that of the film genre he helped create."[61] Bogdanovich, on the other hand, implies that rather than representing an ending, it should be placed at the forefront of the revisionist Western movement of the 1960s when he calls the film

> a serious assault on everything. It tells us our legends are false, that our history is wrong and that everything we believe in is a lie. The revisionist Westerns of [Ford's successor] Sam Peckinpah are not revisionist in that way, they're just more violent.[62]

The transitional nature of this film means that it looks both back and forward, drawing on themes, traditions, and ideologies by this time firmly established in Westerns, but now utilizing them more self-reflectively. Virgil employs a similar strategy in his *Aeneid*, adopting the epic framework made familiar by Homer, but using it not just to reflect and shape national identity, but to scrutinize it consciously as well. Thus while Ford's film shows a relationship to the *Iliad* and *Odyssey*, it has a closer connection to Virgil's later epic, which drew on and reformulated Homer's themes. A similar principle applies to Greek drama, which though a different genre, drew heavily on the foundational myths and legends best known from Homer's works, but self-consciously manipulated them in the service of self-scrutiny.

All three of these works focus on a great hero whose failings reveal him to be a man after all. In each case, the man serves as a representative of the people: Aeneas is both the founder of Rome and the embodiment of what constitutes the ideal Roman character throughout most of the epic; Bernard Knox has argued that Sophocles' play is not simply about its hero, but that the character of Oedipus is equivalent to the character of the Athenian people;[63] and Ransom Stoddard serves as a symbol of the modern America that replaced the Wild West embodied by Tom Doniphon and Liberty Valance. And by problematizing these heroes – Aeneas succumbs to *furor*, Oedipus unwittingly commits heinous transgressions, and Ranse builds his life on a lie to Doniphon's utter detriment – each of these authors then also problematizes the prevailing grand national self-image.

The civic focus of Virgil's work is clear, as it was commissioned by Augustus as a propaganda piece to promote his incipient regime, while that of Sophocles' play is suggested by its performance context at the Great Dionysia, a community occasion where the city was on display, particularly in its "role and image as an international power," as Simon Goldhill has argued.[64] Ford's film is similarly anchored, as Peabody's nomination speech makes clear. Indeed, as Warfield notes, in Johnson's short story Liberty Valance stands alone, but Ford transforms him "into the hired gun of the ranchers in their battle against farmers, fences, *civitas*, and statehood,"[65] shaping the story into one with a much more explicit attention to civic matters.

This civic emphasis, set against its self-reflective construction and the problematic nature of a hero who stands in for the state itself, in each case begins to call the narratives upon which national identity is built into question. As we have seen, Virgil complicates his picture of the glorious nationalistic vision the powers-that-be would promote both by emphasizing the personal sacrifice required to advance the imperial agenda and by foregrounding its violent origins. In Oedipus' tragic downfall, Sophocles offers the Athenian people, who had provoked a protracted war with Sparta through their imperial behavior, a cautionary tale about the dangers of pride, rash action, and arrogance. So too does Ford challenge us to scrutinize our own national character, appropriately through the genre most closely associated with ideas of Manifest Destiny and American identity. By offering up an Aeneas-like protagonist in Tom Doniphon, a larger-than-life hero of epic proportions who exhibits a frontier version of *pietas* by sacrificing his personal needs and desires for the sake of the progress of the larger community, Ford, like Virgil, emphasizes the sacrifice and loss inherent in nation-building. And much as Sophocles did with Oedipus, by offering the morally compromised, self-blinded Ranse as a symbol of modern America, Ford calls our assumption of national greatness into question.

Jim Kitses has argued that in some ways, "the violence of Doniphon's killing of Valance stand[s] in for much darker stains, the slaughter of the native peoples."[66] If so, by highlighting Ranse's willful sweeping of this deed under the rug, Ford prods us to acknowledge the unspoken sins upon which the nation is built. I would point out that this is not entirely unproblematic: although he was generally a friend to Native Americans and the Navajo even adopted him into their tribe,[67] Native Americans are entirely absent from this film, so if Ford intends to call attention to white Americans' denial of the near-total annihilation of the native people, he does so by replicating it.[68] Nonetheless, his film makes a start[69] at the long process of dismantling the portions of America's national mythology which rely on a denial of the history of violence by exposing the reality that the privileges "we" (i.e. post-frontier-era white Americans) enjoy result from the oppression of others – a project that continues even today. As John Ford's culminating statement on the Western genre, this film functions in much the same way as did Virgil's *Aeneid* and Sophocles' *Oedipus*: it holds America's glorious civic identity up for scrutiny, inviting its viewers to see themselves clearly in seeking the self-knowledge without which neither man nor state can truly and fully embrace his or its own identity.[70]

NOTES

1 The film was nominated for a Top Action Drama Laurel but took fifth place; Lee Marvin was nominated for Top Action Performer alongside Wayne but took fourth place. The film's wins in the newly instituted Western Heritage Awards (first given in 1961) include those for Theatrical Motion Picture, for production (to Willis Goldbeck), for direction (to John Ford), for writing (to James Warner Bellah), and five for acting (to Lee Marvin, Edmond O'Brien, James Stewart, Vera Miles, and John Wayne).

2 McBride (2011: 625); see also Pye (1996: 119). Another contributing factor may have been that the film broke considerably from generic expectations (for more on which see Pye 1996: 121–2).

3 Crowther (1962: 121); Gill qtd. in Davis (1995: 310); Callenbach (1963–64: 42).

4 See McBride (2011: 624); Eyman (2014: 362).

5 Sarris (1962: 15); Bogdanovich qtd. in McBride (2011: 625. From the program notes of Bogdanovich's fourteen-film Ford series at Dan Talbot's New Yorker Theater in 1963).

6 McBride (2011: 623).

7 McBride (2011: 633).

8 As many scholars and critics (e.g. Bogdanovich 1968: 34; Gallagher 1986: 409; Pye 1996: 114–22) have noted, Ford touched on this problem, though less forcefully, in his 1948 *Fort Apache*, in which Wayne also starred.

9 Johnson (1953: 37, 40); Warfield (1975: 15–20).

10 Blundell and Ormand (1997: 533, 536).

11 Gallagher (1986: 402).

12 Unlike today, the term "dude" in the last part of the nineteenth century referred to a well-dressed city slicker who was ill-suited to life outside urban locales.

13 Wayne dropped to fourteenth in 1958, but aside from that anomaly,

he stayed in the top ten every year until 1973, and with a record twenty-five of twenty-six years in the top ten, remains the number one money-maker of all time (quigleypublishing.com/MPalmanac/Top10/Top10_lists, accessed July 27, 2015).

14 See Eyman (1999: 488). James Stewart earned $300,000 (like Wayne, plus 7.5% of the gross), and Lee Marvin just $50,000.

15 Qtd. in Hughes (2008: 87).

16 As Robert Meyer pointed out in a 2014 conference presentation, Doniphon too exhibits bullying tendencies, as when he shoots the paint buckets Ranse is placing on fence posts, splattering him with paint, a cruel and unnecessary trick at which he laughs in glee.

17 See Stowell (1986: 98) for discussion of "first-" and "second-cycle pioneers" in *The Man Who Shot Liberty Valance.*

18 Eyman (1999: 492).

19 Stowell (1986: 108), connecting "Liberty" with an attempt to hold onto the freedom of the wilderness, sees the name as suggesting Ford's ambivalence about the progress of civilization. See also Bogdanovich (1968: 34).

20 In Don Siegel's 1976 *The Shootist*, John Wayne's J. B. Books calls attention to this when he tells Gillom Rogers (Ron Howard) that it is usually an inept amateur who kills a master gunfighter (foreshadowing, of course, his own death).

21 Kitses (2007: 123); Eyman (1999: 491). See also Wollen (1972: 101); French (1997: 142); McBride (2011: 632).

22 Pippin (2010: 82).

23 Bogdanovich (1968: 34); McBride (2011: 633).

24 Johnson (1953: 26). Screenwriters James Warner Bellah and Willis Goldbeck took considerable liberties with characterization and storyline, adding, for instance, the characters of Peabody and Pompey, sharpening the political context of the gunfight, and having Ranse confess the truth rather than keeping it concealed (see McBride 2011: 624).

25 Gallagher (1986: 408–9).

26 Gallagher (1986: 408); Pippin (2010: 79). See also Pippin (2010: 78, 83).

27 Gallagher (1986: 409).

28 Noted in Perkell (1981: 355).

29 Gallagher (1986: 406).

30 French (1997: 137).

31 Nugent (1999: 253). See e.g. *Aen.* 1.208–9.

32 See Stowell (1986: 109).

33 In Johnson's short story, Ranse's reputation as the man who shot Liberty Valance is a political liability rather than an asset (1953: 47–8); Ford's shift emphasizes that Ranse's career is built on violence rather than that he succeeded in spite of it. I might also note that Ford includes two character names – that of Doniphon's "boy" Pompey and of the "cattleman's

mouthpiece" Cassius Starbuckle – that may remind the educated viewer of Julius Caesar's once ally and later opponent Pompey the Great and of one of his assassins, Gaius Cassius Longinus, historical figures from the troubled times that led up to Augustus' *Pax Romana*, a connection which tempts me to argue that Ford might be consciously alluding to the sort of problematizing of Augustan propaganda that many see Virgil including in the *Aeneid*.

34 Pippin (2010: 93).

35 Pippin (2010: 96). Blundell and Ormand suggest something similar for Clint Eastwood's *Unforgiven* (1997: 553–60).

36 Ford qtd. in Warfield (1975: 18); Kitses (2007: 118).

37 Pippin (2010: 97).

38 Warfield (1975: 2); Gallagher (1986: 385); McBride (2011: 626).

39 Stowell (1986: 108).

40 French (1997: 140, 146); Kopff (1999: 240); Kitses (2007: 121).

41 Warshow (1954: 193).

42 Gallagher (1986: 384).

43 Trailer available at youtube.com/watch?v=bNoonE09-8c (accessed July 31, 2015).

44 Knox (1979: 97).

45 See Bakewell (2002: 37) for an analysis of parallel generational tensions in *Oedipus Rex* and John Sayles's 1996 *Lonestar*. Bakewell's examination also includes consideration of how each work "deepens into a drama about personal and community identity" (2002: 40), a dynamic also noted here. See Winkler (2008: 75–6) for a very brief overview of Westerns that feature such Oedipal father–son conflicts.

46 This despite the fact that Lee Marvin, who was born in 1924, was more than fifteen years younger than both Wayne and Stewart.

47 Compare *Red River*, in which we observed similar generational tensions played out between Tom Dunson (also played by John Wayne) and Matthew Garth, who, although less problematic, like Ranse represents a softer, more communal approach to leadership. See also Mast (1982: 333), who notes that both *Red River* and this film focus on "the transition from one kind of cultural leader to another" in these "allegor[ies] of historical transition from one kind of law, one kind of virtue, to another."

48 Johnson (1953: 48).

49 Stowell (1986: 108). Nancy Warfield calls the two men "relics of the past" (1975: 19).

50 French has also argued that the answer to the titular question is "unambiguous," reasoning that "Stoddard killed Liberty even if the bullet from his gun never entered the body of Liberty Valance. The easterner's conception of civilization and law and order, the very idea that the wilderness could and should be converted into a garden, destroyed the West" (1997: 138). See also Gallagher (1986: 405).

51 Gallagher (1986: 406).
52 See Pippin (2010: 79); see also Stowell (1986: 11); French (1997: 139).
53 See Bogdanovich (1968: 100).
54 Pippin (2010: 87, 92).
55 Pippin (2010: 92).
56 The ancient audience would have been familiar with the crucial points of Oedipus' story.
57 See again Bakewell (2002: 42–3) for a discussion of a similar reversal of the dramatic irony in Oedipus' play and in *Lonestar*.
58 Yet Oedipus displays what could be considered "willful blindness" in failing to consider what the information given in the oracle and the rumor that sent him there in the first place taken together imply; he thus incurs some blame for killing a man of his father's generation and marrying a woman old enough to be his mother.
59 Pippin (2010: 87).
60 *Cheyenne Autumn*, also featuring James Stewart, was released in 1964.
61 McBride (2011: 632).
62 Qtd. in Brady (2012).
63 Knox (1979: 91).
64 Goldhill (1990: 103–4).
65 Warfield (1975: 10).
66 Kitses (2007: 39).
67 See Gallagher (1986: 341); Day (2008: 37–45).
68 Likewise, several scholars have noted that although in this film Ford tries to call attention to our problematic treatment of black Americans – most explicitly in the scene where Pompey attempts to recite from the Declaration of Independence but stumbles when he gets to "all men are created equal," prompting Ranse to reassure him with, "A lot of people forget that part of it" – he does so by dressing Pompey to look like an "Uncle Remus" type figure. See Gallagher (1986: 399); McBride (2011: 630–1).
69 *The Searchers*, too, might be considered Ford's less explicit initiation into this process.
70 This recommendation of self-scrutiny and self-knowledge recalls a number of Plato's Socratic dialogues in which Plato has Socrates explore the wisdom of this aphorism, which dovetails nicely with Nancy Warfield's identification of Platonic themes in Ford's film.

Conclusion

While the Western genre at a glance may seem to have little in common with the oral poetry of Homer or with Rome's most elite literary epic, they show remarkable similarities in their use of myth and history to reflect and shape national identities and prevailing ideologies. Their close kinship is often suggested in the rhetoric of film scholars, whose descriptions of the function of Westerns often apply equally well to ancient epic, as we see in Robert Pippin's statement that

> one of our mythic forms of self-understanding [in the United States] . . . could be said to be the very best Hollywood Westerns. They deal with a past form of life that is self-consciously treated as gone, unrecoverable (even if still quite powerfully and somewhat mysteriously attractive) and . . . many tell a basic and clearly troubling, complicated story of a traumatic, decisive political transition, the end of one sort of order and self-image and the beginning of another.[1]

Like epic did for antiquity, then, Westerns help us grapple with identity issues in a way that is relevant yet comfortably distanced, and for this reason they have proven remarkably resilient despite occasional pronouncements that the genre is dead.[2] The past decade, for instance, has seen remakes of *3:10 to Yuma* (2007) and *True Grit* (2010), a film adaptation of Cormac McCarthy's novel *No Country for Old Men* (2007), a postmodern re-envisioning of the spaghetti Western in *Django Unchained* (2012), the family-friendly computer-animated feature film *Rango* (2011), as well as at least two popular and acclaimed post-*Deadwood* TV series in FX's *Justified* (2010–15) and A&E/Netflix's *Longmire* (2012–).

Moreover, just as the characterization of the epic hero in Homer and Virgil's works reflected and shaped notions of idealized virtue for men in ancient Greece and Rome, the Western hero as he is presented in film has become a pervasive and persistent model for idealized

6.1a, b, and c At top: Han Solo (Harrison Ford) from *Star Wars Episode V: The Empire Strikes Back* (1980). Lucasfilm. At center: Chris Kyle (Bradley Cooper) in *American Sniper* (2014). Warner Bros. At bottom: Rick Grimes (Andrew Lincoln) in *The Walking Dead* S2E1 (2010–). AMC.

American masculinity more generally. Indeed, we see his influence everywhere, from *Star Wars*' Han Solo[3] to *American Sniper*'s Chris Kyle (a protagonist whom Richard Corliss has called "the Shane of Sadr City")[4] and from *The Walking Dead*'s Rick Grimes to real-world politicians like Barack Obama (Figs 6.1a–c and 6.2)

6.2 "Obama the Cowboy": presidential candidate Barack Obama at a campaign rally in Austin, Texas (Feb. 2007). Copyright Matthew C. Wright.

in scenarios where such figures are, like the heroes of ancient epic, engaged in heroic action directed toward developing, redeeming, or preserving society (or at least wanting to present themselves as such). As these connections suggest, works as varied and diverse as science fiction movies, fantasy narratives,[5] post-apocalyptic tales, gangster[6] and detective stories, and more all utilize mythic themes and "on the edge" settings while drawing on similar and deeply ingrained notions of what constitutes idealized masculine – and correspondingly, feminine – behaviors. My hope, therefore, is that this study opens up a wider discussion, and that readers are able to see similar patterns and concerns in not only other Westerns, but even in other "frontier" genres as well.

This being so, we may ask: how much of the cultural equivalence between the epics of classical antiquity and modern genres like the Western stems from continuity with the Greco-Roman past that forms the foundation of Western civilization more generally? How much from the fact that all three societies are grounded in strong patriarchal structures and notions of ethnic and cultural superiority? I do not intend to assert definitive conclusions on these issues – indeed I do not think they can be definitively decided – but instead to offer them up for consideration in the belief that these parallels are mutually enlightening. I will, however, venture to suggest that whether we watch Westerns or not, the model of masculinity developed in Western film is so deeply embedded in American collective consciousness that it influences the reception of ancient epic, both Greek and Roman, so that some aspects of these works are filtered through a "Westerns" lens, a direction of influence that is often overlooked. Camerini's 1954 *Ulysses*, for instance, includes a scene where the suitors mock Telemachus by tossing spears at his feet, laughing as they tell him to "jump!" – reminiscent of the stock scene in Westerns where the villains bully an inferior by shooting at his feet and ordering him to "dance," as we see Stockburn and his deputies do to Spider in Eastwood's 1985 *Pale Rider*. So too have my students often unprompted seen duels between epic warriors as versions of a Wild West shoot-out. By recognizing this tendency, we can not only become more aware of our own ideological assumptions, but also better grasp how we understand the epics of antiquity as well.

NOTES

1 Pippin (2010: 62).

2 The genre was presumed dead, for instance, after the spectacular failure of Michael Cimino's extravagantly expensive *Heaven's Gate* in 1980, but revived in the early 1990s with Kevin Costner's *Dances With Wolves* (1990) followed by Clint Eastwood's *Unforgiven* in 1992, both Oscar-winning films (see Kitses 2007: 2, 5).

3 Howard Hughes calls *Star Wars* and its ilk "little more than way-out westerns, set in a galaxy far, far away, but with their roots firmly in the American west" (2008: 247), and George Lucas himself has acknowledged that the dearth of Westerns in the late 1970s was a "motivating force in the creation of his series" (Kitses 2007: 3).

4 Corliss (2014). A. O. Scott, likewise, has called *American Sniper* "Less a war movie than a western – the story of a lone gunslinger facing down his nemesis in a dusty, lawless place" (2014).

5 The enormously popular HBO series *Game of Thrones* (2011–), for instance, is set in the mythical land of Westeros; its generic connection to Westerns is well illustrated by several Western-style re-imaginings of the series's introductory theme available on the web (e.g. youtube.com/watch?v=WrooVE6i-XM ("Game of Thrones Theme – Western Cover") and youtube.com/watch?v=roBo85sv7uo ("Game of Thrones Western-Style (The Rains of Castamere) [Red Noon]"), both accessed July 30, 2015).

6 This parallel was recognized as early as 1954 by Robert Warshow.

Bibliography

Anderson, L. (1956). "Film Reviews: *The Searchers*," *Sight and Sound* 26.2: 94–5.

Baker, B. (1996). "*Shane* Through Five Decades," in I. Cameron and D. Pye (eds), *The Book of Westerns*. New York: Continuum, 214–20.

Bakewell, G. W. (2002). "Oedipus Tex: *Lone Star*, Tragedy, and Postmodernism," *Classical and Modern Literature* 22.1: 35–48.

Bazin, A. (1971). *What is Cinema? Vol. 2*, trans. and ed. H. Gray. Berkeley: University of California Press.

Beale, L. (2003). "They're the Presidents' Elect Films," *Los Angeles Times/latimes.com*, November 18, 2014.

Belton, J. (1972). "Hawks and Co.," in J. McBride (ed.), *Focus on Howard Hawks*. Englewood Cliffs, NJ: Prentice-Hall, 94–108.

Belton, J. (1994). *American Cinema/American Culture*. New York: McGraw-Hill.

Biskind, P. (2001). *Seeing is Believing: How Hollywood Taught Us to Stop Worrying and Love the Fifties*. New York: Pantheon Books.

Blondell, R. (2013). *Helen of Troy: Beauty, Myth, Devastation*. Oxford: Oxford University Press.

Blumberg, L. (2006). "The Anachronistic Hero in Sophocles' *Ajax* and Howard Hawks' *Red River*," paper presented at *The Classical Association of the Middle West and South* Annual Meeting: Gainesville, Florida.

Blumberg, L. (2008). "The Sophoclean Hero in Howard Hawks' Westerns," paper presented at *The Classical Association of the Middle West and South* Annual Meeting: Tucson, Arizona.

Blundell, M. W. and K. Ormand (1997). "Western Values, or the Peoples Homer: *Unforgiven* as a Reading of the *Iliad*," *Poetics Today* 18.4: 533–69.

Bogdanovich, P. (1962). *The Cinema of Howard Hawks*. New York: Museum of Modern Art.

Bogdanovich, P. (1968). *John Ford*. Berkeley: University of California Press.

Böhnke, M. (2001). "Myth and Law in the Films of John Ford," *Journal of Law and Society* 28.1: 47–63.

Bolmarcich, S. (2001). "Ὁμοφροσύνη in the *Odyssey*," *Classical Philology* 96.3: 205–13.
Brady, T. (2012). "In Praise of an Old Hollywood Master," *irishtimes.com*, June 19, 2015.
Branson, C. (1987). *Howard Hawks: A Jungian Study.* Santa Barbara: Capra Press.
Broder, M. (2013). "Tradition vs. Reception as Models for Studying the Great Books," *Classical World* 106.3: 505–15.
Brown, H. (1962). *The Stars in Their Courses.* New York: Alfred A. Knopf.
Budelmann, F. and J. Haubold (2011). "Reception and Tradition," in L. Hardwick and C. Stray (eds), *A Companion to Classical Receptions.* Chichester: Wiley-Blackwell, 13–25.
Buscombe, E. (1988). "The Western: A Short History," in E. Buscombe (ed.), *The BFI Companion to the Western.* New York: Da Capo Press, 15–54.
Buscombe, E. (2000). *The Searchers: BFI Film Classics.* London: British Film Institute.
Byron, S. (1979). "*The Searchers*: Cult Movie of the New Hollywood," *New York* 12.10: 45–8.
Callenbach, E. (1963–64). "*The Man Who Shot Liberty Valance* and *Donovan's Reef*," *Film Quarterly* 17.2: 42–4.
Campbell, J. (1973). *The Hero with a Thousand Faces*, 2nd edn. Princeton: Princeton University Press.
Carson, A. (1990). "Putting Her in Her Place: Woman, Dirt, and Desire," in D. M. Halperin, J. J. Winkler, and F. I. Zeitlin (eds), *Before Sexuality: The Construction of Erotic Experience in the Ancient Greek World.* Princeton: Princeton University Press, 135–69.
Carson, A. (1995). *Glass, Irony, & God.* New York: New Directions Books.
Cawelti, J. G. (1971). *The Six-Gun Mystique.* Bowling Green, OH: Bowling Green University Popular Press.
Chase, B. (1946a). "The Chisholm Trail (Part 1)," *Saturday Evening Post* 219.23: 9–10, 147–8, 150, 152, 154, 156, 159–60.
Chase, B. (1946b). "The Chisholm Trail (Part 2)," *Saturday Evening Post* 219.24: 32–3, 56, 58–60, 62, 64–6, 68, 70.
Chase, B. (1946c). "The Chisholm Trail (Part 3)," *Saturday Evening Post* 219.25: 32, 68–72, 74.
Chase, B. (1946d). "The Chisholm Trail (Part 4)," *Saturday Evening Post* 219.26: 32, 54, 56, 58–60.
Chase, B. (1947a). "The Chisholm Trail (Part 5)," *Saturday Evening Post* 219.27: 32, 70–2, 74.
Chase, B. (1947b). "The Chisholm Trail (Part 6)," *Saturday Evening Post* 219.28: 32, 46–8, 50–2.
Chase, B. (1948). *Red River: Blazing Guns on the Chisholm Trail.* New York: Bantam Books.
Clauss, J. J. (1999). "Descent into Hell: Mythic Paradigms in *The Searchers*," *Journal of Popular Film and Television* 27.3: 2–17.

Clauss, J. J. (2008). "*Hercules Unchained: Contaminatio, Nostos, Katabasis,* and the Surreal," *Arethusa* 41.1: 51–66.

Cloutier, J. (2012). "A Country for Old Men: *Unforgiven, The Shootist*, and the Post–Heyday Western," *Cinema Journal* 51.4: 110–29.

Cohen, H. I. (2010). "*Red River* and *The Searchers*: Deception in the Modern Western," *Film Criticism* 35.1: 82–102.

Cohen, T. (2013). "Is it 'High Noon' for Obama on Syria?" *CNN Politics/ cnn.com*, May 4, 2015.

Combs, R. (1986). "When the Big Hand is on Twelve . . . *or 7 Ambiguities of Time*," *Monthly Film Bulletin* 53.269. London: British Film Institute.

Corliss, R. (1996). "Borden Chase, Howard Hawks and *Red River*," in J. Hillier and P. Wollen (eds), *Howard Hawks: American Artist*. London: British Film Institute, 185–9. First published in R. Corliss, *Talking Pictures*. Woodstock, NY: The Overlook Press, 1985.

Corliss, R. (2014). "Review: In *American Sniper*, Clint Eastwood and Bradley Cooper Are Right on Target," *Time.com*, January 19.

Cortese, J. (1976). "Bourgeois Myth and Anti-Myth: The Western Hero of the Fifties," *SubStance* 5.15: 122–32.

Countryman, E. (1988). "Shane," in E. Buscombe (ed.), *The BFI Companion to the Western*, new edn. London: Da Capo, 297.

Cowie, P. (2004). *John Ford and the American West*. New York: Harry N. Abrams.

Crichton, K. (1948). "Collier's Movies: This Week's Preview," *Collier's*, October 9, 64.

Crowther, B. (1956). "Screen: *The Searchers* Find Action," *New York Times*, May 31, 21.

Crowther, B. (1962). "Film Odds and Endings: Reflections Upon Some Surprises and Weaknesses in New Pictures," *The New York Times*, June 3, 121.

Cunningham, J. M. (1947). "The Tin Star," *Collier's*, December 6, 11, 64–73.

Davis, R. L. (1995). *John Ford: Hollywood's Old Master*. Norman: University of Oklahoma Press.

Davis, S. D. (2005). "Augustus Deified or Denigrated? The Political Subtext of Anchises' Speech in *Aeneid* Book VI," Abstract: Conference paper presented at CAMWS in Madison, WI. *camws.org*, April 24, 2015.

Day, K. (2008). "'What Makes a Man to Wander?' *The Searchers* as a Western *Odyssey*," *Arethusa* 41.1: 11–49.

Day, K. (2014). "Experiments in Love: Longus' *Daphnis & Chloe* and Henry de Vere Stacpoole's *The Blue Lagoon*," *Dialogue: The Interdisciplinary Journal of Popular Culture and Pedagogy* 1.1. http://journaldialogue.org/issues/issue-1/experiments-in-love-daphnis-chloe-and-the-blue-lagoon/

De Pourcq, M. (2012). "Classical Reception Studies: Reconceptualizing the Study of the Classical Tradition," *The International Journal of the Humanities* 9.4: 219–25.

Drummond, P. (1997). *High Noon*. London: British Film Institute.

Du Boulay, J. (1994). *Portrait of a Greek Mountain Village*. Limni, Evia, Greece: Denise Harvey.

Dyer, P. J. (1972). "Sling the Lamps Low," in J. McBride (ed.), *Focus on Howard Hawks*. Englewood Cliffs, NJ: Prentice-Hall, 78–93.

Eagleton, T. (1996). *Literary Theory: An Introduction*, 2nd edn. Minneapolis: University of Minnesota Press.

Eckstein, A. M. (1998). "Darkening Ethan: John Ford's *The Searchers* (1956) from Novel to Screenplay to Screen," *Cinema Journal* 38.1: 3–24.

Eckstein, A. M. (2004a). "Introduction: Main Critical Issues in *The Searchers*," in A. M. Eckstein and P. Lehman (eds), *The Searchers: Essays and Reflections on John Ford's Classic Western*. Detroit: Wayne State University Press, 1–45.

Eckstein, A. M. (2004b). "Incest and Miscegenation in *The Searchers* (1956) and *The Unforgiven* (1959)," in A. M. Eckstein and P. Lehman (eds), *The Searchers: Essays and Reflections on John Ford's Classic Western*. Detroit: Wayne State University Press, 197–221.

Erisman, F. (1984). "Growing Up with the American West: Fiction of Jack Schaefer," in J. Schaefer, *Shane: The Critical Edition*, ed. J. C. Work. Lincoln: University of Nebraska Press, 289–99.

Eyman, S. (1999). *Print the Legend: The Life and Times of John Ford*. Baltimore: Johns Hopkins University Press.

Eyman, S. (2004). *John Ford: The Searcher 1894–1973*, ed. P. Duncan. Italy: Taschen Books.

Eyman, S. (2014). *John Wayne: The Life and Legend*. New York: Simon & Schuster.

Felson, N. (1997). *Regarding Penelope: From Character to Poetics*. Princeton: Princeton University Press.

Fenin, G. N. and W. K. Everson (1973). *The Western: From Silents to the Seventies*. New York: Grossman Publishers.

Fiedler, L. A. (1975). *Love and Death in the American Novel*, rev. edn. New York: Stein & Day.

Fisher, M. A. (2004). "A Dollar and Cents Conjecture," in P. Cronin (ed.), *George Stevens: Interviews*. Jackson: University Press of Mississippi, 24–30.

Fitzgerald, R. (1963). "Postscript," in *The Odyssey*, trans. R. Fitzgerald. Garden City, NY: Anchor Books, 465–507.

Fletcher, J. (2014). "The *Catabasis* of Mattie Ross in the Coens' *True Grit*," *Classical World* 107.2: 237–54.

Folsom, J. K. (1984). "*Shane* and *Hud*: Two Stories in Search of a Medium," in J. Schaefer, *Shane: The Critical Edition*, ed. J. C. Work. Lincoln: University of Nebraska Press, 372–92.

Foster, G. (1999). "The Women in *High Noon* (1952): A Metanarrative of Difference," in A. Nolletti, Jr. (ed.), *The Films of Fred Zinnemann: Critical Perspectives*. Albany: State University of New York Press, 93–102.

Frankel, G. (2013). *The Searchers: The Making of an American Legend.* New York: Bloomsbury.

Frauenfelder, D. (2005). "Popular Culture and Classical Mythology," *The Classical World* 98.2: 210–13.

French, P. A. (1997). *Cowboy Metaphysics: Ethics and Death in Westerns.* Lanham, MD: Rowman & Littlefield.

French, P. A. (2001). *The Virtues of Vengeance.* Lawrence: University Press of Kansas.

Frye, N. (1957). *Anatomy of Criticism: Four Essays.* Princeton: Princeton University Press.

Gallagher, T. (1986). *John Ford: The Man and His Films.* Berkeley: University of California Press.

Gamel, M. (2001). "An American Tragedy: *Chinatown*," in M. M. Winkler (ed.), *Classical Myth and Culture in the Cinema.* Oxford: Oxford University Press, 148–71.

Giannetti, L. (1981). *Masters of the American Cinema.* Englewood Cliffs, NJ: Prentice-Hall.

Giannetti, L. and S. Eyman (2001). *Flashback: A Brief History of Film*, 4th edn. Upper Saddle River, NJ: Prentice-Hall.

Girgus, S. B. (1998). *Hollywood Renaissance: The Cinema of Democracy in the Era of Ford, Capra, and Kazan.* Cambridge: Cambridge University Press.

Goldhill, S. (1990). "The Great Dionysia and Civic Ideology," in J. J. Winkler and F. I. Zeitlin (eds), *Nothing to Do with Dionysos? Athenian Drama in Its Social Context.* Princeton: Princeton University Press, 97–129.

Goodwin, M. and N. Wise (1973). "An Interview with Howard Hawks," *Take One* 3.8: 19–25.

Graham, D. (1979). "*High Noon* (1952)," in W. T. Pilkington and D. Graham (eds), *Western Movies.* Albuquerque: University of New Mexico Press, 51–62.

Graham, D. (1980). "The Women of *High Noon*: A Revisionist View," *Rocky Mountain Review of Language and Literature* 34.4: 243–51.

Graves, M. A. and F. B. Engle (2006). "Western," in *Blockbusters: A Reference Guide to Film Genres.* Westport, CT: Greenwood Press, 253–78.

Graziosi, B. (2011). "The Ancient Reception of Homer," in L. Hardwick and C. Stray (eds), *A Companion to Classical Receptions.* Chichester: Wiley-Blackwell, 26–37.

Haas, R. (2011). "Homer on the Range," *Classical World* 104.2: 245–51.

Hardwick, L. (2003). *Reception Studies: Greece & Rome: New Surveys in the Classics* No. 33. Oxford: Oxford University Press.

Hardwick, L. and C. Stray (2011). "Introduction: Making Connections," in L. Hardwick and C. Stray (eds), *A Companion to Classical Receptions.* Chichester: Wiley-Blackwell, 1–9.

Harris, M. (2014). *Five Came Back: A Story of Hollywood and the Second World War.* New York: Penguin Press.

Haskell, M. (1974). "Howard Hawks: Masculine Feminine," *Film Comment* 10.2: 34–9.
Haskell, M. (1980). "Howard Hawks," in R. Roud (ed.), *Cinema: A Critical Dictionary (The Major Film-Makers)*. New York: Viking Press, 473–86.
Haslam, G. (1984). "Jack Schaefer," in J. Schaefer, *Shane: The Critical Edition*, ed. J. C. Work. Lincoln, NE: University of Nebraska Press, 16–55.
Heitman, R. (2005). *Taking Her Seriously: Penelope and the Plot of Homer's Odyssey.* Ann Arbor: University of Michigan Press.
Hoberman, J. (2004). "It's Always 'High Noon' at the White House," *The New York Times/nytimes.com*, May 4, 2015.
Holloway, R. (1956). "Review: *The Searchers*," *variety.com*, July 21, 2015.
Holtsmark, E. B. (2001). "The *Katabasis* Theme in Modern Cinema," in M. M. Winkler (ed.), *Classical Myth and Culture in the Cinema*. Oxford: Oxford University Press, 23–50.
Homer (1995). *Odyssey*, ed. J. Henderson. LCL. Cambridge, MA: Harvard University Press.
Homer (1999). *Iliad*, ed. J. Henderson. LCL. Cambridge, MA: Harvard University Press.
Hughes, R. (2004). "Getting the Belly Laugh," in P. Cronin (ed.), *George Stevens: Interviews*. Jackson, MS: University Press of Mississippi, 54–74.
Hughes, H. (2008). *Stagecoach to Tombstone: The Filmgoers' Guide to the Great Westerns*. London: I. B. Tauris.
Hyams, J. (2004). "Making *Shane*," in P. Cronin (ed.), *George Stevens: Interviews*. Jackson, MS: University Press of Mississippi, 10–12.
Johnson, D. M. (1953). "The Man Who Shot Liberty Valance," in *The Man Who Shot Liberty Valance, and A Man Called Horse, Lost Sister, The Hanging Tree*. Helena, MT: Riverbend Publishing, 25–49.
Kalinak, K. (2004). "'Typically American': Music for *The Searchers*," in A. M. Eckstein and P. Lehman (eds), *The Searchers: Essays and Reflections on John Ford's Classic Western*. Detroit: Wayne State University Press, 109–43.
Katz, M. A. (1981). "The Divided World of *Iliad* VI," in H. P. Foley (ed.), *Reflections of Women in Antiquity*. New York: Gordon and Breach Science Publishers, 19–44.
Keith, A. M. (2000). *Engendering Rome: Women in Latin Epic*. Cambridge: Cambridge University Press.
Kitses, J. (2007). *Horizons West: Directing the Western from John Ford to Clint Eastwood*, new edn. London: British Film Institute.
Knox, B. (1979). *Word and Action: Essays on the Ancient Theater*. Baltimore: Johns Hopkins University Press.
Kopff, E. C. (1999). *The Devil Knows Latin: Why America Needs the Classical Tradition*. Wilmington: Intercollegiate Studies Institute Books.
Lehman, P. (2004). "Preface: A Film That Fits a Lot of Descriptions," in A. M. Eckstein and P. Lehman (eds), *The Searchers: Essays and Reflections*

on John Ford's Classic Western. Detroit: Wayne State University Press, xi–xvi.
LeMay, Alan (2013). *The Searchers*. New York: Pinnacle Books.
Look (1956). "Movie Review: *The Searchers*...," *Look*, June 12, 90, 92–3.
Loraux, N. (1987). *Tragic Ways of Killing a Woman*, trans. A. Forster. Cambridge, MA: Harvard University Press.
McBride, J. (2011). *Searching for John Ford: A Life*. Jackson: University Press of Mississippi.
McBride, J. (2013). *Hawks on Hawks*. Lexington: University Press of Kentucky.
McBride, J. and M. Wilmington (1971). "Prisoner of the Desert," *Sight & Sound* 40.4: 210–14.
McBride, J. and M. Wilmington (1975). *John Ford*. New York: Da Capo Press.
McCarten, J. (1956). "Review of *The Searchers*," *The New Yorker*, June 9: 54.
McCarthy, T. (1997). *Howard Hawks: The Grey Fox of Hollywood*. New York: Grove Press.
McGee, P. (2007). *From Shane to Kill Bill: Rethinking the Western*. Malden, MA: Blackwell Publishing.
McGilligan, P. and J. McBride (2004). "A Piece of the Rock: An Interview with George Stevens," in P. Cronin (ed.), *George Stevens: Interviews*. Jackson: University Press of Mississippi, 105–22.
Marcus, A. (2000). "Uncovering an Auteur: Fred Zinnemann," *Film History* 12.1: 49–56.
Marsden, M. T. (1984a). "The Making of *Shane*: A Story for All Media," in J. Schaefer, *Shane: The Critical Edition*, ed. J. C. Work. Lincoln: University of Nebraska Press, 338–53.
Marsden, M. T. (1984b). "Savior in the Saddle: The Sagebrush Testament," in J. Schaefer, *Shane: The Critical Edition*, ed. J. C. Work. Lincoln: University of Nebraska Press, 393–404.
Mast, G. (1982). *Howard Hawks, Storyteller*. New York: Oxford University Press.
Mench, F. (2001). "Film Sense in the *Aeneid*," in M. M. Winkler (ed.), *Classical Myth and Culture in the Cinema*. Oxford: Oxford University Press, 219–32.
Metcalf, S. (2006). "The Worst Best Movie: Why on Earth did *The Searchers* get Canonized?" *slate.com*, July 26, 2015.
Meyer, R. (2014). "'What Kind of Man Are You?' Masculinity in the Western Films of James Stewart," paper presented at the *Film & History* conference: Madison, WI.
Milch, D. (2006). *Deadwood: Stories of the Black Hills*. New York: Melcher Media.
Moffitt, J. (1956). "*Searchers* Great Picture; *Serenade* Boxoffice Cinch," *Hollywood Reporter*, March 13, 3, 11.

Murray, W. (1972). "*Playboy* Interview: Sam Peckinpah: A Candid Conversation with the Screen's 'Picasso of Violence,' Controversial Creator of *The Wild Bunch* and *Straw Dogs*," *Playboy* 19.8: 65–74, 192.

Myrsiades, K. (2007). "Reading *The Gunfighter* as Homeric Epic," *College Literature* 34.2: 279–300.

Nagy, G. (1979). *The Best of the Achaeans: Concepts of the Hero in Archaic Greek Poetry*. Baltimore: Johns Hopkins University Press.

Neve, B. (1992). *Film and Politics in America: A Social Tradition*. New York: Routledge.

Newsweek (1956). "Admirable Americana," *Newsweek*, May 21, 116–17.

Nolletti Jr., A. (1999). "Introduction," in A. Nolletti Jr. (ed.), *The Films of Fred Zinnemann: Critical Perspectives*. Albany: State University of New York Press, 1–9.

Nugent, S. G. (1999). "The Women of the *Aeneid*: Vanishing Bodies, Lingering Voices," in C. Perkell (ed.), *Reading Vergil's Aeneid: An Interpretive Guide*. Norman, OK: University of Oklahoma Press, 251–70.

Nuwer, H. J. (1984). "An Interview with Jack Schaefer: May 1972," in J. Schaefer, *Shane: The Critical Edition*, ed. J. C. Work. Lincoln: University of Nebraska Press, 277–88.

O'Brien, G. (1998). "The Movie of the Century," *American Heritage* 49.7: 16–22.

O'Brien, S. R. (1996). "Leaving Behind 'The Chisholm Trail' for *Red River* – Or Refiguring the Female in the Western Film Epic," *Literature/Film Quarterly* 24.2: 183–92.

O'Sullivan, J. (2008). "Virtual Metamorphoses: Cosmetic and Cybernetic Revisions of Pygmalion's 'Living Doll,'" *Arethusa* 41.1: 133–56.

Paglia, C. (1990). *Sexual Personae: Art and Decadence from Nefertiti to Emily Dickinson*. New York: Vintage Books.

Paglia, C. (1997). "Homer on Film: A Voyage through *The Odyssey*, *Ulysses*, *Helen of Troy*, and *Contempt*," *Arion*, 3rd series, 5.2: 166–97.

Parks, R. (1982). *The Western Hero in Film and Television: Mass Media Mythology*. Ann Arbor: UMI Research Press.

Paul, J. (2011). "Working with Film: Theories and Methodologies," in L. Hardwick and C. Stray (eds), *A Companion to Classical Receptions*. Chichester: Wiley-Blackwell, 303–14.

Perkell, C. G. (1981). "On Creusa, Dido, and the Quality of Victory in Virgil's *Aeneid*," in H. P. Foley (ed.), *Reflections of Women in Antiquity*, New York: Gordon and Breach Science Publishers, 355–77.

Perkins, V. F. (1962). "An Important Re-Release: George Stevens' *Giant*," *Movie* 4: 31–3.

Pippin, R. B. (2009). "What is a Western? Politics and Self-Knowledge in John Ford's *The Searchers*," *Critical Inquiry* 35: 223–46.

Pippin, R. B. (2010). *Hollywood Westerns and American Myth: The Importance of Howard Hawks and John Ford for Political Philosophy*. New Haven, CT: Yale University Press.

Porter, J. I. (2011). "Reception Studies: Future Prospects," in L. Hardwick and C. Stray (eds), *A Companion to Classical Receptions*. Chichester: Wiley-Blackwell, 469–81.
Powell, B. B. (2012). *Classical Myth, Seventh Edition: Instructor's Review Copy*. Boston: Pearson.
Prince, S. (1999). "Historical Perspective and the Realist Aesthetic in *High Noon* (1952)," in A. Nolletti, Jr. (ed.), *The Films of Fred Zinnemann: Critical Perspectives*. Albany: State University of New York Press, 79–92.
Pye, D. (1996). "Genre and History: *Fort Apache* and *The Man Who Shot Liberty Valance*," in I. Cameron and D. Pye (eds), *The Book of Westerns*. New York: Continuum, 111–22.
Rankin, C. (1984). "Clash of Frontiers: A Historical Parallel to Jack Schaefer's *Shane*," in J. Schaefer, *Shane: The Critical Edition*, ed. J. C. Work. Lincoln: University of Nebraska Press, 3–15.
Rapf, J. E. (1990). "Myth, Ideology, and Feminism in *High Noon*," *Journal of Popular Culture* 23.4: 75–80.
Reeder, R. (1980a). "*Red River*: The Literary Version and the Film," *Ciné-tracts* 3.2: 56–7.
Reeder, R. (1980b). "The Mythic Mode: Archetypal Criticism and *Red River*," *Ciné-tracts* 3.2: 58–67.
Rivette, J. (1972). "The Genius of Howard Hawks," in J. McBride (ed.), *Focus on Howard Hawks*, trans. R. Campbell and M. Pister. Upper Saddle River, NJ: Prentice-Hall, 70–7. First published as "Genie de Howard Hawks," *Cahiers du Cinéma*, May 1953.
Rose, P. W. (1993). "The Case for Not Ignoring Marx in the Study of Women in Antiquity," in N. S. Rabinowitz and A. Richlin (eds), *Feminist Theory and the Classics*. New York: Routledge, 211–37.
Rubino, C. A. (2014). "Wounds That Will Not Heal: Heroism and Innocence in *Shane* and the *Iliad*," in *Dialogue: The Interdisciplinary Journal of Popular Culture and Pedagogy* 1.1. *journaldialogue.org*, September 2.
Sarris, A. (1962). "Cactus Rosebud or *The Man Who Shot Liberty Valance*," *Film Culture* 25: 13–15.
Sarris, A. (1968). *American Cinema: Directors and Directions, 1929–1968*. New York: E.P. Dutton & Co.
Schaefer, J. (1984). *Shane: The Critical Edition*, ed. J. C. Work. Lincoln: University of Nebraska Press.
Schein, H. (1955). "The Olympian Cowboy," trans. Ida M. Alcock, *The American Scholar* 24.3: 309–20.
Schein, S. L. (2011). "'Our Debt to Greece and Rome': Canon, Class and Ideology," in L. Hardwick and C. Stray (eds), *A Companion to Classical Receptions*. Chichester: Wiley-Blackwell, 75–85.
Scott, A. O. (2006). "'The Searchers': How the Western Was Begun," *The New York Times/nytimes.com*, July 31, 2015.

Scott, A. O. (2014). "A Sniper Does His Deeds, but the Battle Never Ends," *The New York Times/nytimes.com*, January 19.

Settis, S. (2006). *The Future of the Classical*, trans. A. Cameron. Cambridge: Polity Press.

Shay, J. (1994). *Achilles in Vietnam: Combat Trauma and the Undoing of Character*. New York: Atheneum.

Sklar, R. (1996). "Empire to the West: *Red River*," in J. Hillier and P. Wollen (eds), *Howard Hawks: American Artist*. London: British Film Institute, 152–62. First published in J. E. O'Connor and M. A. Jackson (eds), *American History/American Film*. New York: Ungar, 1979.

Skulsky, S. (1985). "'Inuitus, Regina…' Aeneas and the Love of Rome," *American Journal of Philology* 106.4: 447–55.

Slotkin, R. (1998). *Gunfighter Nation: The Myth of the Frontier in Twentieth-Century America*. Norman, OK: University of Oklahoma Press.

Smith, R. A. (2003). "Dido as Vatic Diva: A New Voice for the Persona of the Lost Lover," *The Classical Journal* 98.4: 433–6.

Smyth, J. E. (2014). *Fred Zinnemann and the Cinema of Resistance*. Jackson: University Press of Mississippi.

Snierson, D. (2013). "*Breaking Bad*: Creator Vince Gilligan Explains Series Finale," *Entertainment Weekly: ew.com*, July 21, 2015.

Stanford, W. B. (1963). *The Ulysses Theme: A Study in the Adaptability of a Traditional Hero*, 2nd edn. Ann Arbor: University of Michigan Press.

Staten, H. (1993). "The Circulation of Bodies in the *Iliad*," *New Literary History* 24.2: 339–61.

Stevens, Jr., G. (2006). *Conversations with the Great Moviemakers of Hollywood's Golden Age at the American Film Institute*. New York: A. A. Knopf.

Stowell, P. (1986). *John Ford*. Boston: Twayne Publishers.

Suzuki, M. (1989). *The Metamorphosis of Helen: Authority, Difference, and the Epic*. Ithaca, NY: Cornell University Press.

Tatum, S. (1987). "The Classic Westerner: Gary Cooper," in A. P. McDonald (ed.), *Shooting Stars: Heroes and Heroines of Western Film*. Bloomington, IN: Indiana University Press, 60–86.

Time (1956). "The New Pictures," *Time* 67.26: *web.a.ebscohost.com*, July 22, 2015.

Thomas, D. (1996). "John Wayne's Body," in I. Cameron and D. Pye (eds), *The Book of Westerns*. New York: Continuum, 75–87.

Tompkins, J. (1992). *West of Everything: The Inner Life of Westerns*. New York: Oxford University Press.

Tynan, K. (1967). "*Playboy* Interview: Orson Welles," *Playboy* 14: 53–64.

Van Brock, N. (1959). "Substitution Rituelle," *Revue Hittite et Asianique* 55: 117–46.

Virgil (1999). *Aeneid: Books 1–6*, ed. J. Henderson. LCL. Cambridge, MA: Harvard University Press.

Virgil (2000). *Aeneid: Books 7–12*, ed. J. Henderson. LCL. Cambridge, MA: Harvard University Press.
Warfield, N. (1975). "*The Man Who Shot Liberty Valance*: A Study of John Ford's Film," *The Little Film Gazette of N. D. W.* 6.1.
Warshow, R. (1954). "Movie Chronicle: The Westerner," *Partisan Review* 21.2: 190–203.
Weil, S. (1965). "The *Iliad*, or, the Poem of Force," trans. Mary McCarthy, *Chicago Review* 18.2: 5–30. First published under the pseudonym Emile Novis in *Cahiers du Sud*, December 1940–January 1941.
Whitehall, R. (1966–67). "The Heroes Are Tired," *Film Quarterly* 20.2: 12–24.
Whitman, C. H. (1958). *Homer and the Heroic Tradition*. Cambridge, MA: Harvard University Press.
Wills, G. (1997). *John Wayne's America: The Politics of Celebrity*. New York: Simon & Schuster.
Winkler, J. J. (1990). *The Constraints of Desire: The Anthropology of Sex and Gender in Ancient Greece*. New York: Routledge.
Winkler, M. M. (1985). "Classical Mythology and the Western Film," *Comparative Literature Studies* 22.4: 516–40.
Winkler, M. M. (1996). "Homeric *kleos* and the Western Film," *Syllecta Classica* 7: 43–54.
Winkler, M. M. (2001a). "Introduction," in M. M. Winkler (ed.), *Classical Myth and Culture in the Cinema*. Oxford: Oxford University Press, 3–22.
Winkler, M. M. (2001b). "Tragic Features in John Ford's *The Searchers*," in M. M. Winkler (ed.), *Classical Myth and Culture in the Cinema*. Oxford: Oxford University Press, 118–47.
Winkler, M. M. (2004). "Homer's *Iliad* and John Ford's *The Searchers*," in A. M. Eckstein and P. Lehman (eds), *The Searchers: Essays and Reflections on John Ford's Classic Western*. Detroit: Wayne State University Press, 145–70.
Winkler, M. M. (2008). "Oedipus in the Cinema," *Arethusa* 41.1: 67–94.
Winkler, M. M. (2009). *Cinema and Classical Texts: Apollo's New Light*. Cambridge: Cambridge University Press.
Wollen, P. (1972). *Signs and Meaning in the Cinema*, new edn. Bloomington: Indiana University Press.
Wollen, P. (1996). "Introduction," in J. Hillier and P. Wollen (eds), *Howard Hawks: American Artist*. London: British Film Institute, 1–11.
Wood, R. (1967). "Who the Hell is Howard Hawks? Part 2," *Focus!* 2: 8–18.
Wood, R. (1996a). "Retrospect," in J. Hillier and P. Wollen (eds), *Howard Hawks: American Artist*. London: British Film Institute, 163–74. First published in R. Wood, *Howard Hawks*, 2nd edn. London: British Film Institute, 1981.
Wood, R. (1996b). "*Rio Bravo*," in J. Hillier and P. Wollen (eds), *Howard Hawks: American Artist*. London: British Film Institute, 87–102. First published in R. Wood, *Howard Hawks*. London: Secker & Warburg/BFI, 1968.

Wood, R. (2001). "'Shall We Gather at the River?' The Late Films of John Ford," in G. Studlar and M. Bernstein (eds), *John Ford Made Westerns: Filming the Legend in the Sound Era*. Bloomington: Indiana University Press, 23–42.

Work, J. C. (1984). "Settlement Waves and Coordinate Forces in *Shane*," in J. Schaefer, *Shane: The Critical Edition*, ed. J. C. Work. Lincoln: University of Nebraska Press, 307–18.

Wright, W. (1975). *Sixguns & Society: A Structural Study of the Western*. Berkeley: University of California Press.

Wyke, M. (1997). *Projecting the Past: Ancient Rome, Cinema and History*. New York: Routledge.

Wyke, M. (2003). "Are you not entertained? Classicists and Cinema," *International Journal of the Classical Tradition* 9.3: 430–45.

Yamato, J. (2012). "Quentin Tarantino's *Django* Klansmen Inspired by John Ford: 'To Say the Least, I Hate Him,'" *movieline.com*, July 27, 2015.

Zanker, P. (1988). *The Power of Images in the Age of Augustus*, trans. A. Shapiro. Ann Arbor: University of Michigan Press.

Zinnemann, F. (1986). "Fred Zinnemann," *American Film* 11.4: 12–3, 62, 66–7.

Zinnemann, F. (1992). *Fred Zinnemann: An Autobiography: A Life in the Movies*. New York: Charles Scribner's Sons.

Filmography

Feature Films

3:10 to Yuma (1957). Directed by Delmer Daves. Columbia Pictures Corporation.

3:10 to Yuma (2007). Directed by James Mangold. Lionsgate, Tree Line Film.

American Sniper (2014). Directed by Clint Eastwood. Warner Bros.

Big Jake (1971). Directed by George Sherman. Cinema Center Films, Batjac Productions.

Broken Arrow (1950). Directed by Delmer Daves. Twentieth Century Fox Film Corporation.

El Dorado (1966). Directed by Howard Hawks. Paramount Pictures.

A Fistful of Dollars (1964). Directed by Sergio Leone. Jolly Film, Constantin Film Produktion, Ocean Films.

For a Few Dollars More (1965). Directed by Sergio Leone. Produzioni Europee Associati, Arturo González Producciones Cinematográficas, Constantin Film Produktion.

The Good, the Bad, and the Ugly (1966). Directed by Sergio Leone. Produzioni Europee Associati, Arturo González Producciones Cinematográficas, Constantin Film Produktion.

The Gunfighter (1950). Directed by Henry King. Twentieth Century Fox Film Corporation.

High Noon (1952). Directed by Fred Zinnemann. Stanley Kramer Productions.

High Plains Drifter (1973). Directed by Clint Eastwood. Universal Pictures, The Malpaso Company.

Lonestar (1996). Directed by John Sayles. Columbia Pictures Corporation, Castle Rock Entertainment.

The Magnificent Seven (1960). Directed by John Sturges. The Mirisch Company, Alpha Productions.

The Man from Laramie (1955). Directed by Anthony Mann. Columbia Pictures Corporation, William Goetz Productions.

The Man Who Shot Liberty Valance (1962). Directed by John Ford. Paramount Pictures, John Ford Productions.

The Missouri Breaks (1976). Directed by Arthur Penn. Devon/Persky-Bright.
My Darling Clementine (1946). Directed by John Ford. Twentieth Century Fox Film Corporation.
The Naked Spur (1953). Directed by Anthony Mann. Metro-Goldwyn-Mayer.
Once Upon a Time in the West (1968). Directed by Sergio Leone. Rafran Cinematografica, Finanzia San Marco, Paramount Pictures.
The Outlaw Josey Wales (1976). Directed by Clint Eastwood. Warner Bros., The Malpaso Company.
Pale Rider (1985). Directed by Clint Eastwood. The Malpaso Company.
The Quiet Man (1952). Directed by John Ford. Argosy Pictures.
Red River (1948). Directed by Howard Hawks. Monterey Productions.
Rio Bravo (1959). Directed by Howard Hawks. Warner Bros., Armada Productions.
The Searchers (1956). Directed by John Ford. Warner Bros., C. V. Whitney Pictures.
Shane (1953). Directed by George Stevens. Paramount Pictures.
The Shootist (1976). Directed by Don Siegel. Paramount Pictures.
The Sons of Katie Elder (1965). Directed by Henry Hathaway. Paramount Pictures, Hal Wallis Productions.
Stagecoach (1939). Directed by John Ford. Walter Wanger Productions.
Star Wars Episode V: The Empire Strikes Back (1980). Directed by Irvin Kerschner. Lucasfilm.
True Grit (1969). Directed by Henry Hathaway. Paramount Pictures, Hal Wallis Productions.
True Grit (2010). Directed by Ethan and Joel Coen. Paramount Pictures, Skydance Productions, Scott Rudin Productions.
Ulysses (1954). Directed by Mario Camerini. Lux Film, Paramount Pictures, Producciones Ponti-de Laurentiis.
Unforgiven (1992). Directed by Clint Eastwood. Warner Bros., Malpaso Productions.
The Virginian (1929). Directed by Victor Fleming. Paramount Pictures.
Wagon Master (1950). Directed by John Ford. Argosy Pictures.
The Wild Bunch (1969). Directed by Sam Peckinpah. Warner Bros./Seven Arts.
Will Penny (1967). Directed by Tom Gries. Paramount Pictures.
Winchester '73 (1950). Directed by Anthony Mann. Universal International Pictures.
The Wings of Eagles (1957). Directed by John Ford. Metro-Goldwyn-Mayer.

Television Series

Deadwood (2004–6). Created by David Milch. HBO.
Justified (2010–15). Created by Graham Yost. FX Network.
Longmire (2012–). Created by Hunt Baldwin, John Coveny. A&E Television Networks, Netflix.

The Sopranos (1999–2007). Created by David Chase. HBO.
The Walking Dead (2010–). Created by Frank Darabont. AMC.

Songs

"High Noon (Do Not Forsake Me)," from *High Noon*. Words by Ned Washington. Music by Dimitri Tiomkin. Copyright © 1952 Volta Music Corp., Catharine Hinen Music, and Patti Washington Music Copyright renewed. All Rights for Volta Music Corp. controlled and administered by Universal Music Corp. All Rights for Catharine Hinen Music administered worldwide by Shapiro, Bernstein & Co. All rights reserved; used by permission. Reprinted by permission of Hal Leonard Corporation and Alfred Music

"The Searchers." Composed by Stan Jones. Copyright © 1956 (Renewed) Warner Music Corp. All Rights Reserved. Used By Permission of Alfred Music.

Index

Page numbers in *italics* refer to illustrations.

EU Authorised Representative:
Easy Access System Europe Mustamäe tee 50, 10621 Tallinn, Estonia
gpsr.requests@easproject.com

Printed and bound by CPI Group (UK) Ltd, Croydon, CR0 4YY
29/09/2026
02224986-0004